FOOTBALL LEAGUE

MAINE

MINNESOTA

Minnesota Vikings

Green Bay Packers

WISCONSIN

Detroit Lions

MICHIGAN

IOWA

Cleveland Browns

Chicago Bears

ILLINOIS

Indianapolis Colts

INDIANA

Cincinnati Bengals

OHIO

NEW YORK

VT.

N.H.

New England Patriots

MASS.

CONN.

R.I.

Buffalo Bills

GIANTS

New York Giants

New York Jets

PENNSYLVANIA

N.J.

Philadelphia Eagles

Pittsburgh Steelers

MD.

DEL.

Washington Redskins

D.C.

Chiefs

St. Louis Cardinals

MISSOURI

KENTUCKY

WEST VIRGINIA

VIRGINIA

NORTH CAROLINA

ARKANSAS

TENNESSEE

SOUTH CAROLINA

Atlanta Falcons

ALABAMA

MISSISSIPPI

LOUISIANA

GEORGIA

New Orleans Saints

FLORIDA

Tampa Bay Buccaneers

Miami Dolphins

THE AMERICAN FOOTBALL

BOOK 3

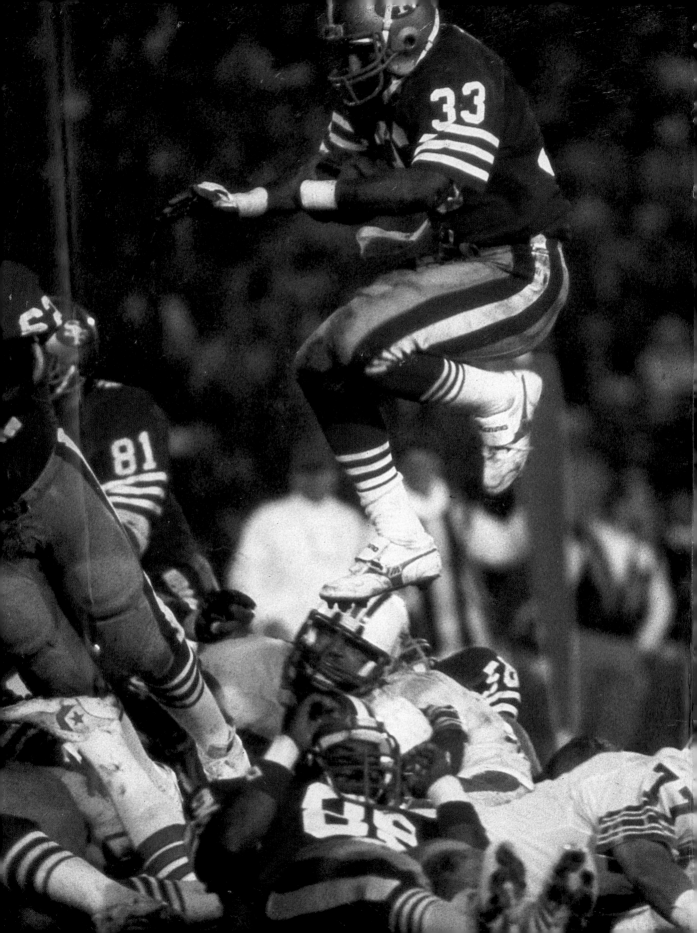

THE AMERICAN FOOTBALL

BOOK 3

KEN THOMAS

ORBIS · LONDON

In association with Channel Four Television Company Limited

ACKNOWLEDGEMENTS

Having reached the stage where survival means nothing more than meeting the next deadline, I find myself now almost totally dependent on those people without whose kindness and consideration this annual could not be written. Nick Wridgway has been of invaluable assistance, preparing text, proof reading, suggesting amendments and discovering errors. The all-time statistics were hammered out by Roger Smith, with an efficiency I now take for granted. And Louise Payne of NFL Properties Inc., Los Angeles, no doubt now takes for granted my last-minute telephone calls for photographic material. To both Louise and Beau Riffenburgh, the latter who works in the same office, I extend my thanks. Mike Niblock, of *Touchdown* magazine, kindly allowed full access to his library of NFL slides, several of which are reproduced: 'Thanks Mike'. Mrs. Susanna Yager, the Publishing and Merchandising Manager of Channel Four Television, continues to insulate me from the harsh realities of the business world and has my sincere gratitude. The Orbis lads, editor Richard Wigmore and designers Mike Moule and Simon Webb, have somehow taken rough text and transformed it into, at least, something worth a glance. Finally to my wife Janie who, in addition to extending me her limitless tolerance, has contributed more than a few ideas: 'Thanks again, love.'

First published in Great Britain by Orbis Publishing Limited, London 1985.
© 1985 by Ken Thomas

ISBN 0-85613-822-3

The American Football Annual is associated with Channel Four Television's coverage of the sport produced by Cheerleader Productions Limited.

Typeset in Great Britain by SX Composing Ltd.
Printed in Spain by Cayfosa, Barcelona
Dep. Legal B. 26.856/85

PHOTOGRAPHS
All photographs have been supplied by courtesy of the NFL. In addition, the following photographers took the pictures on the pages indicated: The Allens 41, 49; John Biever 20, 32, 81, 150-151; Vernon Biever 27, 145; Dave Boss 21, 59; Rob Brown 48, 91; Christine Cotter 121; D. Cross 85; Scott Cunningham 141, 149; Jay Dickman 18; Malcolm Emmons Title page, 9, 55, 63, 70; Nate Fine 15, 22, 87; Jim Flores, 60; L.D. Fullerton 95; G. Gojkovich 45; Peter Groh 23, 155; Andy Hayto 6; Paul Jasienski 24, 39, 113; R. Mackson 30, 119; Mike Marten 44; Robert Mayer 86; John McDonough 17; Al Messerschmidt 9, 38, 42, 65, 89, 101, 117, 133; P.R. Miller 25, 62, 157; Darryl Norenberg 36; Russ Reed 54; Frank Rippon 56, 57, 58, 65; George Rose 51, 147; Ron Ross 11; Manny Rubio 29, 35, 47, 126, 139, 153; Alan Schwartz 134-135; Bill Smith 29; Robert L. Smith 33; Chuck Solomon 12, 129; Paul Spinelli 97; R.H. Stagg 8, 27; Vic Stein 78; Tony Tomsic 40, 51, 75(2); Corky Trewin 26, 43, 123; Jim Turner 10, 14, 105; Fred Vuich 88; Michael Zagaris 47.

CONTENTS

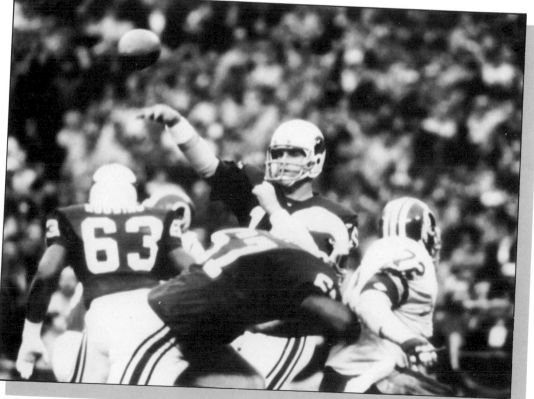

Neil Lomax, St Louis Cardinals quarterback

INTRODUCTION

Not very long ago, the man wearing the Pittsburgh Steelers sweatshirt would be taking photographs of some derelict castle 'just to show the folks back home'. These days he'll be in the supermarket buying the groceries – he'll be one of the six million Brits who stayed up until 2 am to watch Super Bowl XIX. American Football has arrived, and the 170 teams who form part of one of the four British leagues are bent on making sure that it stays. Recognizing this, the National Football League owners have decreed that the city of London will be included in the world-wide programme of exhibition games which will begin in 1987. It is just conceivable that the NFL will establish a franchise here in the U.K. In 1970, the very thought of that would have been laughable, and it would have raised more than a little mirth in 1980.

The lion's share of the credit for popularising NFL football must go to Channel Four Television, through its programme maker, Cheerleader Productions, and that company's producers, successively, Elaine Rose, Chris Hayden and, latterly, Gary Franses. Not surprisingly, several British publishing houses have flooded the bookshelves with their products – but in this context, Orbis Publishing was the first, closely followed by Michael Philips Productions, the publishers of *Touchdown* magazine.

This Annual, the third in the series, follows the pattern established by the second. It is meant to allow the reader to savour the 1984 season whilst preparing for 1985. There have been some minor alterations, such as listing each team's previous championships in greater detail, but it remains as an attempt to assist television fans in their enjoyment of the sport. If that can be achieved, then the effort which went into the production of this book will have been worthwhile.

San Diego's Dan Fouts, who has passed for over 4,000 yards in a season three times

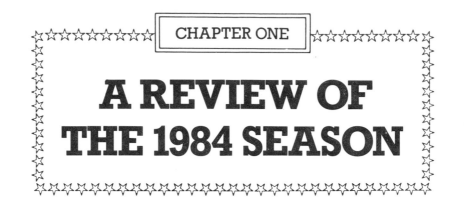

CHAPTER ONE

A REVIEW OF THE 1984 SEASON

Prologue

The clamour surrounding the Raiders' stunning victory over the Washington Redskins, in Super Bowl XVIII, had barely subsided as the teams gathered for the NFL's sixty-fifth campaign. Three rookie head coaches joined the other twenty-four, who spent the offseason plotting the overthrow of the defending NFL Champion 'Silver and Black'. Les Steckel had the unenviable responsibility of filling the shoes of the retired Bud Grant, up in Minnesota. At the tender age of thirty-eight, Steckel, a former Marine Lieutenant with combat experience in Vietnam, was the youngest of the active head coaches. Hugh Campbell, formerly the head coach of the Canadian Football League team, the Edmonton Eskimos, and latterly with the USFL's Los Angeles Express, took charge of the Houston Oilers. He was reunited with his strong-armed quarterback, Warren Moon, with whom he had enjoyed remarkable success, notably winning five Grey Cup Championships (this is Canada's equivalent of the Vince Lombardi Trophy) in consecutive years (1978-82). The former University of Washington quarterback, Moon, was voted MVP in his team's 27-20 Rose Bowl victory over the Michigan Wolverines but, until now, had opted for earning his living north of the border. Entering his first year in the NFL, he would be the league's highest-paid player. Forrest Gregg who, for four years had been the head coach at Cincinnati, resigned to take the top job at Green Bay. Gregg was a key member of the Packers team which won five NFL Championships in seven years, in the 1960s. He was going home. Gregg's departure gave Sam Wyche his first chance and for Wyche, too, it was a homecoming. A former NFL quarterback, he had begun his ten-year pro career with the Bengals in 1968 and was returning to a club which was well-equipped to take advantage of his particular philosophy – he promised to install a wide-open offense.

New England showed no hesitation in making the University of Nebraska's Irving Fryar the first selection, overall, in the May 1 collegiate draft. He was considered to be the best of four wide receivers picked in round one. Outside of these, the only offensive strike players to go in the first round were tight end David Lewis (Detroit) and running back Greg Bell (Buffalo). The balance was made up of five offensive linemen and defense, defense, defense (six linemen, six linebackers and five in the secondary). For the first quarterback to emerge, we had to wait until the tenth pick of round two, when Cincinnati acquired 'Boomer' Esiason.

By releasing the veteran running back, Franco Harris, during the preseason after unsuccessful contract negotiations, the Pittsburgh Steelers eliminated Walter Payton's only competitor in the race to surpass Jim Brown's career rushing record of

Jim Plunkett, Raiders quarterback

12,312 yards. For Payton and the rest of us willing him on, it was now only a question of how soon he would gain the necessary 688 yards. San Diego wide receiver Charlie Joiner needed 54 pass receptions to move ahead of the retired Charley Taylor's NFL career best of 649 but, for a veteran entering his sixteenth season, it was asking rather a lot. Atlanta's Billy 'White Shoes' Johnson seemed certain to become the all-time punt return leader (he needed just 207 yards), and 78 punts would take Houston's John James ahead of the existing career record of 1,072, set by Jerrel Wilson over a career with Kansas City and New England. Washington's John Riggins would surely become the fifth player in NFL history to score 100 career touchdowns (he required six) and Cincinnati quarterback Ken Anderson was all set to complete the 48 passes he needed to become only the fourth man to log a career total of 2,500.

The Jets' Mark Gastineau in classic pose after one of his many quarterback sacks

Looking at the prospects for the twenty-eight teams, the Raiders were the popular favourites to retain their Super Bowl Championship but firstly, they would have to dispense with their rivals in the AFC Western division which, as in 1983 when it produced the two wild cards, appeared to be the most closely fought in that conference. Miami were fancied to come out on top in the AFC Eastern division but might feel the heat from a New England team, whose offense now had no weaknesses. The Pittsburgh Steelers were always going to be under pressure from both Cleveland and Cincinnati to retain their title in the AFC Central division, and they could not afford to ignore Houston, who might well be ignited by the arrival of quarterback Warren Moon.

Of the NFC Western division teams, it was felt that the multi-talented San Francisco 49ers, guided by their innovative head coach, Bill Walsh, were good enough to stay ahead of the Los Angeles Rams. A severe, preseason training injury, to running back William Andrews, was a bitter blow to Atlanta's hopes, and New Orleans had yet to have a net winning season. The NFC Eastern division promised to be more competitive than in recent years, with St Louis predicted to join Dallas and Washington in the scramble. As usual, the NFC Central division was a puzzle but a good case could be made on behalf of Detroit, who were probably going to retain their title, under pressure from Chicago and, perhaps, a Green Bay team roused by new head coach Gregg.

After due consideration, then, most of the 'experts' opted for the Raiders as the AFC's representative in Palo Alto (the site for Super Bowl XIX), and few people looked beyond Washington to represent the NFC.

Minnesota head coach Bud Grant

WEEK ONE

American Football Conference
Cincinnati 17 at Denver 20
Cleveland 0 at Seattle 33
Kansas City 37 at Pittsburgh 27
Los Angeles Raiders 24 at Houston 14
New England 21 at Buffalo 17
New York Jets 23 at Indianapolis 14

National Football Conference
Atlanta 36 at New Orleans 28
Dallas 20 at Los Angeles Rams 13
Philadelphia 27 at New York Giants 28
St Louis 23 at Green Bay 24
San Francisco 30 at Detroit 27
Tampa Bay 14 at Chicago 34

Interconference Games
Miami 35 at Washington 17
San Diego 42 at Minnesota 13

Interconference Play
AFC 2, NFC 0

With few exceptions, everything went according to plan on Week One. All five AFC West teams opened with victories, the most impressive being that of Seattle, who sacked Browns quarterback Paul McDonald seven times in handing Cleveland its first shutout for 93 regular season games. Sadly for the Seahawks, however, they lost their star running back, Curt Warner, whose season ended with a knee injury after he had rushed for just 40 yards. The Chargers were only marginally less commanding in victory at Minnesota, where quarterback Dan Fouts passed for 292 yards and two touchdowns before withdrawing with, still, 7:32 remaining in the third quarter. The Raiders were given a few problems by Houston and even trailed 7-0 at halftime, before restoring a little sanity to the proceedings. Perhaps the most disappointed pair in the NFL were Pittsburgh's wide receivers, rookie Louis Lipps and veteran John Stallworth who, between them, caught fourteen passes for 350 yards and yet finished on the losing side.

There were several close games in the NFC, where both the Giants and Green Bay won by the narrowest of margins. For the Giants, quarterback Phil Simms threw for 409 yards (the second highest total in the club's history) and four touchdowns, whilst over in Green Bay, wide receiver James Lofton caught seven passes for 134 yards against St Louis. At Anaheim, Dallas quarterback Gary Hogeboom confirmed the wisdom of head coach Tom Landry, who had installed the fifth-year man as starter ahead of Danny White. Hogeboom completed a team-record 33 passes as the Cowboys gained some measure of revenge for their 1983 wild card loss to the Rams. As usual, the 49ers struggled against Detroit (they had won only three of the last nine meetings) but came out on top thanks to Ray Wersching's 22-yard field goal with only four seconds of regulation time remaining. The day's top performance came in the interconference matchup between Miami and Washington. The Redskins, who led 10-7 at one stage in the second

quarter, went down under a withering hail of passes from Miami's second-year quarterback, Dan Marino. Completing three-quarters of his passes for 311 yards and a personal best five touchdowns, Marino had set a standard below which he would fall only rarely, throughout the regular season and beyond.

Outstanding Individual Performances

Gerald Riggs (Atlanta) rushed for a personal best 202 yards on 35 carries and scored two touchdowns.

Eric Dickerson (Los Angeles Rams) rushed for 138 yards on 21 carries and scored one touchdown.

Dan Marino (Miami) completed 21 of 28 passes for 311 yards and five touchdowns.

Phil Simms (New York Giants) completed 23 of 30 passes for a personal best 409 yards and four touchdowns.

Louis Lipps (Pittsburgh) caught six passes for 183 yards and two touchdowns, one of which covered 80 yards.

Mark 'Super' Duper (Miami) caught six passes for 178 yards and scored two touchdowns, one of which covered 74 yards.

Byron Williams (New York Giants) caught five passes for 167 yards including a 65-yard touchdown reception.

John Stallworth (Pittsburgh) caught eight passes for 167 yards and scored one touchdown.

Mark Gastineau (New York Jets) registered 4.0 quarter-back sacks.

Joey Browner (Minnesota) returned a fumble recovery 63 yards for a touchdown.

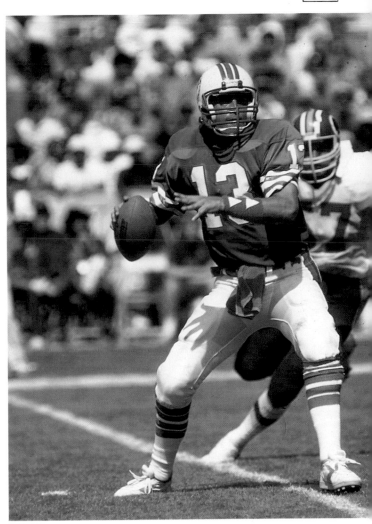

Dan Marino

◀ *Phil Simms delivers*

STANDINGS

AFC East	W	L	T	PF	PA	NFC East	W	L	T	PF	PA
Miami	1	0	0	35	17	Dallas	1	0	0	20	13
New England	1	0	0	21	17	N.Y. Giants	1	0	0	28	27
N.Y. Jets	1	0	0	23	14	Philadelphia	0	1	0	27	28
Buffalo	0	1	0	17	21	St Louis	0	1	0	23	24
Indianapolis	0	1	0	14	23	Washington	0	1	0	17	35
AFC Central						**NFC Central**					
Cincinnati	0	1	0	17	20	Chicago	1	0	0	34	14
Cleveland	0	1	0	0	33	Green Bay	1	0	0	24	23
Houston	0	1	0	14	24	Detroit	0	1	0	27	30
Pittsburgh	0	1	0	27	37	Minnesota	0	1	0	13	42
AFC West						Tampa Bay	0	1	0	14	34
Denver	1	0	0	20	17	**NFC West**					
Kansas City	1	0	0	37	27	Atlanta	1	0	0	36	28
L.A. Raiders	1	0	0	24	14	San Francisco	1	0	0	30	27
San Diego	1	0	0	42	13	L.A. Rams	0	1	0	13	20
Seattle	1	0	0	33	0	New Orleans	0	1	0	28	36

WEEK TWO

American Football Conference
Indianapolis 35 at Houston 21
Kansas City 27 at Cincinnati 22
New England 7 at Miami 28
Pittsburgh 23 at New York Jets 17
San Diego 17 at Seattle 31

National Football Conference
Dallas 7 at New York Giants 28
Detroit 27 at Atlanta 24 (OT)
Minnesota 17 at Philadelphia 19
Tampa Bay 13 at New Orleans 17
Washington 31 at San Francisco 37

Interconference Games
Buffalo 7 at St Louis 37
Cleveland 17 at Los Angeles Rams 20
Denver 0 at Chicago 27
Green Bay 7 at Los Angeles Raiders 28

Interconference Play
AFC 3, NFC 3

Bobby Humphery (#84) after his 97-yard touchdown return

The Redskins' tale of woe continued at San Francisco, where quarterback Joe Montana passed for the second-highest yardage total in 49ers history. But there were signs of encouragement in a gritty Washington fight-back which saw them lose by only six points after they had trailed 27-0 in the second quarter. The Patriots can be forgiven for feeling that the journey to Miami is hardly worthwhile – they had lost on their last sixteen consecutive visits – and they duly made it seventeen. After a slow start on Week One, Chicago's Walter Payton lopped a 179-yard chunk off his target at the expense of Denver, who could never recover from a 27-point first-half hammering. The Bears were looking good, as were the Detroit Lions, for whom running back Billy Sims gained 140 yards on 23 carries. Even so, it took a 48-yard field goal by Eddie Murray, in overtime, to break the deadlock with Atlanta. Another team to issue a reminder of its presence after several years, most of which have been spent in decline, was the New York Giants who beat Dallas by the biggest margin since their 41-10 victory in 1962. With St Louis rattling up 37 points in fine style against Buffalo, clearly, the NFC East was going to be at least a four-way fight.

The Seahawks, who signed running back Franco Harris as a replacement for the injured Curt Warner, continued to impress, with four interceptions, four fumble recoveries and two quarterback sacks in a 31-17 come-from-behind victory over San Diego. Rushing for 46 yards on 14 carries, Harris eased himself back into the race with Payton. Down the Pacific coast in Los Angeles, the Raiders had little difficulty controlling the Packers' feared wide receivers, James Lofton and John Jefferson, after an early injury to Green Bay quarterback Lynn Dickey. But doubts were beginning to grow about a 'Silver and Black' offense which, though scoring points, continued to stutter.

Outstanding Individual Performances

Walter Payton (Chicago) rushed for 179 yards on 20 carries and scored a 72-yard touchdown.

Billy Sims (Detroit) rushed for 140 yards on 23 carries and scored one touchdown.

Joe Montana (San Francisco) completed 24 of 40 passes for 381 yards and two touchdowns.

Warren Moon (Houston) completed 23 of 43 passes for 365 yards.

Art Monk (Washington) caught ten passes for 200 yards to exceed his previous best in both categories.

Bobby Humphery (New York Jets) returned a kickoff 97 yards for a touchdown.

LeRoy Irvin (Los Angeles Rams) returned an interception 81 yards for a touchdown.

Andy Headen (New York Giants) returned a fumble recovery 81 yards for a touchdown.

STANDINGS

AFC East	W	L	T	PF	PA	NFC East	W	L	T	PF	PA
Miami	2	0	0	63	24	N.Y. Giants	2	0	0	56	34
Indianapolis	1	1	0	49	44	Dallas	1	1	0	27	41
New England	1	1	0	28	45	Philadelphia	1	1	0	46	45
N.Y. Jets	1	1	0	40	37	St Louis	1	1	0	60	31
Buffalo	0	2	0	24	58	Washington	0	2	0	48	72
AFC Central						**NFC Central**					
Pittsburgh	1	1	0	50	54	Chicago	2	0	0	61	14
Cincinnati	0	2	0	39	47	Detroit	1	1	0	54	54
Cleveland	0	2	0	17	53	Green Bay	1	1	0	31	51
Houston	0	2	0	35	59	Minnesota	0	2	0	30	61
AFC West						Tampa Bay	0	2	0	27	51
Kansas City	2	0	0	64	49	**NFC West**					
L.A. Raiders	2	0	0	52	21	San Francisco	2	0	0	67	58
Seattle	2	0	0	64	17	Atlanta	1	1	0	60	55
Denver	1	1	0	20	44	L.A. Rams	1	1	0	33	37
San Diego	1	1	0	59	44	New Orleans	1	1	0	45	49

Pittsburgh's Weegie Thompson catches a touchdown pass against the Jets

LeRoy Irvin

WEEK THREE

American Football Conference
Cincinnati 23 at New York Jets 43
Denver 24 at Cleveland 14
Houston 14 at San Diego 31
Los Angeles Raiders 22 at Kansas City 20
Seattle 23 at New England 38
Miami 21 at Buffalo 17

National Football Conference
Atlanta 20 at Minnesota 27
Chicago 9 at Green Bay 7
Detroit 17 at Tampa Bay 21
New Orleans 20 at San Francisco 30
New York Giants 14 at Washington 30
Philadelphia 17 at Dallas 23

Interconference Games
Los Angeles Rams 14 at Pittsburgh 24
St Louis 34 at Indianapolis 33

Interconference Play
AFC 4, NFC 4

Freeman McNeil (#24)

The New York Giants came down to earth, at least temporarily, against the Redskins who capitalised on Giants errors to chalk up their first win of the season. Cornerback Vernon Dean returned one of his three interceptions of the game 36 yards for a touchdown, and safety Curtis Jordan did likewise after recovering a fumble on the Giants 29-yard line. Two other fast starters, Miami and San Francisco, maintained their unbeaten records but only after suffering major frights against Buffalo and New Orleans respectively. Though the Dolphins never trailed, they allowed Buffalo back into the game, after establishing a 14-0 lead, and for their survival could thank an alert Don McNeal, who recovered a late fumble by the Bills' wide receiver, Byron Franklin. The 49ers established a comfortable 17-0 lead over the Saints but saw it steadily evaporate and, at one stage in the third quarter, they fell behind 20-17. Furthermore, quarterback Joe Montana had left the game with injured ribs. But a 23-yard touchdown pass, by reserve quarterback Matt Cavanaugh to tight end Earl Cooper, steadied

the boat, before a brace of field goals by Ray Wersching put the result beyond doubt.

Fourth-quarter touchdown passes of 47 and 56 yards, both to wide receiver Roy 'Jetstream' Green, and a Neil O'Donoghue field goal with just seven seconds remaining, gave St Louis a one-point victory over Indianapolis. But that comeback was nothing compared with an astonishing performance by New England, who overcame a 23-0 deficit against Seattle, scoring 38 unanswered points for a victory which kept them in touch with the Dolphins in the AFC East.

Outstanding Individual Performances

Freeman McNeil (New York Jets) rushed for 150 yards on 26 carries and scored two touchdowns.

Ken Anderson (Cincinnati) completed 16 of 22 passes for 316 yards and two touchdowns, one of which covered 80 yards.

Roy 'Jetstream' Green (St Louis) caught eight passes for 183 yards and scored two touchdowns, one of which covered 56 yards.

Tim Smith (Houston) caught five passes for 159 yards, including a 75-yard touchdown reception.

Drew Hill (Los Angeles Rams) caught four passes for 152 yards.

Kellen Winslow (San Diego) caught ten passes for 146 yards.

Phil Smith (Indianapolis) returned a kickoff 96 yards for a touchdown.

Kevin Ross (Kansas City) returned an interception 71 yards for a touchdown.

Vernon Dean (Washington) intercepted three passes and returned one 36 yards for a touchdown.

Ed Nelson (Pittsburgh) registered 5.0 quarterback sacks.

Randy Holloway (Minnesota) registered 4.5 quarterback sacks.

STANDINGS

AFC East	W	L	T	PF	PA
Miami	3	0	0	84	41
New England	2	1	0	66	68
N.Y. Jets	2	1	0	83	60
Indianapolis	1	2	0	82	78
Buffalo	0	3	0	41	79
AFC Central					
Pittsburgh	2	1	0	74	68
Cincinnati	0	3	0	62	90
Cleveland	0	3	0	31	77
Houston	0	3	0	49	90
AFC West					
L.A. Raiders	3	0	0	74	41
Denver	2	1	0	44	58
Kansas City	2	1	0	84	71
San Diego	2	1	0	90	58
Seattle	2	1	0	87	55
NFC East	**W**	**L**	**T**	**PF**	**PA**
Dallas	2	1	0	50	58
N.Y. Giants	2	1	0	70	64
St Louis	2	1	0	94	64
Philadelphia	1	2	0	63	68
Washington	1	2	0	78	86
NFC Central					
Chicago	3	0	0	70	21
Detroit	1	2	0	71	75
Green Bay	1	2	0	38	60
Minnesota	1	2	0	57	81
Tampa Bay	1	2	0	48	68
NFC West					
San Francisco	3	0	0	97	78
Atlanta	1	2	0	80	82
L.A. Rams	1	2	0	47	61
New Orleans	1	2	0	65	79

◄ *Ken Anderson*

Vernon Dean (#32) scoring

WEEK FOUR

American Football Conference
Indianapolis 7 at Miami 44
Kansas City 0 at Denver 21
New York Jets 28 at Buffalo 26
Pittsburgh 10 at Cleveland 20
San Diego 30 at Los Angeles Raiders 33

National Football Conference
Green Bay 6 at Dallas 20
Minnesota 29 at Detroit 28
St Louis 24 at New Orleans 34
San Francisco 21 at Philadelphia 9
Tampa Bay 14 at New York Giants 17

Interconference Games
Chicago 9 at Seattle 38
Houston 10 at Atlanta 42
Los Angeles Rams 24 at Cincinnati 14
Washington 26 at New England 10

Interconference Play
AFC 5, NFC 7

In beating the Pittsburgh Steelers, the Browns recorded their first victory of the campaign and, remarkably, were now only one game out of first place in the AFC Central division. After four weeks of play, the AFC Central teams had a grand total of just three wins. This was still one fewer than each of Miami, San Francisco and the Raiders, all three of whom retained their unbeaten records. There were no scares this week for Miami, who blasted the Colts, and San Francisco kept Philadelphia out of the end zone whilst reserve quarterback Matt Cavanaugh threw three touchdown passes in a flawless performance. The Raiders–San Diego game was a typical shootout, finished off characteristically by Marcus Allen, two of whose four touchdowns of the night came late in the fourth quarter. The Minnesota Vikings took advantage of Chicago's first loss of the season, drawing to within one game of the lead in the NFC Central division with a one-point victory over Detroit. Lions quarterback Gary Danielson could hardly be blamed for the loss – he completed 24 of 30 passes for 218 yards and four touchdowns, without an interception. But he could only watch from the sidelines as the 40-year-old Jan Stenerud, who has probably forgotten what it feels like to be nervous, chipped five field goals without a failure.

Wide receiver Wesley Walker made a welcome return to form, with three touchdown receptions in the Jets' 28-26 victory over the luckless Buffalo Bills. It was good enough to take them into second place in the AFC East, following New England's loss to Washington, for whom John Riggins duly scored his 100th career touchdown. A peerless display by

Outstanding Individual Performances

Earnest Jackson (San Diego) rushed for 155 yards on 29 carries and scored one touchdown.

Sammy Winder (Denver) rushed for 139 yards on 31 carries and scored one touchdown.

Mark Duper (Miami) caught seven passes for 173 yards and two touchdowns, one of which covered 80 yards.

Henry Marshall (Kansas City) caught eight passes for 148 yards.

Marcus Allen (Los Angeles Raiders) scored four touchdowns.

Jan Stenerud (Minnesota) was successful on all five field goal attempts.

Sam Washington (Pittsburgh) returned an interception 69 yards for a touchdown.

Lawrence Taylor (New York Giants) registered 4.0 quarterback sacks.

Giants' linebacker Lawrence Taylor made it a day for double celebration in New York city. Taylor had six unassisted tackles and four quarterback sacks in his team's 17-14 win over Tampa Bay. The Giants, too, were now in second place in their division.

Sammy Winder

STANDINGS

AFC East	W	L	T	PF	PA	NFC East	W	L	T	PF	PA
Miami	4	0	0	128	48	Dallas	3	1	0	70	64
N.Y. Jets	3	1	0	111	86	N.Y. Giants	3	1	0	87	78
New England	2	2	0	76	94	St Louis	2	2	0	118	98
Indianapolis	1	3	0	89	122	Washington	2	2	0	104	96
Buffalo	0	4	0	67	107	Philadelphia	1	3	0	72	89
AFC Central						**NFC Central**					
Pittsburgh	2	2	0	84	88	Chicago	3	1	0	79	59
Cleveland	1	3	0	51	87	Minnesota	2	2	0	86	109
Cincinnati	0	4	0	76	114	Detroit	1	3	0	99	104
Houston	0	4	0	59	132	Green Bay	1	3	0	44	80
AFC West						Tampa Bay	1	3	0	62	85
L.A. Raiders	4	0	0	107	71	**NFC West**					
Denver	3	1	0	65	58	San Francisco	4	0	0	118	87
Seattle	3	1	0	125	64	Atlanta	2	2	0	122	92
Kansas City	2	2	0	84	92	L.A. Rams	2	2	0	71	75
San Diego	2	2	0	120	91	New Orleans	2	2	0	99	103

Marcus Allen (#32) scores his fourth touchdown

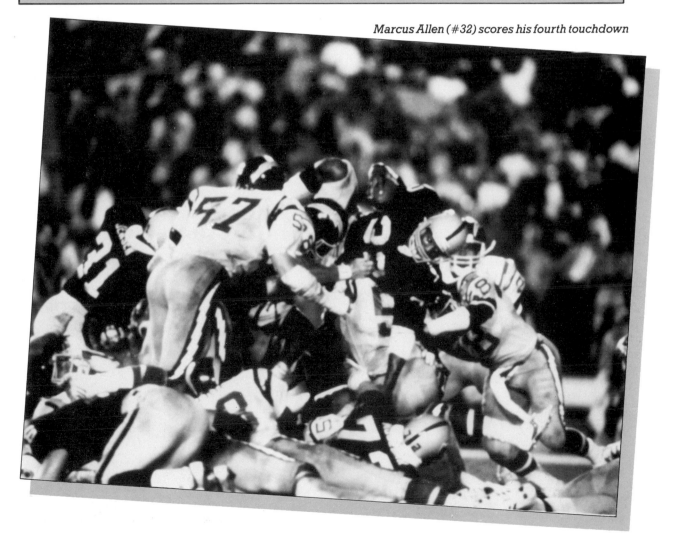

WEEK FIVE

American Football Conference
Buffalo 17 at Indianapolis 31
Cleveland 6 at Kansas City 10
Los Angeles Raiders 13 at Denver 16
New England 28 at New York Jets 21
Cincinnati 17 at Pittsburgh 38

National Football Conference
Atlanta 5 at San Francisco 14
Dallas 23 at Chicago 14
Green Bay 27 at Tampa Bay 30 (OT)
New York Giants 12 at Los Angeles Rams 33
Philadelphia 0 at Washington 20

Interconference Games
Detroit 24 at San Diego 27
Miami 36 at St Louis 28
New Orleans 27 at Houston 10
Seattle 20 at Minnesota 12

Interconference Play
AFC 8, NFC 8

Norwood Vann blocks a Dave Jennings punt
immediately prior to one of three Rams safeties

The Miami Dolphins powered on, with quarterback Dan Marino taking full advantage of a weakened St Louis Cardinals defensive secondary to pass for a Miami team record 429 yards, in a victory which was gained more easily than the scoreline suggests. One team which managed to win, despite being in a similar predicament on defense, was the 49ers. They, too, fielded the walking wounded in the secondary and, on offense, quarterback Joe Montana wore a flak jacket to protect his sore ribs. Despite yielding 136 yards rushing to Atlanta's Gerald Riggs, for the second consecutive week the 49ers did not give up a touchdown. Five times the Falcons were at first-and-ten inside the 49ers 20-yard line, but were restricted to just a Mick Luckhurst field goal and a safety, when punter Max Runager was forced out of the end zone by Atlanta's Scott Case. The third, hitherto unbeaten team fared less well – so less well that they lost. It was, of course, the Raiders, who had been unimpressive for most of the season. They went down to a well-drilled Denver team which stifled its opponent's famed big play offense and, alarmingly, was able to rush for a mammoth 233 yards against a defense which isn't used to being treated that way. The win took Denver into a three-way tie with the Raiders and Seattle on top of the AFC Western division.

Against the Cowboys, the Chicago Bears dominated possession and outgained Tom Landry's men by 400 yards to 313 but, with quarterback Jim McMahon virtually incapable of passing, they were unable to capitalise on their statistical supremacy. However, Walter Payton scampered, twisted, turned and swerved to within 66 yards of his immediate goal, that 12,312 yards. The only NFC Central team to notch a win on Week Five was the Buccaneers, for whom running back James Wilder gained 172 yards rushing and equalled the NFL single-game record with 43 carries. But for victory over Green Bay they had to thank their Nigerian-born kicker, Obed Ariri, whose 48-yard field goal came with 4:22 remaining in overtime. The day's most extraordinary events took place in Anaheim, where the Rams logged an NFL record three safeties in beating the Giants – and even the goal posts fell down!

Henry Ellard (Los Angeles Rams)

Outstanding Individual Performances

James Wilder (Tampa Bay) rushed for 172 yards on 43 carries and scored one touchdown.

Walter Payton (Chicago) rushed for 155 yards on 25 carries and scored one touchdown.

Greg Bell (Buffalo) rushed for 144 yards on 29 carries.

Dan Marino (Miami) completed 24 of 36 passes for 429 yards and three touchdowns.

Tony Eason (New England) completed 28 of 42 passes for 354 yards and three touchdowns.

Mark Duper (Miami) caught eight passes for 164 yards.

Mark Clayton (Miami) caught five passes for 143 yards and one touchdown.

Steve Largent (Seattle) caught eight passes for 130 yards and a touchdown.

Henry Ellard (Los Angeles Rams) returned a punt 83 yards for a touchdown.

Mark Kafentzis (Indianapolis) returned an interception 59 yards for a touchdown.

STANDINGS

AFC East	W	L	T	PF	PA
Miami	5	0	0	164	76
New England	3	2	0	104	115
N.Y. Jets	3	2	0	132	114
Indianapolis	2	3	0	120	139
Buffalo	0	5	0	84	138
AFC Central					
Pittsburgh	3	2	0	122	105
Cleveland	1	4	0	57	97
Cincinnati	0	5	0	93	152
Houston	0	5	0	69	159
AFC West					
Denver	4	1	0	81	71
L.A. Raiders	4	1	0	120	87
Seattle	4	1	0	145	76
Kansas City	3	2	0	94	98
San Diego	3	2	0	147	115
NFC East	**W**	**L**	**T**	**PF**	**PA**
Dallas	4	1	0	93	78
N.Y. Giants	3	2	0	99	111
Washington	3	2	0	124	96
St Louis	2	3	0	146	134
Philadelphia	1	4	0	72	109
NFC Central					
Chicago	3	2	0	93	82
Minnesota	2	3	0	98	129
Tampa Bay	2	3	0	92	112
Detroit	1	4	0	123	131
Green Bay	1	4	0	71	110
NFC West					
San Francisco	5	0	0	132	92
L.A. Rams	3	2	0	104	87
New Orleans	3	2	0	126	113
Atlanta	2	3	0	127	106

WEEK SIX

American Football Conference
Houston 3 at Cincinnati 13
Miami 31 at Pittsburgh 7
New England 17 at Cleveland 16
New York Jets 17 at Kansas City 16
Seattle 14 at Los Angeles Raiders 28

National Football Conference
Atlanta 30 at Los Angeles Rams 28
Minnesota 31 at Tampa Bay 35
New Orleans 7 at Chicago 20
St Louis 31 at Dallas 20
San Francisco 31 at New York Giants 10

Interconference Games
Denver 28 at Detroit 7
Philadelphia 27 at Buffalo 17
San Diego 34 at Green Bay 28
Washington 35 at Indianapolis 7

Interconference Play
AFC 10, NFC 10

▼ *Nick Lowery (Kansas City) became the NFL career accuracy leader with 100 field goals from 131 attempts*

Tight end Kellen Winslow set a club single-game record with 15 pass receptions ▶

Walter Payton duly stepped into unknown territory when, on his 17th carry of the day, he swept round left end for the six yards which took him to the new NFL career rushing record. And he just kept on going, ending up with 154 yards in the game, taking his total of career 100-yard rushing games to 59, again relegating Jim Brown to second best. Furthermore, though in all common sense it was a little premature to think of it, he was on a schedule which would take him beyond even the single-season rushing record of 2,003 yards, held by O.J. Simpson. Chicago's victory over New Orleans halted a two-game losing streak and kept the Bears ahead of Tampa Bay. Elsewhere around the league, the teams were sorting themselves out into a not unfamiliar pecking order. A reassuring victory over Seattle kept the Raiders level with the Broncos on top of the AFC West, and Miami maintained its two-game cushion in the East by inflicting on the Steelers their heaviest home defeat since they moved to Three Rivers Stadium in 1970. Despite suffering this humiliation, the Steelers remained two

STANDINGS

AFC East	W	L	T	PF	PA	NFC East	W	L	T	PF	PA
Miami	6	0	0	195	83	Dallas	4	2	0	113	109
New England	4	2	0	121	131	Washington	4	2	0	159	103
N.Y. Jets	4	2	0	149	130	N.Y. Giants	3	3	0	109	142
Indianapolis	2	4	0	127	174	St Louis	3	3	0	177	154
Buffalo	0	6	0	101	165	Philadelphia	2	4	0	99	126
AFC Central						**NFC Central**					
Pittsburgh	3	3	0	129	136	Chicago	4	2	0	113	89
Cincinnati	1	5	0	106	155	Tampa Bay	3	3	0	127	143
Cleveland	1	5	0	73	114	Minnesota	2	4	0	129	164
Houston	0	6	0	72	172	Detroit	1	5	0	130	159
AFC West						Green Bay	1	5	0	99	144
Denver	5	1	0	109	78	**NFC West**					
L.A. Raiders	5	1	0	148	101	San Francisco	6	0	0	163	102
San Diego	4	2	0	181	143	Atlanta	3	3	0	157	134
Seattle	4	2	0	159	104	L.A. Rams	3	3	0	132	117
Kansas City	3	3	0	110	115	New Orleans	3	3	0	133	133

games clear in the AFC Central, where, with their first win of the season, the Bengals moved into a tie for second place.

In the NFC West, a 37-yard field goal by Mick Luckhurst, as time ran out, gave the Falcons their first away victory over the Rams at the 17th attempt. But there were now three games of daylight between San Francisco and the pack. The 49ers had dispatched the Giants with a display of clinical efficiency that was to become their trade mark by the end of the season – establish a comfortable lead and then play high percentage defensive football. The Giants' loss put a little extra gloss on a handsome 31-20 victory by St Louis over Dallas. The Cardinals moved into a tie with New York behind the 'old firm', Dallas and Washington, who drew level right on cue – they were scheduled to renew their feud on Week Seven.

Stacey Bailey

Outstanding Individual Performances

Walter Payton (Chicago) rushed for 154 yards on 32 carries and scored one touchdown.

Lynn Cain (Atlanta) rushed for 145 yards on 35 carries and scored three touchdowns.

Tommy Kramer (Minnesota) completed 27 of 47 passes for 386 yards and two touchdowns.

Neil Lomax (St Louis) completed 19 of 29 passes for 354 yards and three touchdowns.

Roy Green (St Louis) caught eight passes for 189 yards and two touchdowns, one of which covered 70 yards.

Marcus Allen (Los Angeles Raiders) caught four passes for 173 yards and one touchdown.

James Lofton (Green Bay) caught five passes for 158 yards and one touchdown.

Stacey Bailey (Atlanta) caught seven passes for 158 yards.

Kellen Winslow (San Diego) caught fifteen passes for 157 yards.

WEEK SEVEN

American Football Conference
Buffalo 28 at Seattle 31
Cincinnati 14 at New England 20
Houston 10 at Miami 28
New York Jets 24 at Cleveland 20
San Diego 13 at Kansas City 31

National Football Conference
Chicago 21 at St Louis 38
Dallas 14 at Washington 34
Los Angeles Rams 28 at New Orleans 10
New York Giants 19 at Atlanta 7
Tampa Bay 7 at Detroit 13 (OT)

Intercoference Games
Green Bay 14 at Denver 17
Indianapolis 7 at Philadelphia 16
Minnesota 20 at Los Angeles Raiders 23
Pittsburgh 20 at San Francisco 17

Interconference Play
AFC 13, NFC 11

Riggins takes a breather

Ozzie Newsome is just too quick for Lance Mehl (#56) ▶

In the day's major upset, the Pittsburgh Steelers confounded every known form-line by beating San Francisco in Candlestick Park. A spectacular one-handed interception and 43-yard return by Pittsburgh linebacker Bryan Hinkle set up Gary Anderson's game-winning 21-yard field goal, which came with 1:42 left to play. The 49ers' day was summed up when kicker Ray Wersching subsequently missed a 37-yard field goal which would have taken the game into overtime. Miami remained the NFL's only unbeaten team with a victory over the luckless Houston Oilers who, periodically, were adding an extra notch to their NFL team record for consecutive away defeats – it now stood at 22. All season, it had seemed that Marino had merely to put the ball in the air and someone would catch it, probably for a touchdown. And now, head coach Don Shula turned loose his rookie running back, Joe Carter, who became the first Miami player to rush for over 100 yards in a game since the 1982 season (he gained 105 yards).

There were all the ingredients for a rushing spectacular in the Louisiana Superdome, where coach 'Bum' Phillips unveiled his midweek acquisition from Houston, the great Earl Campbell. However, the combined talents of Campbell and George Rogers came nowhere close to matching the performance of the Rams' Eric Dickerson, who had his best day of the year so far, rushing for 175 yards on just 20 carries. Someone observed that Dickerson, too, had a shot at breaking O.J. Simpson's single-season rushing record – but nobody thought

it possible. A cocktail of John Riggins, Joe Theismann and Calvin Muhammad was just too much for the Cowboys in RFK Stadium, where a 34-14 victory put Washington on top of the NFC Eastern division. Riggins rushed for 165 yards and Theismann threw three touchdown passes, one of which was an 80-yarder to Muhammad, a recent arrival from the Raiders. Another wide receiver, Green Bay's James Lofton, put on a remarkable show, catching 11 passes for 206 yards in a Colorado blizzard. But it was not enough to save his team, which slumped to its sixth consecutive loss.

Outstanding Individual Performances

Eric Dickerson (Los Angeles Rams) rushed for 175 yards on 20 carries.

John Riggins (Washington) rushed for 165 yards on 32 carries.

James Lofton (Green Bay) caught eleven passes for 206 yards and a touchdown.

Ozzie Newsome (Cleveland) caught fourteen passes for 191 yards.

Roy Green (St Louis) caught six passes for 166 yards.

Carlos Carson (Kansas City) caught seven passes for 165 yards.

Calvin Muhammad (Washington) caught five passes for 104 yards, including an 80-yarder for a touchdown.

Gill Byrd (San Diego) returned an interception 99 yards for a touchdown.

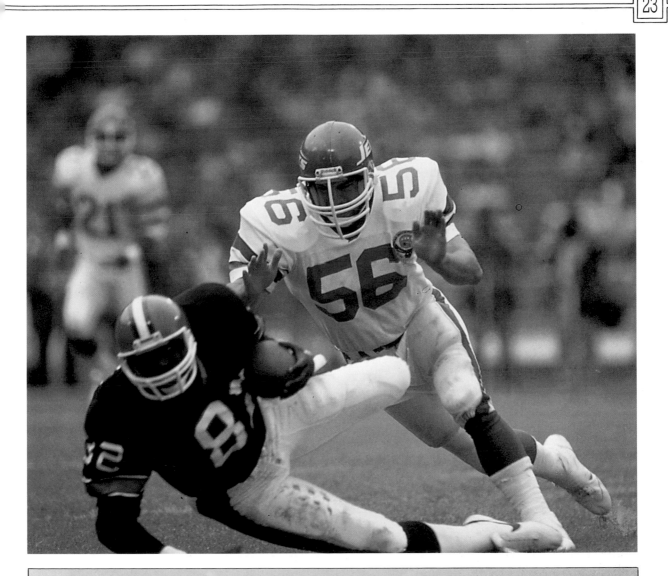

STANDINGS

AFC East	W	L	T	PF	PA	NFC East	W	L	T	PF	PA
Miami	7	0	0	223	93	Washington	5	2	0	193	117
New England	5	2	0	141	145	Dallas	4	3	0	127	143
N.Y. Jets	5	2	0	173	150	N.Y. Giants	4	3	0	128	149
Indianapolis	2	5	0	134	190	St Louis	4	3	0	215	175
Buffalo	0	7	0	129	196	Philadelphia	3	4	0	115	133
AFC Central						**NFC Central**					
Pittsburgh	4	3	0	149	153	Chicago	4	3	0	134	127
Cincinnati	1	6	0	120	175	Tampa Bay	3	4	0	134	156
Cleveland	1	6	0	93	138	Detroit	2	5	0	143	166
Houston	0	7	0	82	200	Minnesota	2	5	0	149	187
						Green Bay	1	6	0	113	161
AFC West						**NFC West**					
Denver	6	1	0	126	92						
L.A. Raiders	6	1	0	171	121	San Francisco	6	1	0	180	122
Seattle	5	2	0	190	132	L.A. Rams	4	3	0	160	127
Kansas City	4	3	0	141	128	Atlanta	3	4	0	164	153
San Diego	4	3	0	194	174	New Orleans	3	4	0	143	161

WEEK EIGHT

American Football Conference
Cleveland 9 at Cincinnati 12
Denver 37 at Buffalo 7
Kansas City 7 at New York Jets 28
Los Angeles Raiders 44 at San Diego 37
Miami 44 at New England 24
Pittsburgh 16 at Indianapolis 17

National Football Conference
Chicago 44 at Tampa Bay 9
Detroit 16 at Minnesota 14
Los Angeles Rams 24 at Atlanta 10
New Orleans 27 at Dallas 30 (OT)
New York Giants 10 at Philadelphia 24
Washington 24 at St Louis 26

Interconference Games
San Francisco 34 at Houston 21
Seattle 30 at Green Bay 24 (played in Milwaukee)

Interconference Play
AFC 14, NFC 12

The Cowboys averted a third consecutive loss with a comeback which was heroic even by their standards. Trailing New Orleans by the score of 27-6, in the final quarter, they recovered to tie the game in regulation time and win it, 30-27, on Rafael Septien's 41-yard field goal, 3:42 into overtime. As a bonus, they regained a share of the lead in the NFC Eastern division for, earlier in the day, Philadelphia had surprisingly beaten the Giants and St Louis had won a nail-biter with Washington. St Louis kicker Neil O'Donoghue, who had been out of touch for most of the game, popped over the winning 21-yard field goal, with just three seconds of regulation time remaining. The Chicago Bears gained a two-game lead in the NFC Central, mauling the Buccaneers 44-9, and the 49ers regrouped to beat Houston and keep ahead of the Rams by the same margin.

Miami quarterback Dan Marino was beginning to murder the opposition and, with four touchdown passes in the victory over New England, now stood only twelve short of equalling the all-time NFL single-season record with, still, half the regular

James Lofton breaks free from cover against Seattle

season remaining. However, the Dolphins had not yet broken clear of the Jets who, though two games back, were proving to be unexpectedly tenacious. Quarterback Pat Ryan, who threw three touchdown passes against Kansas City, had shown himself to be a more-than-adequate replacement for the departed Richard Todd. Cincinnati beat Cleveland in the battle for sole occupancy of second place in the AFC Central division and, though with only two wins, were still in contention. Over in the AFC West, the Raiders scored 44 points but needed an end zone interception by Ted Watts to hold off San Diego. For the Chargers, defeat was all the more bitter for the loss of their All-Pro tight end, Kellen Winslow, whose season ended with severe knee ligament damage.

For two head coaches, Week Eight was the end of the line. Sam Rutigliano was replaced in Cleveland by the team's former defensive coordinator, Marty Schottenheimer. In New England, the Hall of Fame end, Raymond Berry, took over in place of Ron Meyer.

Dan Fouts during his best day of the season

STANDINGS

AFC East	W	L	T	PF	PA
Miami	8	0	0	267	117
N.Y. Jets	6	2	0	201	157
New England	5	3	0	165	189
Indianapolis	3	5	0	151	206
Buffalo	0	8	0	136	233
AFC Central					
Pittsburgh	4	4	0	165	170
Cincinnati	2	6	0	132	184
Cleveland	1	7	0	102	150
Houston	0	8	0	103	234
AFC West					
Denver	7	1	0	163	99
L.A. Raiders	7	1	0	215	158
Seattle	6	2	0	220	156
Kansas City	4	4	0	148	156
San Diego	4	4	0	231	218
NFC East	**W**	**L**	**T**	**PF**	**PA**
Dallas	5	3	0	157	170
St Louis	5	3	0	241	199
Washington	5	3	0	217	143
N.Y. Giants	4	4	0	138	173
Philadelphia	4	4	0	139	143
NFC Central					
Chicago	5	3	0	178	136
Detroit	3	5	0	159	180
Tampa Bay	3	5	0	143	200
Minnesota	2	6	0	163	203
Green Bay	1	7	0	137	191
NFC West					
San Francisco	7	1	0	214	143
L.A. Rams	5	3	0	184	137
Atlanta	3	5	0	174	177
New Orleans	3	5	0	170	191

Outstanding Individual Performances

Eric Dickerson (Los Angeles Rams) rushed for 145 yards on 24 carries and scored one touchdown.

Dan Fouts (San Diego) completed 24 of 45 passes for 410 yards and three touchdowns.

Roy Green (St Louis) caught six passes for 163 yards and two touchdowns, one of which covered 83 yards.

James Lofton (Green Bay) caught five passes for 162 yards and two touchdowns, one of which covered 79 yards.

Steve Cox (Cleveland) kicked a 60-yard field goal.

Kenny Jackson (Philadelphia) caught an 83-yard touchdown pass.

Mitchell Brookins (Buffalo) caught a 70-yard touchdown pass.

WEEK NINE

American Football Conference
Buffalo 7 at Miami 38
Cincinnati 31 at Houston 13
Denver 22 at Los Angeles Raiders 19 (OT)
New York Jets 20 at New England 30
Seattle 24 at San Diego 0

National Football Conference
Detroit 9 at Green Bay 41
Minnesota 7 at Chicago 16
St Louis 34 at Philadelphia 14
San Francisco 33 at Los Angeles Rams 0
Washington 13 at New York Giants 37

Interconference Games
Atlanta 10 at Pittsburgh 35
Indianapolis 3 at Dallas 22
New Orleans 16 at Cleveland 14
Tampa Bay 20 at Kansas City 24

Interconference Play
AFC 16, NFC 14

Kenny Easley homes in on another interception.

In a 38-7 drubbing of Buffalo, Miami's Dan Marino passed for three more touchdowns, two of which were to wide receiver Mark Clayton. The second-year player, Clayton, who entered the season with only six pass receptions to his credit, was making his bid for an NFL single-season record – after nine games, he was averaging one touchdown per game and the record stood at 17. New England came back into contention with a solid 30-20 victory over the Jets. The Patriots could not sensibly hope to catch the Dolphins but there was certainly a wild card spot to play for. There would be no wild cards emerging from the AFC Central division where both the Steelers and the Bengals eased further away from Cleveland. The Broncos confirmed their supremacy over the Raiders and showed a good deal of mettle doing it. Trailing at one stage 19-6, they came back to tie the score in regulation time and won with Rich Karlis's 35-yard field goal as overtime ran out. The Raiders dropped into a tie with Seattle, who had held the Chargers scoreless – and that takes extraordinarily good defense.

Had there been any remaining doubts about the Giants, they were dispelled by a comprehensive 37-13 victory over Washington. The Redskins were never in it. St Louis dealt similarly with Philadelphia to remain in a tie for first place with the Cowboys. If you're going to snap a six-game losing streak there's no better way of doing it than beating a rival of 55 years by the score of 41-9. That's what happened in Green Bay where the Packers made a late attempt to salvage something from the season. The Bears sacked Minnesota quarterback Archie Manning a Chicago team record eleven times in opening up a three-game lead in the NFC Central division. Not since 1971 had the Bears made such a good start to the season. The 49ers, too, were well and truly back on track with their biggest victory over the Rams since winning 35-0 in 1961.

Outstanding Individual Performances

Sammy Winder (Denver) rushed for 126 yards on 34 carries.

Joe Montana (San Francisco) completed 21 of 31 passes for 365 yards and three touchdowns.

Ron Jaworski (Philadelphia) completed 22 of 38 passes for 340 yards and two touchdowns.

Mike Quick (Philadelphia) caught six passes for 170 yards, including a 90-yarder for a touchdown.

Dwayne Woodruff (Pittsburgh) returned a recovered fumble 65 yards for a touchdown.

Steve Largent (Seattle) caught three touchdown passes.

Kenny Easley (Seattle) intercepted three passes.

Tom Flynn (Green Bay) intercepted three passes.

▲ Tony Dorsett (Dallas)

Tom Flynn returning an interception

STANDINGS

AFC East	W	L	T	PF	PA	NFC East	W	L	T	PF	PA
Miami	9	0	0	305	124	Dallas	6	3	0	179	173
New England	6	3	0	195	209	St Louis	6	3	0	275	213
N.Y. Jets	6	3	0	221	187	N.Y. Giants	5	4	0	175	186
Indianapolis	3	6	0	154	228	Washington	5	4	0	230	180
Buffalo	0	9	0	143	271	Philadelphia	4	5	0	153	177
AFC Central						**NFC Central**					
Pittsburgh	5	4	0	200	180	Chicago	6	3	0	194	143
Cincinnati	3	6	0	163	197	Detroit	3	6	0	168	221
Cleveland	1	8	0	116	166	Tampa Bay	3	6	0	163	224
Houston	0	9	0	116	265	Green Bay	2	7	0	178	200
AFC West						Minnesota	2	7	0	170	219
Denver	8	1	0	185	118	**NFC West**					
L.A. Raiders	7	2	0	234	180	San Francisco	8	1	0	247	143
Seattle	7	2	0	244	156	L.A. Rams	5	4	0	184	170
Kansas City	5	4	0	172	176	New Orleans	4	5	0	186	205
San Diego	4	5	0	231	242	Atlanta	3	6	0	184	212

WEEK TEN

American Football Conference
Cleveland 13 at Buffalo 10
Houston 7 at Philadelphia 35
Kansas City 0 at Seattle 45
Miami 31 at New York Jets 17
New England 19 at Denver 26
San Diego 38 at Indianapolis 10

National Football Conference
Atlanta 14 at Washington 27
Green Bay 23 at New Orleans 13
Los Angeles Rams 16 at St Louis 13
New York Giants 19 at Dallas 7
Philadelphia 23 at Detroit 23 (OT)
Tampa Bay 24 at Minnesota 27

Interconference Games
Los Angeles Raiders 6 at Chicago 17
Cincinnati 17 at San Francisco 23

Interconference Play
AFC 16, NFC 16

At the end of an hour's helmet banging at Chicago's Soldier Field, the Bears had increased their lead on top of the NFC Central division to three and a half

Cornerback Dave Brown, an original Seahawk

games, but they had lost starting quarterback Jim McMahon for the rest of the season. The Raiders saw their quarterbacks, one by one, go down and out under the weight of nine Chicago sacks, 4.5 of which were by defensive end Richard Dent. Furthermore, they had slipped dangerously to third place in the AFC West. Seattle had mounted a show of astonishing pass defense against Kansas City, setting an NFL team record by returning four of their six interceptions for touchdowns. For the second week in a row, they held their opponent scoreless. The only comfort for the Raiders came from losses by both New England and the Jets, who were shaping up as competitors for wild card spots. With the Bengals going down after a good battle with San Francisco, Pittsburgh took a giant stride with a resounding 35-7 victory over Houston, whose sequence of consecutive away defeats now extended to 23.

The Canadians would call it a log-jam – football fans called it the NFC Eastern division, where four teams were tied with 6-4 records and the fifth, Philadelphia, was still in touch at 4-5-1, after tying 23-23 with Detroit. Not since 1963, the year of their last title of any kind, had the Giants done the regular season 'double' over Dallas. With several key intra-divisional games remaining, it began to look as if ten victories might be enough to take the division title. Over in the NFC West, the Rams did their wild card chances a great deal of good by knocking off an obvious contender, St Louis. And Eric Dickerson didn't harm his record ambitions with a personal best 208 yards rushing on 21 carries. He needed to average 139 yards over the remaining six games – it was still not quite on.

Outstanding Individual Performances

Eric Dickerson (Los Angeles Rams) rushed for 208 yards on 21 carries.

Boyce Green (Cleveland) rushed for 156 yards on 29 carries.

James Wilder (Tampa Bay) rushed for 146 yards on 30 carries.

Dan Marino (Miami) completed 23 of 42 passes for 422 yards and two touchdowns.

Butch Johnson (Denver) caught nine passes for 156 yards and two touchdowns.

Mark Duper (Miami) caught seven passes for 155 yards.

Richard Dent (Chicago) registered 4.5 quarterback sacks, caused and recovered the same fumble, and had six solo tackles.

Dave Brown (Seattle) intercepted two passes, each of which he returned for touchdowns covering 95 and 58 yards respectively.

STANDINGS

AFC East	W	L	T	PF	PA	NFC East	W	L	T	PF	PA
Miami	10	0	0	336	141	Dallas	6	4	0	186	192
New England	6	4	0	214	235	N.Y. Giants	6	4	0	194	193
N.Y. Jets	6	4	0	238	218	St Louis	6	4	0	288	229
Indianapolis	3	7	0	164	266	Washington	6	4	0	257	194
Buffalo	0	10	0	153	284	Philadelphia	4	5	1	176	200
AFC Central						**NFC Central**					
Pittsburgh	6	4	0	235	187	Chicago	7	3	0	211	149
Cincinnati	3	7	0	180	220	Detroit	3	6	1	191	244
Cleveland	2	8	0	129	176	Green Bay	3	7	0	201	213
Houston	0	10	0	123	300	Minnesota	3	7	0	197	243
AFC West						Tampa Bay	3	7	0	187	251
Denver	9	1	0	211	137	**NFC West**					
Seattle	8	2	0	289	156	San Francisco	9	1	0	270	160
L.A. Raiders	7	3	0	240	197	L.A. Rams	6	4	0	200	183
Kansas City	5	5	0	172	221	New Orleans	4	6	0	199	228
San Diego	5	5	0	269	252	Atlanta	3	7	0	198	239

Chicago defensive end Richard Dent (#95) beating L.A.'s Bruce Davis en route to another quarterback sack

Eric Dickerson in his first 200-yard rushing game in the pros

WEEK ELEVEN

American Football Conference
Buffalo 10 at New England 38
Denver 16 at San Diego 13
Houston 17 at Kansas City 16
Indianapolis 9 at New York Jets 5
Los Angeles Raiders 14 at Seattle 17
Pittsburgh 20 at Cincinnati 22

National Football Conference
Chicago 13 at Los Angeles Rams 29
Dallas 24 at St Louis 17
Detroit 14 at Washington 28
Minnesota 17 at Green Bay 45 (played in Milwaukee)
New Orleans 17 at Atlanta 13
New York Giants 17 at Tampa Bay 20

Interconference Games
Philadelphia 23 at Miami 24
San Francisco 41 at Cleveland 7

Interconference Play
AFC 17, NFC 17

Freddie Solomon safe in the end zone

Gerry Ellis

Miami remained the NFL's only unbeaten team but only just, after a tense finish in the game against Philadelphia. They had come back from 14-0 down to lead 24-17, with time running out. However, a 38-yard touchdown pass from Ron Jaworski to wide receiver Mel Hoover gave Philadelphia the opportunity to take the game into overtime. But rookie Paul McFadden's attempted extra point kick was blocked by Miami defensive end Doug Betters to preserve a one-point victory. New England kept in the hunt with a 38-10 stroll over Buffalo and nosed ahead of the Jets, who sagged to their third straight loss. Cincinnati took closer order in the AFC Central with a 22-20 win over division leaders Pittsburgh, trimming the deficit to two games. And, at last, the Houston Oilers managed a win (away from home too), beating Kansas City 17-16. In the AFC West, Denver came from behind to beat San Diego and Seattle beat the Raiders. Realistically, the Raiders' division title hopes had disappeared – they were now looking at a possible wild card spot.

In the NFC, the Cowboys reasserted themselves over St Louis with a victory which kept them in a tie for first place in the East. They were joined by Washington for whom rookie running back Keith Griffin rushed for 114 yards, and the veteran Otis Wonsley scored three touchdowns, in the victory over Detroit. The Giants continued to defy analysis, losing to the Buccaneers. It was no surprise when San Francisco blew the Browns away but the ease with which Eric Dickerson ran over the NFL's top-rated defense raised a few eyebrows. Rushing for 149 yards on 28 carries and scoring two touchdowns, Dickerson kept the Rams in contention for a wild card spot in the playoffs. The defeat was hardly a death blow to the Bears, who retained a comfortable lead in the NFC Central. Nonetheless, they would do well to keep an eye on the Packers, who had found their rhythm and barbecued Minnesota for their third consecutive victory.

STANDINGS

AFC East	W	L	T	PF	PA	NFC East	W	L	T	PF	PA
Miami	11	0	0	360	164	Dallas	7	4	0	210	209
New England	7	4	0	252	245	Washington	7	4	0	285	208
N.Y. Jets	6	5	0	243	227	N.Y. Giants	6	5	0	211	213
Indianapolis	4	7	0	173	271	St Louis	6	5	0	305	253
Buffalo	0	11	0	163	322	Philadelphia	4	6	1	199	224
AFC Central						**NFC Central**					
Pittsburgh	6	5	0	255	209	Chicago	7	4	0	224	178
Cincinnati	4	7	0	202	240	Green Bay	4	7	0	246	230
Cleveland	2	9	0	136	217	Tampa Bay	4	7	0	207	268
Houston	1	10	0	140	316	Detroit	3	7	1	205	272
AFC West						Minnesota	3	8	0	214	288
Denver	10	1	0	227	150	**NFC West**					
Seattle	9	2	0	306	170	San Francisco	10	1	0	311	167
L.A. Raiders	7	4	0	254	214	L.A. Rams	7	4	0	229	196
Kansas City	5	6	0	188	238	New Orleans	5	6	0	216	241
San Diego	5	6	0	282	268	Atlanta	3	8	0	211	256

Larry Moriarty (#30) sweeps right

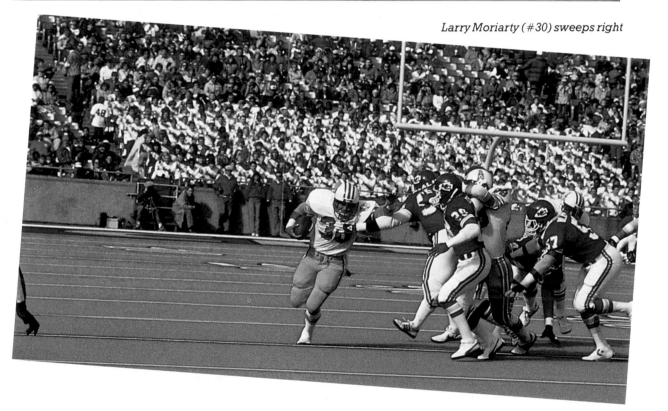

Outstanding Individual Performances

Eric Dickerson (Los Angeles Rams) rushed for 149 yards on 28 carries and scored two touchdowns.

Gerry Ellis (Green Bay) rushed for 107 yards on 10 carries and scored one touchdown.

Lynn Dickey (Green Bay) completed 22 of 40 passes for 303 yards and four touchdowns.

James Lofton (Green Bay) caught four passes for 119 yards, including a 63-yarder for a touchdown.

Freddie Solomon (San Francisco) caught five passes for 105 yards and two touchdowns, one of which covered 60 yards.

Donnell Thompson (Indianapolis) registered 5.0 quarterback sacks.

WEEK TWELVE

American Football Conference
Kansas City 7 at Los Angeles Raiders 17
Miami 28 at San Diego 34 (OT)
New England 50 at Indianapolis 17
New York Jets 20 at Houston 31
Seattle 26 at Cincinnati 6

National Football Conference
Detroit 14 at Chicago 16
Los Angeles Rams 6 at Green Bay 31 (in Milwaukee)
St Louis 10 at New York Giants 16
Tampa Bay 17 at San Francisco 24
Washington 10 at Philadelphia 16

Interconference Games
Cleveland 23 at Atlanta 7
Dallas 3 at Buffalo 14
Minnesota 21 at Denver 42
Pittsburgh 24 at New Orleans 27

Interconference Play
AFC 20, NFC 18

On a day which had more than its share of surprises, Buffalo's victory over Dallas counted as a major shock. Bills rookie running back Greg Bell rushed

Green Bay cornerback Tim Lewis, ready to pounce

for 206 yards, 85 of which were ripped off in scoring the longest rushing touchdown ever yielded by the Dallas defense. Bell also scored Buffalo's second touchdown, on a three-yard pass reception. The Cowboys could muster just three points in reply. The Giants' victory over St Louis and Washington's loss to Philadelphia, made a nonsense of the cosy pattern which had been emerging in the NFC East. Even the Eagles, in fifth place, could still win the division title.

Over on the West coast, Miami's first defeat of the season, in overtime to San Diego, was only a little less unexpected than Buffalo's victory over Dallas. Touchdown passes of 19 and 3 yards from quarterback Dan Fouts to Charlie Joiner and Eric Sievers respectively, brought the Chargers back from 28-14 down, and rookie running back Buford McGee finished the job with a 25-yard touchdown run in the extra period. Four pass receptions by veteran wide receiver Charlie Joiner left him needing just five more to beat Charley Taylor's NFL career record of 649. Elsewhere, the Oilers doubled their tally for the season, severely denting the Jets' playoff ambitions, and the Green Bay Packers continued their return to form (it was their fourth consecutive win) at the expense of the Rams.

San Francisco's victory over Tampa Bay, coupled with the Rams' loss, gave the 49ers at least a wild card spot in the playoffs. The Raiders halted the slide with a 17-7 victory over Kansas City. It was as well for, not only did both Seattle and Denver win but also, New England gave signs of coming into their best form against Indianapolis, where quarterback Tony Eason threw four touchdown passes.

Outstanding Individual Performances

Greg Bell (Buffalo) rushed for 206 yards on 27 carries and scored an 85-yard touchdown.

Eric Dickerson (Los Angeles Rams) rushed for 132 yards on 25 carries.

Dan Fouts (San Diego) completed 37 of 56 passes for 380 yards and four touchdowns.

Gerald Carter (Tampa Bay) caught nine passes for 166 yards and one touchdown.

Eric Sievers (San Diego) caught twelve passes for 119 yards and two touchdowns.

Rod Martin (Los Angeles Raiders) returned a fumble 77 yards for a touchdown, caused a fumble which set up another touchdown, and had a quarterback sack.

Andre Waters (Philadelphia) returned a kickoff 89 yards for a touchdown.

Tim Lewis (Green Bay) returned an interception 99 yards for a touchdown.

STANDINGS

AFC East	W	L	T	PF	PA	NFC East	W	L	T	PF	PA
Miami	11	1	0	388	198	Dallas	7	5	0	213	223
New England	8	4	0	302	262	N.Y. Giants	7	5	0	227	223
N.Y. Jets	6	6	0	263	258	Washington	7	5	0	295	224
Indianapolis	4	8	0	190	321	St Louis	6	6	0	315	269
Buffalo	1	11	0	177	325	Philadelphia	5	6	1	215	234
AFC Central						**NFC Central**					
Pittsburgh	6	6	0	279	236	Chicago	8	4	0	240	192
Cincinnati	4	8	0	208	266	Green Bay	5	7	0	277	236
Cleveland	3	9	0	159	224	Tampa Bay	4	8	0	224	292
Houston	2	10	0	171	336	Detroit	3	8	1	219	288
AFC West						Minnesota	3	9	0	235	330
Denver	11	1	0	269	171	**NFC West**					
Seattle	10	2	0	332	176	*San Francisco	11	1	0	335	184
L.A. Raiders	8	4	0	271	221	L.A. Rams	7	5	0	235	227
San Diego	6	6	0	316	296	New Orleans	6	6	0	243	265
Kansas City	5	7	0	195	255	Atlanta	3	9	0	218	279

* Qualified for playoffs

Buffalo's rookie running back, Greg Bell (#28), ripping into the Cowboys

WEEK THIRTEEN

American Football Conference
Houston 10 at Cleveland 27
Indianapolis 7 at Los Angeles Raiders 21
New York Jets 17 at Miami 28
San Diego 24 at Pittsburgh 52
Seattle 27 at Denver 24

National Football Conference
Chicago 34 at Minnesota 3
Green Bay 28 at Detroit 31
Los Angeles Rams 34 at Tampa Bay 33
Philadelphia 16 at St Louis 17
San Francisco 35 at New Orleans 3

Interconference Games
Atlanta 14 at Cincinnati 35
Buffalo 14 at Washington 41
Kansas City 27 at New York Giants 28
New England 17 at Dallas 20

Interconference Play
AFC 21, NFC 21

On Week Thirteen, three teams clinched division titles, a fourth made certain of reaching the playoffs, one NFL record was broken, another was equalled and two more came under increased threat. In handing the Jets their fifth consecutive loss, the Dolphins clinched the AFC East and, with four touchdown passes on the day, Dan Marino equalled the single-season record of 36. The Bears won their first title of any kind since 1963, the year of their last NFL Championship, and San Francisco wrapped up the NFC West. The Seahawks moved into a tie for first place in the AFC West after a tense struggle with Denver. The Broncos could have tied the score, with 39 seconds remaining in the game, but Karlis's 25-yard field goal attempt hit the uprights. Curiously, even in defeat, the Broncos made certain of reaching the playoffs – at worst they would be in a tie with New England and the Raiders for the second wild card spot and, having previously beaten both these teams, they would go through because of head-to-head superiority in the tie-breaking procedure. The Seahawks, even though in a tie for first place with

Steve Largent

Dave Krieg ▲

Denver, had lost to New England on Week Three and were not yet certain of a playoff berth.

The Chargers were on the wrong end of a 52-24 massacre but their veteran wide receiver, Charlie Joiner, raised his number of career pass receptions to a new NFL record 651. The Rams needed every one of Eric Dickerson's 191 yards rushing to win a thriller against Tampa Bay. Raising his total rushing yardage for the season to 1,643, Dickerson needed to average just 120 yards over the remaining three games for his place in history. Washington wide receiver Art Monk caught eleven passes in the Redskins' 41-14 victory over Buffalo. With 82 on the year, Monk was within striking distance of the NFL single-season record of 101, established by Houston's Charley Hennigan way back in 1964.

Outstanding Individual Performances

Eric Dickerson (Los Angeles Rams) rushed for 191 yards on 28 carries and scored three touchdowns.

Dave Krieg (Seattle) completed 30 of 44 passes for 406 yards and three touchdowns, one of which covered 80 yards.

Steve Largent (Seattle) caught twelve passes for 191 yards and one touchdown.

Carlos Carson (Kansas City) caught five passes for 153 yards and a touchdown.

Cris Collinsworth (Cincinnati) caught six passes for 134 yards and two touchdowns, one of which covered 57 yards.

Art Monk (Washington) caught eleven passes for 104 yards and a touchdown.

Johnie Cooks (Indianapolis) registered 4.5 quarterback sacks.

STANDINGS					
AFC East	**W**	**L**	**T**	**PF**	**PA**
†Miami	12	1	0	416	215
New England	8	5	0	319	282
N.Y. Jets	6	7	0	280	286
Indianapolis	4	9	0	197	342
Buffalo	1	12	0	191	366
AFC Central					
Pittsburgh	7	6	0	331	260
Cincinnati	5	8	0	243	280
Cleveland	4	9	0	186	234
Houston	2	11	0	181	363
AFC West					
*Denver	11	2	0	293	198
Seattle	11	2	0	359	200
L.A. Raiders	9	4	0	292	228
San Diego	6	7	0	340	348
Kansas City	5	8	0	222	283
NFC East	**W**	**L**	**T**	**PF**	**PA**
Dallas	8	5	0	233	240
N.Y. Giants	8	5	0	255	250
Washington	8	5	0	336	238
St Louis	7	6	0	332	285
Philadelphia	5	7	1	231	251
NFC Central					
†Chicago	9	4	0	274	195
Green Bay	5	8	0	305	267
Detroit	4	8	1	250	316
Tampa Bay	4	9	0	257	326
Minnesota	3	10	0	238	364
NFC West					
†San Francisco	12	1	0	370	187
L.A. Rams	8	5	0	269	260
New Orleans	6	7	0	246	300
Atlanta	3	10	0	232	314

† Division Champions
* Qualified for playoffs

Cris Collinsworth hangs on to another pass

WEEK FOURTEEN

American Football Conference
Cincinnati 20 at Cleveland 17 (OT)
Denver 13 at Kansas City 16
Indianapolis 15 at Buffalo 21
Los Angeles Raiders 45 at Miami 34
Pittsburgh 20 at Houston 23 (OT)

National Football Conference
Dallas 26 at Philadelphia 10
New Orleans 21 at Los Angeles Rams 34
Washington 31 at Minnesota 17
San Francisco 35 at Atlanta 17
Tampa Bay 14 at Green Bay 27

Interconference Games
Chicago 7 at San Diego 20
Detroit 17 at Seattle 38
New York Giants 20 at New York Jets 10
St Louis 33 at New England 10

Interconference Play
AFC 23, NFC 23

In the NFC East saga, Philadelphia's loss to Dallas meant the end of their playoff hopes but, outside of that, decision time was deferred for another week. Three thousand miles away, in Los Angeles, the Rams maintained the pace in their bid for a wild card berth in the playoffs with a steady victory over New Orleans. Their one-man offense, Eric Dickerson, eased 149 yards closer to his goal, leaving a balance of 212 yards to be gathered in the last two games – it was all downhill from here. The day's significant action took place in the AFC, where Seattle made certain of a playoff spot, Denver lost again, Cincinnati put Pittsburgh under real pressure and the Raiders, at last, gave us a sample of their brand of big-play football.

Quarterback Dave Krieg threw five touchdown passes as Seattle put Detroit to the sword. The Seahawks went on top of the AFC West following Denver's carbon copy of their defeat on Week Thirteen. Trailing the Chiefs 16-13, the Broncos had the opportunity to tie the score with ten seconds remaining but, again, Karlis hit the upright with his field goal attempt from 42 yards out. On a day reserved for domestic competition in the AFC Central, both games went into overtime. But whereas the Steelers went down to Houston, a 35-yard field goal by Jim Breech gave Cincinnati a victory over Cleveland. Pittsburgh could not now afford one slip since, in the event of a tie at the end of the regular season, Cincinnati's superior intradivisional record would give them the division title. Against the Raiders in the Orange Bowl, Dan Marino surpassed even his previous best, passing for 470 yards and, with the first of his four touchdown passes, established a new single-season NFL record. Before that, however, Raiders cornerback

Seattle's Daryl Turner making a touchdown reception

Mike Haynes had returned the first of two pass interceptions 97 yards for a touchdown. Subsequently, wide receiver Dokie Williams hauled in a 75-yard Marc Wilson pass for a touchdown, and running back Marcus Allen rushed for 155 yards and three touchdowns, the last, a 52-yarder, icing the game when the Dolphins had threatened to steal it.

The Raiders' All-Pro cornerback, Mike Haynes

Dan Marino

Outstanding Individual Performances

Marcus Allen (Los Angeles Raiders) rushed for 155 yards on 20 carries and scored three touchdowns.

Eric Dickerson (Los Angeles Rams) rushed for 149 yards on 33 carries and scored one touchdown.

Dan Marino (Miami) completed 35 of 57 passes for 470 yards and four touchdowns.

Bobby Duckworth (San Diego) caught three passes for 179 yards, including an 88-yarder for a touchdown.

Mike Haynes (Los Angeles Raiders) intercepted two passes, one of which he returned 97 yards for a touchdown.

Lee Williams (San Diego) returned an interception 66 yards for a touchdown.

STANDINGS

AFC East	W	L	T	PF	PA
†Miami	12	2	0	450	260
New England	8	6	0	329	315
N.Y. Jets	6	8	0	290	306
Indianapolis	4	10	0	212	363
Buffalo	2	12	0	212	381
AFC Central					
Pittsburgh	7	7	0	351	283
Cincinnati	6	8	0	263	297
Cleveland	4	10	0	203	254
Houston	3	11	0	204	383
AFC West					
*Seattle	12	2	0	397	217
*Denver	11	3	0	306	214
L.A. Raiders	10	4	0	337	262
San Diego	7	7	0	360	355
Kansas City	6	8	0	238	296

NFC East	W	L	T	PF	PA
Dallas	9	5	0	259	250
N.Y. Giants	9	5	0	275	260
Washington	9	5	0	367	255
St Louis	8	6	0	365	295
Philadelphia	5	8	1	241	277
NFC Central					
†Chicago	9	5	0	281	215
Green Bay	6	8	0	332	281
Detroit	4	9	1	267	354
Tampa Bay	4	10	0	271	353
Minnesota	3	11	0	255	395
NFC West					
†San Francisco	13	1	0	405	204
L.A. Rams	9	5	0	303	281
New Orleans	6	8	0	267	334
Atlanta	3	11	0	249	349

† Division Champions
* Qualified for playoffs

WEEK FIFTEEN

American Football Conference
Buffalo 17 at New York Jets 21
Cleveland 20 at Pittsburgh 23
Miami 35 at Indianapolis 17
San Diego 13 at Denver 16
Seattle 7 at Kansas City 34

National Football Conference
Atlanta 6 at Tampa Bay 23
Green Bay 20 at Chicago 14
Minnesota 7 at San Francisco 51
New York Giants 21 at St Louis 31
Washington 30 at Dallas 28

Interconference Games
Cincinnati 24 at New Orleans 21
Houston 16 at Los Angeles Rams 27
Los Angeles Raiders 24 at Detroit 3
New England 17 at Philadelphia 27

Interconference Play
AFC 25, NFC 25

Joe Montana in determined mood

At the end of Week Fifteen, everything in the NFC East remained to be decided but Washington struck Dallas a blow which, though not mortal, made it virtually obligatory for the Cowboys to beat Miami on Week Sixteen. The Redskins, meanwhile, had one hand on the division title and one foot in the playoffs. The Cardinals underlined their threat by handling the Giants without too much bother, to set up their Week Sixteen match with the Redskins – the winner of that one would take the division title. Eric Dickerson reserved the best performance of his two-year NFL career for the day on which he became the all-time single-season rushing record holder. With 215 yards on 27 carries, Dickerson took his total to 2,007 yards with one game to spare. The Rams' victory over Houston, though not ensuring a playoff spot, left them in a comfortable position.

The Raiders came back from Detroit with the victory that guaranteed a wild card spot in the playoffs. With no hope of winning the division title, they nonetheless had every chance of gaining home-field advantage in the playoffs following Seattle's unexpected loss to Kansas City. Earlier in the season, the Seahawks had grabbed six pass interceptions against the Chiefs and now, in the rematch, Kansas City evened the tally with six of their own. Seattle's loss and Denver's victory over San Diego (this time Karlis did kick the winning field goal with 2:08 remaining) meant that their meeting on the final weekend would decide the destination

of the AFC Western division title – whoever wrote the schedule deserves a bonus. Entering the final week, then, only two NFC playoff spots were decided but in the AFC there was just one place remaining. It would go to the winner of the Central division title. Here was a nice one. If Cincinnati won its final game, the Steelers would have to win theirs to retain the title – all they had to do was travel to Los Angeles and beat the Raiders.

Outstanding Individual Performances

Eric Dickerson (Los Angeles Rams) rushed for 215 yards on 27 carries and scored two touchdowns.

Walter Payton (Chicago) rushed for 175 yards on 35 carries and scored one touchdown.

Dan Marino (Miami) completed 29 of 41 passes for 404 yards and four touchdowns.

Henry Marshall (Kansas City) caught eight passes for 166 yards and one touchdown.

Renaldo Nehemiah (San Francisco) caught six passes for 125 yards, including a 59-yarder for a touchdown.

Cle Montgomery (Los Angeles Raiders) returned a punt 69 yards for a touchdown.

Del Rodgers (Green Bay) returned a kickoff 97 yards for a touchdown.

Bill Pickel (Los Angeles Raiders) registered 3.5 quarterback sacks.

STANDINGS

AFC East	W	L	T	PF	PA	NFC East	W	L	T	PF	PA
†Miami	13	2	0	485	277	Washington	10	5	0	397	283
New England	8	7	0	346	342	Dallas	9	6	0	287	280
N.Y. Jets	7	8	0	311	323	N.Y. Giants	9	6	0	296	291
Indianapolis	4	11	0	229	398	St Louis	9	6	0	396	316
Buffalo	2	13	0	229	402	Philadelphia	6	8	1	268	294
AFC Central						**NFC Central**					
Pittsburgh	8	7	0	374	303	†Chicago	9	6	0	295	235
Cincinnati	7	8	0	287	318	Green Bay	7	8	0	352	295
Cleveland	4	11	0	223	277	Tampa Bay	5	10	0	294	359
Houston	3	12	0	220	410	Detroit	4	10	1	270	378
AFC West						Minnesota	3	12	0	262	446
*Denver	12	3	0	322	227	**NFC West**					
*Seattle	12	3	0	404	251	†San Francisco	14	1	0	456	211
*L.A. Raiders	11	4	0	361	265	L.A. Rams	10	5	0	330	297
Kansas City	7	8	0	272	303	New Orleans	6	9	0	288	358
San Diego	7	8	0	373	271	Atlanta	3	12	0	255	372

† Division Champions
* Qualified for playoffs

Action from the Bears/Packers game. All-Pro Dan Hampton (#99) sacks Green Bay quarterback Rich Campbell

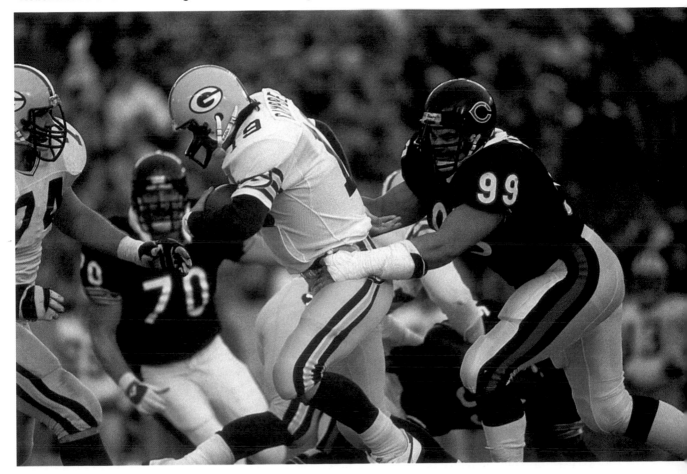

WEEK SIXTEEN

American Football Conference
Buffalo 21 at Cincinnati 52
Cleveland 27 at Houston 20
Denver 31 at Seattle 14
Indianapolis 10 at New England 16
Kansas City 42 at San Diego 21
Pittsburgh 13 at Los Angeles Raiders 7

National Football Conference
Chicago 30 at Detroit 13
Green Bay 38 at Minnesota 14
Los Angeles Rams 16 at San Francisco 19
New Orleans 10 at New York Giants 3
Philadelphia 10 at Atlanta 26
St Louis 27 at Washington 29

Interconference Games
Dallas 21 at Miami 28
New York Jets 21 at Tampa Bay 41

Interconference Play
AFC 26, NFC 26

Roy Green (#81) beating Washington's Darrell Green

Of the NFC East Teams, the Giants made the first bid to reach the playoffs, meeting New Orleans on Saturday. Even they would admit that their performance was most unlike that of a contender and they went down meekly to the Saints. Curiously though, the defeat didn't matter, for, as a result of the Rams' loss to San Francisco on the previous evening, their destiny was in the hands of others. (It was all down to the vagaries of the tie-breaking system.) What was for certain is that, should the Redskins lose to St Louis, the Giants were out, any way you looked at it. The Redskins didn't lose. With Art Monk establishing a new single-season record of 106 pass receptions, they beat St Louis by two points after all had seemed lost. The Redskins retained their division title at the expense of a very gallant loser. That loss eliminated the Cardinals and assured the Rams of a wild card spot. All that remained in the NFC was to settle the final wild card position – it would belong to the Cowboys if they could beat Miami on Monday evening. In the event, despite matching the Dolphins strike-for-strike for most of the game, they lost to a (by now) typical touchdown reception by Miami wide receiver Mark Clayton. The 63-yarder was his third of the game and gave him the new single-season record for touchdown receptions. Dallas was out and the Giants were in.

In the AFC, Denver settled its score with Seattle though the Seahawks would later blame themselves for giving up too many penalties and failing to capitalise on superior possession and field position. Denver was the champion and Seattle was a wild

Neil Lomax

card. Home-field advantage for the AFC Wild Card game would go to the Raiders – if they could beat Pittsburgh. By game time, the Steelers knew they had to win for, earlier in the day, Cincinnati had smashed poor Buffalo, 52-21. And win they did. It wasn't pretty but, after grubbing out a 13-0 lead, they closed down on a Raiders offense which could generate only the one touchdown. The Raiders would have to renew their bid to retain the Super Bowl Championship in Seattle's Kingdome.

Outstanding Individual Performances

Earnest Byner (Cleveland) rushed for 188 yards on 21 carries and scored two touchdowns.

Neil Lomax (St Louis) completed 37 of 46 passes for 468 yards and two touchdowns, one of which covered 75 yards.

Roy Green (St Louis) caught eight passes for 196 yards and two touchdowns, one of which covered 75 yards.

Tim Smith (Houston) caught seven passes for 167 yards.

Stacey Bailey (Atlanta) caught eight passes for 140 yards.

Ottis Anderson (St Louis) caught twelve passes for 124 yards.

Art Monk (Washington) caught eleven passes for 136 yards and two touchdowns.

Tampa Bay running back James Wilder (#32) striving for a few extra yards against the Jets

STANDINGS

AFC East	W	L	T	PF	PA	NFC East	W	L	T	PF	PA
†Miami	14	2	0	513	298	†Washington	11	5	0	426	310
New England	9	7	0	362	352	*N.Y. Giants	9	7	0	299	301
N.Y. Jets	7	9	0	332	364	St Louis	9	7	0	423	345
Indianapolis	4	12	0	239	414	Dallas	9	7	0	308	308
Buffalo	2	14	0	250	454	Philadelphia	6	9	1	278	320
AFC Central						**NFC Central**					
†Pittsburgh	9	7	0	387	310	†Chicago	10	6	0	325	248
Cincinnati	8	8	0	339	339	Green Bay	8	8	0	390	309
Cleveland	5	11	0	250	297	Tampa Bay	6	10	0	335	380
Houston	3	13	0	240	437	Detroit	4	11	1	283	408
AFC West						Minnesota	3	13	0	276	484
†Denver	13	3	0	353	241	**NFC West**					
*Seattle	12	4	0	418	282	†San Francisco	15	1	0	475	227
*L.A. Raiders	11	5	0	368	278	*L.A. Rams	10	6	0	346	316
Kansas City	8	8	0	314	324	New Orleans	7	9	0	298	361
San Diego	7	9	0	394	413	Atlanta	4	12	0	281	382

† Division Champions
* Wild Card

WEEK SEVENTEEN – WILD CARD WEEKEND

AFC   Los Angeles Raiders 7 at Seattle 13

Seattle is one of the few clubs which can point to a series record close to par with the Raiders – they entered this game with seven wins against eight losses in a rivalry which dates back to 1977. More than this, however, they had a score to settle – in last year's AFC Championship Game, they were humiliated 30-14. In more ways than one then, the AFC Wild Card game was a chance to get even. Surprisingly, with wide receivers Steve Largent and Daryl Turner at his disposal, Seattle quarterback Dave Krieg passed only sparingly, and of the ten he attempted, only four were completed. But one was to Turner, who beat the Raiders All-Pro cornerback, Lester Hayes, to latch onto a 26-yarder for the opening touchdown after 10:41 of the second quarter. Meanwhile, Seattle running back Dan Doornink was pounding away en route to his best day in the pros. Norm Johnson's field goals of 35 and 44 yards extended the lead to 13-0 and though Marcus Allen hauled in a 46-yard touchdown pass on one of the few occasions Plunkett was given time

to set up, with just over five minutes to go, there would be no dramatic Raiders comeback this time – Kenny Easley's interception of a late desperation pass by Plunkett saw to that.

NFC
New York Giants 16 at Los Angeles Rams 13

Losses in their last two regular season games could have done little for the Giants' confidence. Moreover, during the season, the Rams had given them a 33-12 licking. But it is a measure, both of Bill Parcells' coaching and the New Yorkers' team spirit, that they regrouped to pull off a surprising victory over the powerhouse Rams, in Anaheim Stadium. The key, of course, was to stop Eric Dickerson and, whilst they didn't exactly achieve that, they restricted him to 107 yards rushing and a longest single gain of 24 yards. The Giants, too, found the going hard against a Rams defense which kept them to just 40 yards rushing and sacked quarterback Phil Simms four times. But they took advantage of their opportunities, notably to score their only touchdown nine plays after recovering a Dickerson fumble on the Rams 23-yard line. Dickerson made amends, and appeared to have sparked a revival, with a 14-yard touchdown

Seattle's Jacob Green (#79) and Kenny Easley ▶

Seattle head coach Chuck Knox

Lawrence Taylor, a fearsome sight

run in the third quarter that left the Rams trailing 13-10. Haji-Sheikh's third field goal widened the gap to six points but it didn't look enough when the Rams subsequently lined up on first-and-goal on the Giants 7-yard line. Once more, however, the Giants barred the way and the Rams had to settle for a field goal. One last chance for the Rams came to nought when the Giants' All-Pro linebacker, Lawrence Taylor, forced a fourth-down fumble, deep in Los Angeles territory.

Outstanding Individual Performances

Dan Doornink (Seattle) rushed for 126 yards on 29 carries.

Eric Dickerson (Los Angeles Rams) rushed for 107 yards on 23 carries and scored one touchdown.

Ali Haji-Sheikh (New York Giants) was successful on all three field goal attempts.

Zeke Mowatt (New York Giants) caught seven passes for 73 yards.

WEEK EIGHTEEN –
DIVISIONAL PLAYOFFS
American Football Conference

Seattle 10 at Miami 31

Miami lived through a few first-half scares before overcoming the Seahawks and gaining revenge for their loss at the same stage last year. The Seahawks came with a pass defense rated best in the entire league for interceptions, and safety John Harris showed why by picking off two of Miami quarterback Dan Marino's first-half attempts. But the remarkable second-year player brushes that kind of thing aside and, even though less commanding than usual, still ended the day with three touchdown passes. The Seahawks never could take advantage of Miami's suspect rushing defense but quarterback Dave Krieg had little difficulty completing his passes, and even exceeded Marino's best on the day with a 56-yard touchdown heave to wide receiver Steve Largent. But that score, which brought Seattle to within four points at 14-10 down, was to be their last success. Third-quarter touchdown receptions by Bruce Hardy and Mark Clayton had already made the game safe long before Uwe von Schamann's field goal in the final period.

Pittsburgh 24 at Denver 17

The relentless rushing of Walter Abercrombie and Frank Pollard, a composed performance from quarterback Mark Malone (after two early fumbles)

and, of course, typical Pittsburgh fighting spirit, brought the Steelers an upset victory in Mile High Stadium. They were helped by an out-of-form Denver quarterback, John Elway, who might have punished Pittsburgh errors more severely. And he would wish to forget the two critical pass interceptions, one deep in Pittsburgh territory, the other which was returned down to the Denver two-yard line and led to the winning touchdown plunge. Just before the latter, Pittsburgh kicker Gary Anderson had failed on a 27-yard field goal attempt which would have broken a 17-17 deadlock. But the Steelers did not pass up the second opportunity with Frank Pollard scoring the winning touchdown, his second of the game, to take them into their seventh AFC Championship Game.

◀ *Washington's John Riggins (#44) held up by Richard Dent (#95) and Dan Hampton*

Steve Watson

National Football Conference

New York Giants 10 at San Francisco 21

At the end of this game, the 49ers could look back with relief at an opening burst which produced two touchdowns in the first seven minutes for, beyond that, they were given as much as they could handle by the wild-card Giants who refused to give up. At one time, the Giants even threatened to overhaul their more fancied opponents. Linebacker Harry Carson had just returned an interception 14 yards for a touchdown and they trailed by only four points, still in the first half. But 49ers quarterback Joe Montana needed only five plays from scrimmage to extend the lead, passing 29 yards for a touchdown to wide receiver Freddie Solomon. That was the last time either defense would crack, though the 49ers squandered more than one second-half opportunity.

Chicago 23 at Washington 19

In a tense struggle at Washington's RFK Stadium, the Bears took full advantage of all their chances to open up a lead, and then played heroic defense to keep out the Redskins. With starting quarterback Steve Fuller clearly nursing his suspect shoulder, running back Walter Payton put his arm to good use, throwing for the Bears' first touchdown, a 19-yard halfback option pass to tight end Pat Dunsmore. But Fuller was later able to pick out Willie Gault with a short pass, which the wide receiver turned into a 75-yard touchdown play. Again, he found Dennis McKinnon with a 16-yard pass, raising the score to 23-10. Inbetween times, Washington's John Riggins had scored on a one-yard dive and he went in again, from the two-yard line, bringing the Redskins to within six points with five seconds remaining in the third quarter. But an intentional two-point safety was all they could gather in the final quarter as the Bears held on and earned the right to play in their first championship game of any kind since 1963.

Outstanding Individual Performances

Walter Payton (Chicago) rushed for 104 yards on 24 carries.

Joe Montana (San Francisco) completed 25 of 39 passes for 309 yards and three touchdowns.

Steve Watson (Denver) caught eleven passes for 177 yards and one touchdown.

Art Monk (Washington) caught ten passes for 122 yards.

Willie Gault (Chicago) caught a 75-yard touchdown pass.

Rich Milot (Washington) registered 3.5 quarterback sacks.

Richard Dent (Chicago) registered 3.0 quarterback sacks.

WEEK NINETEEN –
CONFERENCE CHAMPIONSHIPS
American Football Conference

Pittsburgh 28 at Miami 45

The Pittsburgh Steelers did everything one might reasonably expect of a championship contender. They scored a touchdown in each of the four quarters, they didn't commit many errors, they outrushed their opponents and didn't trail by much in the passing statistics. But they never solved the problems presented by Miami quarterback Dan Marino, who established a new AFC Championship Game record with four touchdown passes and fell only 12 short of Dan Fouts' playoff record of 433 yards passing. Marino exercised his arm with a 40-yard pass to Mark Clayton for the opening touchdown and, after Rich Erenberg's 7-yard touchdown run had brought the teams level at 7-7, he completed key passes to Clayton and Nathan to place von Schamann in position for his 26-yard field goal. There was a moment of minor crisis when Pittsburgh wide receiver John Stallworth caught a 65-yard touchdown pass – the Steelers led 14-10. However, it took less than one and a half minutes for Miami to reply with Mark Duper's 41-yard touchdown reception. And in even shorter time (under a minute), they were a further seven points in front after Tony Nathan had capitalised on Lyle Blackwood's pass interception, by scoring from the two-yard line. Duper's second touchdown reception of the game, 1:48 into the second half, stretched the lead to 31-14 – the Dolphins were almost out of sight. Stallworth's second touchdown reception brought them into focus but two more time-consuming Miami touchdowns had settled the issue long before Wayne Capers' last-minute consolation score.

National Football Conference

Chicago 0 at San Francisco 23

The likelihood always was that there would be few points scored when San Francisco entertained Chicago. The Bears had given up the fewest yards in the league and, in the same company, the 49ers had conceded the fewest points. On offense, the Bears were expecting to be outgunned at quarterback but their rushing attack was more productive even than that of the Eric Dickerson-led Rams. They were reasonably satisfied, then, to be trailing only 6-0 at the end of the first half. Joe Montana had driven his offense down to the Bears' five-, two- and four-yard lines, the first three times he had the ball. But San Francisco had come away with just six points from two Ray Wersching field goals. One big play would

put Chicago in front. But it never came as the 49ers defense repeatedly denied Chicago on first-down plays, forcing quarterback Steve Fuller to chance his arm – a risky business against a ball-hawking 49ers secondary. 49ers running back Wendell Tyler scored on a nine-yard run after 6:33 of the third quarter, making the score 13-0. It stimulated a promising Chicago response which saw wide receiver Dennis McKinnon catch three first-down passes. But they advanced no closer than the San Francisco 22-yard line before back-pedalling under the pressure of sacks by Dwaine Board and Gary Johnson. Wide receiver Freddie Solomon's 10-yard touchdown reception came 3:45 into the final quarter, at which time the Bears were forced into playing four-down football. And it was after they had failed to gain the necessary yards that Wersching kicked the 34-yard field goal which completed the scoring.

Outstanding Individual Performances

Dan Marino (Miami) completed 21 of 32 passes for 421 yards and four touchdowns.

Mark Malone (Pittsburgh) completed 20 of 36 passes for 312 yards and three touchdowns.

Mark Duper (Miami) caught five passes for 148 yards.

John Stallworth (Pittsburgh) caught four passes for 111 yards and two touchdowns, one of which covered 65 yards.

Tony Nathan (Miami) caught eight passes for 114 yards.

Chicago's Walter Payton (#34) rushing for some of his 92 yards, in vain, against the 49ers ▶

◀ *Dan Marino drops back*

Mark Duper

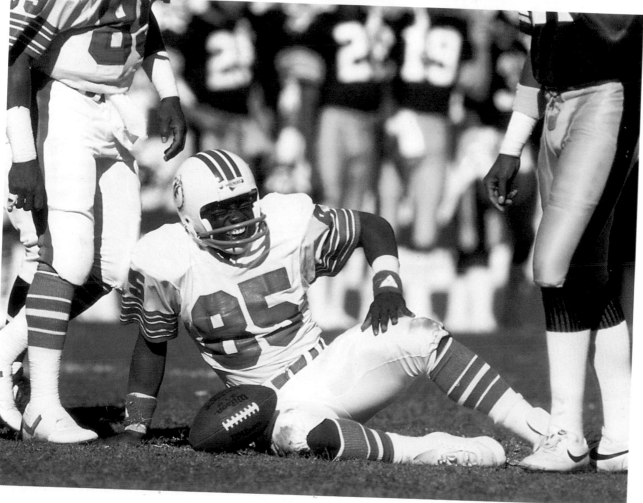

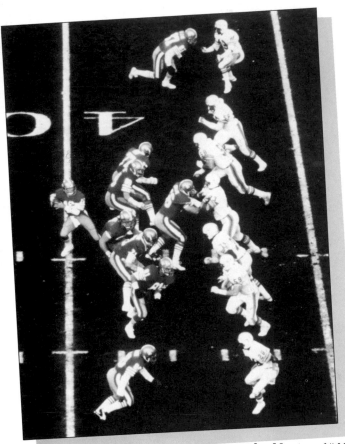

Joe Montana (#16)

Roger Craig tackled by William Judson

SUPER BOWL XIX

San Francisco 49ers 38 – Miami Dolphins 16

Palo Alto, California, January 20th, 1985

In 1984, his first full season as a starter, Miami's Dan Marino had rewritten the manual on quarterback play. The first and only quarterback in NFL history to pass for over 5,000 yards on the year, he threw for 48 touchdowns, banishing the old record by the enormous margin of twelve. The opposition knew he was coming, but no-one had yet figured a way of stopping him. One way might be to attack the problem at source – sack him before he could pass. But that had proved unsuccessful, protected as he was by an offensive line featuring the two Pro Bowlers, right guard Ed Newman and center Dwight Stephenson. He had been sacked just 14 times compared with the next best of 27 given up by Miami's Super Bowl XIX opponents, the 49ers. Thriving on a continuous stream of pin-point passes, the second-year wide receiver, Mark Clayton, had quickly risen to the class of his partner, Mark Duper, and that was the class of superstar. Clayton, too, had etched his name in the record books with an NFL all-time best 18 touchdown receptions in the regular season. The Dolphins' rushing game was less productive than many around the league and served rather to amplify the passing offense, with Tony Nathan an ever-present danger in the medium range. In partnership with Woody Bennett he was

not expected to be a danger when it came to trench warfare.

But the latter kind of game was never likely to develop for, like Miami's Don Shula, San Francisco's well-respected head coach, Bill Walsh, had built an expressive offense around his special star, quarterback Joe Montana. Though not as prolific as Marino, Montana has few equals when it comes to reading defenses. He had worked his way around, through or over the opposition with little difficulty in the regular season. Some said that he should have put the Giants away earlier than he did in the divisional playoffs, and he was careless at times against Chicago in the NFC Championship Game. There were no doubts, however, that he was a winner. Furthermore, he had experienced all this before and emerged as the MVP when quarterbacking the 49ers to victory in Super Bowl XVI. He did have some advantages over his Miami counterpart. The pairing of Wendell Tyler and Roger Craig, at running back, would surely create problems for a Miami defense against the rush which rated dead last in the NFL (yards conceded per carry). When it came to stopping Marino, the 49ers would present a bewildering variety of front-seven formations and players (they could almost perm any seven players from eleven). And after the pass rush had slowed the man down, he would face the problem of beating a defensive secondary which had remained unchanged since performing with distinction in Super Bowl XVI.

By game time, the pundits had installed San Francisco as favourites by anywhere from two to four points. In other words, they felt that San Francisco were the better team but were scared stiff of what Marino might do.

THE GAME

Scoring By Quarters

1st Quarter
Miami: von Schamann, 37-yard field goal with 7:24 remaining.
San Francisco 0 – Miami 3
San Francisco: Monroe, 33-yard pass from Montana; Wersching kick with 3:12 remaining.
San Francisco 7 – Miami 3
Miami: Dan Johnson, 2-yard pass from Marino; von Schamann kick with 0:45 remaining.
San Francisco 7 – Miami 10

2nd Quarter
San Francisco: Craig, 8-yard pass from Montana; Wersching kick with 11:34 remaining.
San Francisco 14 – Miami 10
San Francisco: Montana, 6-yard run; Wersching kick with 6:58 remaining.

Miami's Doug Betters fails to stop Montana passing

San Francisco 21 – Miami 10
San Francisco: Craig, 2-yard run; Wersching kick with 2:05 remaining.
San Francisco 28 – Miami 10
Miami: von Schamann, 31-yard field goal with 0:12 remaining.
San Francisco 28 – Miami 13
Miami: von Schamann, 30-yard field goal with 0:00 remaining.
San Francisco 28 – Miami 16

3rd Quarter
San Francisco: Wersching, 27-yard field goal with 10:12 remaining.
San Francisco 31 – Miami 16
San Francisco: Craig, 16-yard pass from Montana; Wersching kick with 6:18 remaining.
San Francisco 38 – Miami 16

'This is one of the best teams of all time,' said the victorious head coach, Bill Walsh, whilst Don Shula reflected, 'Offensively, it was our poorest game. . . . We hadn't been stopped all year, but we were stopped today.'

It would be difficult to dispute the words of either man after a 49ers performance which left Miami in disarray and the record books in tatters. The Dolphins had started out in fine style and, despite leading by only three points at the end of the first

quarter, had done enough to suggest that the game would be one of those which went 'down to the wire', as they say. In that quarter, Marino completed nine of ten passes, including a key 25-yarder to set up the first field goal, and all five attempts in a 70-yard drive culminating in Dan Johnson's two-yard touchdown reception. But then it all fell apart. Joe Montana had already exposed a weakness in the Miami defense, with a 15-yard scramble in the 49ers' first touchdown drive. He did it again, this time scrambling for 19 yards, in the drive which led to Roger Craig's 8-yard touchdown reception. All told, he went on to gain 59 yards rushing, a Super Bowl record for a quarterback. In addition he established records for most yards passing (331), career completion percentage (66.7), lowest interception percentage (0.00 – he shares this with the Raiders' Jim Plunkett) and most attempts in a single game without being intercepted (35).

Miami's fading prospects were given a boost when slack play by the 49ers allowed von Schamann to kick a field goal as time ran out in the first half. That brought the Dolphins to within two touchdowns. However, it was their last act of defiance as, gradually, the 49ers defense took over (they sacked Marino four times and intercepted two of his passes).

49ers running back Roger Craig established a single-game record with three touchdowns and must have been considered for the MVP award. However, it went to Joe Montana, as much, one felt, for his field-generalship as for the records he established.

Marino did not go empty-handed – he established records for most passing attempts (50) and completions (29), and perhaps more than these, he impressed 49ers coach Walsh, who proffered the words of warning, 'Marino will have his day.'

◀ Stanford Stadium

▲ Ronnie Lott (#42)
smothers Mark Clayton

Bubba Paris (#77)
wards off Kim
Bokamper (#58)

ANATOMY OF SUPER BOWL XIX
QUARTER BY QUARTER

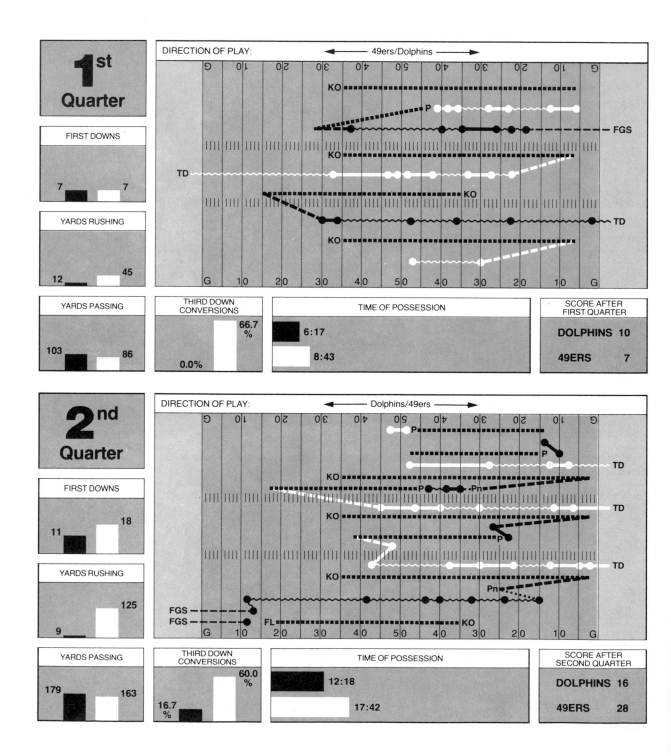

1st Quarter

DIRECTION OF PLAY: ←— 49ers/Dolphins —→

FIRST DOWNS
7 — 7

YARDS RUSHING
12 — 45

YARDS PASSING
103 — 86

THIRD DOWN CONVERSIONS
66.7%
0.0%

TIME OF POSSESSION
6:17
8:43

SCORE AFTER FIRST QUARTER
DOLPHINS 10
49ERS 7

2nd Quarter

DIRECTION OF PLAY: ←— Dolphins/49ers —→

FIRST DOWNS
11 — 18

YARDS RUSHING
9 — 125

YARDS PASSING
179 — 163

THIRD DOWN CONVERSIONS
60.0%
16.7%

TIME OF POSSESSION
12:18
17:42

SCORE AFTER SECOND QUARTER
DOLPHINS 16
49ERS 28

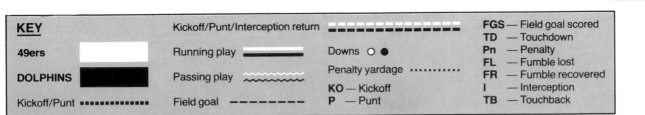

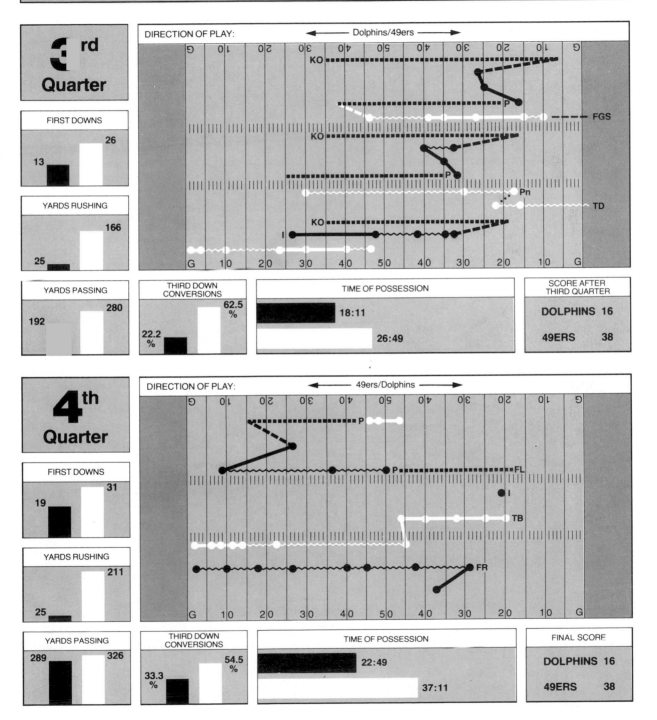

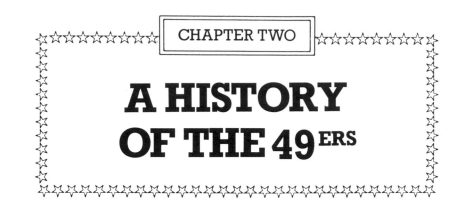

CHAPTER TWO

A HISTORY OF THE 49ERS

In early June of 1944, the Allied armies were consolidating their landings along the coast of Normandy and, even though there were still many battles to be fought, victory in the Second World War was in sight. There was a feeling of euphoria. Around the world, people were making plans, in readiness for the era of prosperity which peace would surely bring.

For over a year before then, a group of visionaries from cities across the United States had been making their own plans and, coincidentally, in that same June, they and other interested parties met in St Louis, Missouri. One man was in the lumber transporting business; another was in oil. Arthur McBride owned a fleet of taxicabs; Don Ameche was a Hollywood filmstar and Arch Ward was the disgruntled sports editor of the *Chicago Tribune*.

It was a long-standing friendship between Ameche and Ward which had led to the meeting in the first place. Ward was a man of some influence with the National Football League. It was Ward who had organized the annual Chicago All-Star Game, which matched the NFL Champion with a team made up of the best players in college football. (Beginning in 1934, there were 42 All-Star Games. There was no game in 1974 and the series ended in 1976.) He had even been proposed for the post of NFL Commissioner in 1940 and again in 1941. After declining the opportunity for the second time, he suggested that Elmer Layden be given the job – and he was. That's the measure of Ward's influence.

Imagine his anger when he was unable to obtain an NFL franchise for his best mate, Ameche, after repeated attempts. 'Right . . .' he said, '. . . let's organize our own league.'

The new league would begin play once the war had ended and would be known as the All-America Football Conference. The name was appropriate since it would be the first pro football organization which stretched across the USA,

though, by the time they started operating, the NFL's Rams had moved to Los Angeles from Cleveland.

You'd have to say that Ameche really did want a place in pro football – his team, in Los Angeles, was nicknamed the 'Dons'. The Oilman, James F. Brueil, of Buffalo, had shown more than a passing interest in obtaining an NFL franchise (he had deposited $25,000 with the NFL) but chose to enter the AAFC with his 'Bisons'. McBride's company was based in the city of Cleveland and so would be his 'Browns', though, at that time, they hadn't yet been given a nickname. Tony Morabito was the man in the lumber business, and he was from San Francisco.

Though Morabito can fairly be called the team's founding father, at the time he was in partnership with two others and it was one of these, either Allen

Frankie Albert

Current star quarterback Joe Montana

Tony Morabito

E. Sorrell or E.J. Turre (no-one is sure which), who thought of the team nickname, 'Forty-Niners'. It commemorated the time, 1849, when the city of San Francisco was the jumping off point for tens of thousands of adventurers who went out in search of gold. One of these wild men was depicted in the team's first emblem, which is described as being, 'A booted prospector with lumberjack shirt, checkered pants, hat blown off, moustache and hair askew, splayed feet and pair of six-shooters in full fire.' 'He was drunk,' a subsequent President of the club, Lou Spadia, confirmed.

Across the USA, more than one observer thought that the men involved in the AAFC were in the same state of intoxication and viewed their prospects with scorn. NFL Commissioner Layden didn't hide his feelings and, after Morabito had borrowed $100,000 to buy out his partners, in 1947, a well-known sportscaster, Harry Wismer, was particularly cruel when he said, 'There's this nut with a hearing aid in San Francisco who is putting his own money into his damn team.' He was referring to Morabito, who was partially deaf. Some years later, Wismer tried his own hand at owning a pro football team, when he obtained an AFL franchise for New York City (the team later became known as the Jets). In 1962, the team's third season, he went broke.

Perhaps more than any other AAFC owner, Morabito was determined to succeed. He was the son of an immigrant father, whose business had failed during the Great Depression. Tony had worked himself up from an ordinary lorry driver to ownership of a transport company. He had a formula for success. Furthermore, he had been rebuffed by the NFL on the two occasions he had tried to obtain a franchise for San Francisco. There is little doubt that he took the rejections personally.

When it came to assembling his squad for the inaugural 1946 season, he went to war against the NFL. All told, twelve players on his first squad had previously been with NFL teams. One of them, returning serviceman Norm Standlee, had been outstanding in his only year in the NFL, as a rookie fullback for the Chicago Bears in 1941. For the quarterback position, he acquired the diminutive (5ft 9in) Frankie Albert, who had been given his chance at Stanford University by the innovative Clark Shaughnessy. Morabito's master stroke was to lure Lawrence T. 'Buck' Shaw away from Santa Clara (a University in the San Francisco area) and into pro football. Shaw was regarded as one of the top ten college coaches in the nation. He brought five former Santa Clara players with him, including the prolific pass receiver, Alyn Beals.

It's interesting to look at the final standings for that first season.

Eastern Division	W	L	T
N.Y. Yankees	10	3	1
Brooklyn Dodgers	3	10	1
Buffalo Bisons	3	10	1
Miami Seahawks	3	11	0
Western Division	**W**	**L**	**T**
Cleveland Browns	12	2	0
San Francisco 49ers	9	5	0
Los Angeles Dons	7	5	2
Chicago Rockets	5	6	3

In the Western division, for three seasons, the final order of teams remained the same and even in the AAFC's final season, 1949, when the teams were grouped into one division, Cleveland beat San Francisco into second place. The 49ers were always competitive and, in the first of two 1949 meetings with the Browns, scored 56 points, a total which has never been exceeded by any other team against Cleveland. But they never did dethrone the Browns, who went on to win all four AAFC Championships.

By the end of the four-year lifetime of the AAFC, the Browns were quite a team. Arthur 'Mickey' McBride, their original owner, was a great lad – he looked after his players. If they couldn't make the roster, rather than coldly discarding them, he gave them jobs, driving his taxicabs around Cleveland. Of course, if he was short of a player, he had a ready-made squad of reserves, driving his cars. This group of reserves has since become known as the 'Taxi Squad'. He had gathered together several outstanding players. Six of the 1946 squad have subsequently been elected to the Pro Football Hall of Fame. They are quarterback Otto Graham, tackle-kicker Lou Groza, running back Marion Motley, guard Bill Willis, center Frank Gatski and end Dante Lavelli. Cleveland's original head coach, Paul Brown, after whom the team was nicknamed, also is in the Hall of Fame.

The 49ers weren't quite that well-blessed with talent but Beals was selected to the AAFC all-star team (the equivalent of being a consensus all-pro in the NFL) three times out of a possible four, and in 1948 the judges were unable to separate quarterbacks Albert and Otto Graham, and they shared the title of AAFC co-Most Valuable Player. It was in 1948 that the 49ers acquired a punishing running back by the name of Joe Perry. By the end of 1949, he too had become an all-star. All told, 49ers players occupied four of the eleven places on the 1949 AAFC all-star squad. At least the 49ers' claim to be second-best was undisputed.

When the hitherto rival leagues, the NFL and the AAFC, came around to settling their differences, in time for the 1950 season, the 49ers were one of just three former AAFC teams accepted for membership of the expanded NFL. The third team, the Baltimore Colts, is connected only in name with that of the current NFL team which plays in Indianapolis.

San Francisco and Baltimore were placed in the National Conference, joining the likes of Detroit, Green Bay, the Los Angeles Rams and the Chicago Bears. Life in the NFL was never going to be easy – and for twenty seasons it wasn't. But there were many exciting moments and, once or twice, they came close to winning a title. Despite bringing together some of the game's all-time great players, however, team honours remained exasperatingly elusive. As a long-standing devotee once remarked to me, 'In those days you had to have a sense of humour to be a 49ers fan.' Some fans went further – they once threw beer cans.

The first of their truly outstanding gridiron heroes, running back Joe Perry, was already on the squad. Leo Nomellini, an earth-moving offensive tackle, was drafted to provide the blocking in 1950. Quarterback Y.A. Tittle came from the Baltimore Colts after that organization had folded at the end of the 1950 season. Then, in 1952, came running back Hugh McElhenny. In 1954, running back John Henry Johnson arrived from Pittsburgh to complete what most experts described as, potentially, the most awesome offensive backfield in pro football. Collectively, Tittle, Perry, McElhenny and Johnson became known as the 'Million Dollar Backfield'.

Hugh McElhenny (#39) with Joe Perry

Over a fourteen-year NFL career, Perry rushed for 8,378 yards at an average of 4.8. He was the first man to rush for over 1,000 yards in consecutive seasons (1953 and 1954). After the first of these, owner Morabito gave him a bonus cheque for $5,090, which was $5 for every yard. Nicknamed 'the Jet' for his speed, Perry was also a very tough man – in 1954, he played with a specially constructed face mask to protect his broken jaw.

McElhenny never did rush for 1,000 yards in a season but came close, with 916 yards in 1956, and was well on the way in 1954, when he was stopped with a shoulder dislocation after gaining 515 yards at the astonishing average of 8.0 per carry. But he will be remembered more as a brilliant open-field runner; many would assert him to be the best the game has ever seen. With an uncanny instinct for the impending tackle, direction meant nothing to him. He'd run across the field and even back, towards his own goal line, often beating the same players more than once, before breaking clear for yet another big-play touchdown. On his first carry as a 49er, in the 1952 preseason, he took a pitchout from Albert and ran 60 yards for a touchdown. It didn't matter that the play wasn't in coach Shaw's book, McElhenny just made it up as he went along. In the fourth game of the regular season, he scored three touchdowns, one on a 94-yard punt return, and had two others disallowed for infractions by his team-mates. After that game, Albert nicknamed him 'The King'. Injuries restricted his appearances and, in retrospect, he stayed on the gridiron a couple of seasons too long as, sadly, the great ones often do. Even so, he gained his 5,281 career rushing yards at the average of 4.7 per carry. In addition, he caught passes for 3,247 yards at the average of 12.3, a figure remarkably high for a running back, returned 83 kickoffs at an average of 23.1 yards and, in total, scored 60 touchdowns.

Tittle was a good one but, it's fair to say, he had his best years when with the New York Giants from 1961 to 1964. (When he retired, the NFL career passing yardage record of 28,339 went with him.) However, one of many memories which will remain of his ten-year stay in San Francisco, was that of his partnership with R.C. Owens, a rookie end in 1957. Obviously feeling rather bored at practice, early in the regular season, Tittle put an aimless pass 'up for grabs', as they would say in today's parlance. The 6ft 5in Owens simply outjumped everyone and came down with the ball. That was the first ever 'Alley-Oop' pass, as assistant coach 'Red' Hickey named it. It was an exciting, high-risk play, but that was the style of the 49ers – and that's why it found its way into the playbook.

Johnson, too, reserved his finest years for the

Lions, whom he joined in 1957, and later, the Steelers (1960-65). He's the only one of the 1954 backfield foursome who has not found his way into the Pro Football Hall of Fame.

The sad memory of 1957 was the death of owner Morabito, who succumbed to a heart attack during a home game against the Chicago Bears. The grief-stricken players, who heard the news midway through the third quarter, responded in the only way they knew how. Ripping into the Bears, they over-came a 17-7 halftime deficit to win, 27-17. The end of that regular season found them in a tie for first place in the conference with Detroit – there would have to be a playoff game. It produced one of the greatest comebacks in NFL history but not by the 49ers. Leading Detroit by the score of 24-7 at halftime, the 49ers went further ahead, 27-7, before the Lions finally clicked into gear. Three Detroit touchdowns, in a nightmare spell of four and a half minutes, gave them a one-point lead, which was topped up by a subsequent field goal.

Lawrence T. 'Buck' Shaw

The 1960s was a decade of disappointment for the 49ers and yet, it had opened with a bang, to the sound of a 'Shotgun' indeed. With the 49ers drifting through the season, head coach Howard 'Red' Hickey, who had taken over from Albert in 1959, devised a new offensive arrangement which he termed the 'Shotgun' formation. In this, the quarterback stood several yards back from the line of scrimmage to receive the direct snap from center. It gave him just that bit longer time to survey the downfield options before passing and still did not exclude the possibility of a rushing play.

The results were promising, as the 49ers won four of their last five games. By the beginning of 1961 the system had been perfected and, in the first five games, brought four victories. Two of those were real shockers, 49-0 over Detroit and 35-0 against the Rams. Yet, even more quickly than it had been developed, it was destroyed – the Bears had tumbled to its weakness. Simply, they observed that, because he had to make a longer snap, the center's effectiveness as a blocker was reduced and, they guessed, he would have difficulty controlling a good middle linebacker. In Bill George, the Bears certainly had one of these and, on Week Six, he repeatedly penetrated the 49ers' backfield, where the quarterback was unprotected and vulnerable. The 49ers didn't score a point and the Bears scored 31.

As far as the 49ers were concerned, that was the end of the shotgun, not because Hickey had lost confidence in it but rather, because the players had. However, fourteen years later, in 1975, Hickey's innovation was revived to good effect by Tom Landry's Dallas Cowboys and, these days, it is used widely as an alternative to the varieties of the 'T' formation.

A combination of Hickey's initial commitment to the shotgun and the developing maturity of the 1957 rookie, John Brodie, led to the departure of Tittle. For eleven of his seventeen years in San Francisco, Brodie was the club's leading passer. He, too, knew how to find wide receiver R.C. 'Alley-Oop' Owens who, in 1961, caught 55 passes for 1,032 yards. After Owens' departure came Bernie Casey and then Dave Parks, the latter whose 1,344 yards pass receiving, in 1965, was the best in the NFL. For the early part of the 1960s, J.D. Smith did well at running back, and the standard was maintained for the remainder by the gutsy Ken Willard. Both men made Pro Bowl appearances. On defense, there were several top-class players, such as defensive tackle Charlie Krueger, defensive backs Abe Woodson and Kermit Alexander, and linebackers Matt Hazeltine and Dave Wilcox, Pro Bowlers all. Woodson, Wilcox and cornerback Jimmy Johnson attained All-Pro status.

R.C. 'Alley-Oop' Owens   *All-Pro Jimmy Johnson* ▶

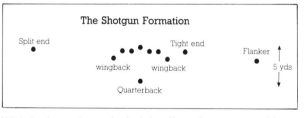

The Shotgun Formation

Split end   Tight end   Flanker

wingback   wingback   5 yds

Quarterback

With the formation at the height of its refinement, in 1961, Hickey rotated three players in the position of quarterback. They were, John Brodie, Billy Kilmer and Bobby Waters.

But the closest they came to a title was a tie for second place in the Western conference in 1960. Sadly, Vic Morabito, who had become the club owner on the death of his brother, Tony, died in 1964 at the age of 44.

At last, in 1970, the 49ers fought their way to a title. It was the championship of the four-team NFC Western division in the reorganized NFL, and was all the sweeter for having been clinched by a 38-7 victory over their near neighbours, the Oakland Raiders, on the final weekend. In that year they established the existing NFL team record for fewest sacks yielded, with eight. Once they had broken the ice for their first title, a second and third came in consecutive years. They were playing under the club's sixth head coach, Dick Nolan, who had taken control in 1968. Over the three title-winning years,

twelve different 49ers players went to the AFC-NFC Pro Bowl one or more times. It was a case of 'standing room only' in Candlestick Park, which had been their new home since the beginning of 1971. Of course, the Division Championship was the ticket to the playoffs and a shot at Pro Football's greatest prize, the Super Bowl Championship. In both 1970 and 1971 they were eliminated in the NFC Championship Game, and in 1972, went out in the divisional playoffs. On all three occasions, Nolan lost to his former mentor, Tom Landry. Back in the AAFC days, the 49ers had been thwarted by Cleveland and now, they had come across a new bogey team, the Dallas Cowboys.

In the first game, the Cowboys won more comfortably than the 17-10 scoreline suggests. San Francisco could not stop Duane Thomas, who rushed for 143 yards and a touchdown. In the second, a 14-3 loss, they could not find a way through the Dallas 'Doomsday Defense'. The third game was much closer, in fact, it was a heartbreaker and must have evoked memories of their 1957 Conference Championship playoff loss to Detroit. Quarterback Roger Staubach came off the bench, late in the third quarter, to pass for 174 yards and two touchdowns as Dallas overcame a fourth-quarter 28-13 deficit, to win by the score of 30-28.

This last depressing loss marked the beginning of a slide into relative obscurity. Some people might call it a slump. Certainly, they had only one winning season (they went 8-6-0 in 1976) out of the next eight. At the end of the 1973 season, both Brodie and Krueger retired, to be followed a year later by Wilcox. At the end of 1975, Dick Nolan was replaced as head coach by Monte Clark, who had been an assistant coach of the Miami Dolphins. Over eight regular seasons, Nolan compiled a good 54-53-5 record, but nine of the losses had come in his final campaign.

Clark appeared to have found the successful formula when, with ex-Patriot Jim Plunkett at quarterback, the 49ers won six of their first seven games. But they won just two of the remaining seven and slipped quietly out of contention.

There were wholesale changes in 1977, starting at the top where the 31-year-old Edward J. DeBartolo, Jr., became the NFL's youngest outright owner. There was a new vice president-general manager, Joe Thomas, and even a new head coach, Ken Meyer, who had been the offensive coordinator of the Rams. He couldn't have had a more disheartening start, with the 49ers losing the first five games. Hopes were raised by victories in the next four

consecutive games but, with only one more win in the last five games, the 49ers were back to where they had been in 1975, 5-9-0.

A new head coach, Pete McCulley, and even the acquisition of running back O.J. Simpson from Buffalo, couldn't halt the decline, which had now become precipitous. Their record in 1978 was 2-14-0, the worst in the league. And they couldn't look forward to what usually comes with that lowly status, the first pick in the subsequent collegiate draft. That option had been traded to Buffalo as just part of the deal which brought Simpson to San Francisco. Through the early part of the season, Simpson was on course for a rushing total of 1,054 yards, with 593 in nine games, before going out with injury. Figures like that sound good but, in truth, the great O.J. had lost his magic. He returned for one more season, under yet another head coach, Bill Walsh, but that too ended ignominiously with the 49ers tied for last place in the NFL with Detroit. At the end of the season, Simpson retired with the NFL's second-best career rushing total of 11,236 yards.

The ownership showed a great deal of confidence in Walsh. Perhaps they could read the signs. Even though only two games were won in 1979, they had scored 308 points (they ranked 16th in the league in this category). Quarterback Steve DeBerg's arm worked overtime as he passed a league-leading 578 times. Walsh also had made a couple of good picks in the 1979 collegiate draft. Quarterback Joe Montana came in round three and wide receiver Dwight Clark was a 'steal' in round ten.

The 1980 draft was even better, producing six starters, instant or future, including running back Earl Cooper, who led the NFC with 83 pass receptions. Clark was just one reception behind him. For over half the season, DeBerg and Montana shared time at quarterback but Walsh indicated his preference by opting for Montana to start the last five games. He responded by directing the team to three straight wins, including an NFL record come-from-behind victory against New Orleans. Trailing 35-7 at halftime, the 49ers drew level in regulation time and won 38-35 with an overtime field goal.

Again, in 1981, the 49ers drafted well, particularly for the defense. Cornerbacks Ronnie Lott and Eric Wright, and safety Carlton Williamson, became instant starters. The other safety, Dwight Hicks, was already a good one.

In the years since then, it has appeared that the club can do no wrong with its selections. Tackle 'Bubba' Paris came in 1982 and the dual-purpose backfield player, Roger Craig, in 1983. Both players were second-round picks. Six rookies from the 1984 collegiate draft gained places on that year's roster. Twenty-five players on the squad which ended the

John Brodie, the 49ers' longest serving quarterback

1984 season came via the collegiate draft. In addition, the city by the bay has become 'home' for several players who were unable to settle with other teams. Players such as wide receiver Freddie Solomon, tight end Russ Francis, quarterback Matt Cavanaugh and running back Wendell Tyler, have all helped the club on offense. And the Chargers may well regret not hanging on to all three of defensive ends Fred Dean and Gary Johnson, and nose tackle Louie Kelcher. Together with the former Seattle player, nose tackle Manu Tuiasosopo, they'd form an effective four-man line if need be. There are others, such as free agents Lawrence Pillers, Jack 'Hacksaw' Reynolds, Dwight Hicks, Dwaine Board, Ray Wersching and Mike Wilson.

It is a squad, which has been designed, constructed and refined by the man they now call a football genius, Bill Walsh. Only seven of the current players were with the team before he made the move from Stanford in 1979. In just six years, he has transformed a 2-14-0 team into the winner of two Super Bowl Championships. In 1981, they lost two of the first three games but, over the rest of the regular season, lost just one more, 15-12 to Cleveland (shades of the AAFC). The Giants were swept aside 38-24 in the divisional playoffs and then, in the NFC Championship Game, came some sort of revenge when they beat Dallas, 28-27, on a dramatic, late touchdown reception by Dwight Clark. If he hadn't already coined the phrase in 1957, 'Red' Hickey might well have called that one an 'Alley-Oop' pass. Against Cincinnati in Super Bowl XVI, they opened up a 20-point lead and then took things steady to win, 26-21. A loss to Washington, in the 1983 AFC Championship Game, was tough to take after they had fought back to tie the scores at 21-21. They didn't have the best of luck. They didn't need any luck in Super Bowl XIX, when the Miami Dolphins were systematically destroyed, 38-16.

It is difficult not to imagine them representing the NFC in Super Bowl XX.

Dwight Clark scores the winner against Dallas

Defensive tackle Charlie Krueger (#70)

49ers RECORD 1946-84

Year	Won	Lost	Tied	PF	PA	Postseason Losses
1946*	9	5	0	307	189	
1947*	8	4	2	327	264	
1948*	12	2	0	495	248	
1949*	9	3	0	416	227	Cleveland 21 – San Francisco 7: AAFC Championship Game
1950	3	9	0	213	300	
1951	7	4	1	255	205	
1952	7	5	0	285	221	
1953	9	3	0	372	237	
1954	7	4	1	313	251	
1955	4	8	0	216	298	
1956	5	6	1	233	284	
1957	8	4	0	260	264	
1958	6	6	0	257	324	
1959	7	5	0	255	237	
1960	7	5	0	208	205	
1961	7	6	1	346	272	
1962	6	8	0	282	331	
1963	2	12	0	198	391	
1964	4	10	0	236	330	
1965	7	6	1	421	402	
1966	6	6	2	320	325	
1967	7	7	0	273	337	
1968	7	6	1	303	310	
1969	4	8	2	277	319	
1970 (a)	10	3	1	352	267	Dallas 17 – San Francisco 10: NFC Championship Game
1971 (a)	9	5	0	300	216	Dallas 14 – San Francisco 3: NFC Championship Game
1972 (a)	8	5	1	353	249	Dallas 30 – San Francisco 28: Divisional Playoffs
1973	5	9	0	262	319	
1974	6	8	0	226	236	
1975	5	9	0	255	286	
1976	8	6	0	270	190	
1977	5	9	0	220	260	
1978	2	14	0	219	350	
1979	2	14	0	308	416	
1980	6	10	0	320	415	
1981 (a)(b)	13	3	0	357	250	
1982	3	6	0	209	206	
1983 (a)	10	6	0	432	293	Washington 24 – San Francisco 21: NFC Championship Game
1984 (a)(b)	15	1	0	475	227	

*　AAFC
(a) NFC Western Division Champion
(b) Super Bowl Champion

49ers Players in the Pro Football Hall of Fame

Leo Nomellini, Offensive and Defensive Tackle (1950-63) 1969*
Joe Perry, Running Back (1948-60, 1963) 1969*
Hugh McElhenny, Running Back (1952-60) 1970*
Y.A. Tittle, Quarterback (1951-60) 1971*
O.J. Simpson, Running Back (1978-79) 1985*

* Year of induction

49ers Head Coaches

Lawrence 'Buck' Shaw	1946-54
Norman 'Red' Strader	1955
Frankie Albert	1956-58
Howard 'Red' Hickey*	1959-63
Jack Christiansen	1963-67
Dick Nolan	1968-75
Monte Clark	1976
Ken Meyer	1977
Pete McCulley**	1978
Fred O'Connor	1978
Bill Walsh	1979-

*Resigned after three games in 1963
**Replaced after nine games in 1978

49ers head coach Bill Walsh

Quarterback Y.A. Tittle

CHAPTER THREE

HOW THE SEASON WORKS

The National Football League consists of twenty-eight teams divided into two Conferences, the American Football Conference (AFC) and the National Football Conference (NFC). Each conference has fourteen teams, and is subdivided into two five-team Divisions and one four-team Division. These are essentially based on sensible geographical considerations but also take into account the traditional rivalries which were in existence when the expanded NFL was restructured in 1970. The teams are listed below in order of their final 1984 division standings since this is of importance in arriving at a team's schedule (fixture list) for 1985.

AMERICAN FOOTBALL CONFERENCE

Eastern Division

	W	L	T
Miami	14	2	0
New England	9	7	0
New York Jets	7	9	0
Indianapolis	4	12	0
Buffalo	2	14	0

Central Division

	W	L	T
Pittsburgh	9	7	0
Cincinnati	8	8	0
Cleveland	5	11	0
Houston	3	13	0

Western Division

	W	L	T
Denver	13	3	0
Seattle	12	4	0
Los Angeles Raiders	11	5	0
Kansas City	8	8	0
San Diego	7	9	0

NATIONAL FOOTBALL CONFERENCE

Eastern Division

	W	L	T
Washington	11	5	0
New York Giants	9	7	0
St Louis	9	7	0
Dallas	9	7	0
Philadelphia	6	9	1

Central Division

	W	L	T
Chicago	10	6	0
Green Bay	8	8	0
Tampa Bay	6	10	0
Detroit	4	11	1
Minnesota	3	13	0

Western Division

	W	L	T
San Francisco	15	1	0
Los Angeles Rams	10	6	0
New Orleans	7	9	0
Atlanta	4	12	0

THE SCHEDULE

When considering a team's schedule, it's best to set aside the four teams who each finished the 1984 season in fifth place in their divisions. Looking at the remaining twenty-four, every team plays twelve games against others from its own conference.

Again, excluding the four fifth-placed teams, every team will play four games against teams from the rival conference (known as Interconference games), specifically to allow fans in the cities of one conference the opportunity of seeing the star players and teams of the other conference. The structure of a team's schedule depends on whether it plays in a four-team or a five-team division.

Four-Team Division

A typical schedule, e.g. for the Pittsburgh Steelers, appears below. It is set out deliberately not in chronological order, to emphasise that the schedule has a quite definite structure.

PITTSBURGH STEELERS (AFC Central)

Cincinnati Bengals	AFC Central	Home
Cincinnati Bengals	AFC Central	Away
Cleveland Browns	AFC Central	Home
Cleveland Browns	AFC Central	Away
Houston Oilers	AFC Central	Home
Houston Oilers	AFC Central	Away
Buffalo Bills	AFC East	Home
Indianapolis Colts	AFC East	Home
Miami Dolphins	AFC East	Away
Denver Broncos	AFC West	Home
Kansas City Chiefs	AFC West	Away
San Diego Chargers	AFC West	Away
Dallas Cowboys	NFC East	Away
New York Giants	NFC East	Away
St Louis Cardinals	NFC East	Home
Washington Redskins	NFC East	Home

The Steelers will always play their division rivals, Cincinnati, Cleveland and Houston, both home and away. The flavour of intraconference competition is maintained by six games, every year, against teams from outside their division but within their conference. There will always be three games against the AFC East and three against the AFC West. Again, every year, there will be four games against teams from a particular division of the rival conference, based on a three-year cycle. In 1985, they play against the NFC East; in 1986 they will play teams from the NFC Central and in 1987, the NFC West. For every team in the NFL, a complete list of opponents, other than those within a team's own division, is arrived at by applying the following formula. The letters and numbers refer to Conference, Division and final standing in that division. Thus, the Miami Dolphins, who are in the American Conference Eastern Division and finished first in that division, are identified as AE-1. Equally, the Atlanta Falcons, who are in the National Conference Western Division and finished fourth in that division, are identified by NW-4.

AFC EAST-AE

AE-1		AE-2		AE-3		AE-4		AE-5	
H	**A**	**H**	**A**	**H**	**A**	**H**	**A**	**H**	**A**
NC-1	NC-2	NC-2	NC-1	NC-1	NC-2	NC-2	NC-1	AC-2	AC-1
NC-3	NC-4	NC-4	NC-3	NC-3	NC-4	NC-4	NC-3	AC-4	AC-3
AC-1	AC-4	AC-2	AC-3	AC-3	AC-2	AC-4	AC-1	NC-5	NE-5
AW-4	AW-1	AW-3	AW-2	AW-2	AW-3	AW-1	NW-4	AW-5	AW-5

AFC CENTRAL-AC

AC-1		AC-2		AC-3		AC-4	
H	**A**	**H**	**A**	**H**	**A**	**H**	**A**
NE-1	NE-2	NE-2	NE-1	NE-1	NE-2	NE-2	NE-1
NE-3	NE-4	NE-4	NE-3	NE-3	NE-4	NE-4	NE-3
AE-4	AE-1	AE-3	AE-2	AE-2	AE-3	AE-1	AE-4
AE-5	AW-4	AW-2	AE-5	AE-5	AW-2	AW-4	AE-5
AW-1	AW-5	AW-5	AW-3	AW-3	AW-5	AW-5	AW-1

AFC WEST-AW

AW-1		AW-2		AW-3		AW-4		AW-5	
H	**A**	**H**	**A**	**H**	**A**	**H**	**A**	**H**	**A**
NW-1	NW-2	NW-2	NW-1	NW-1	NW-2	NW-2	NW-1	NE-5	NC-5
NW-3	NW-4	NW-4	NW-3	NW-3	NW-4	NW-4	NW-3	AE-5	AE-5
AE-1	AE-4	AE-2	AE-3	AE-3	AE-2	AE-4	AE-1	AC-1	AC-2
AC-4	AC-1	AC-3	AC-2	AC-2	AC-3	AC-1	AC-4	AC-3	AC-4

NFC EAST-NE

	NE-1		NE-2		NE-3		NE-4		NE-5	
	H	A	H	A	H	A	H	A	H	A
	AC-2	AC-1	AC-1	AC-2	AC-2	AC-1	AC-1	AC-2	AE-5	AW-5
	AC-4	AC-3	AC-3	AC-4	AC-4	AC-3	AC-3	AC-4	NC-5	NC-5
	NC-4	NC-1	NC-3	NC-2	NC-2	NC-3	NC-1	NC-4	NW-2	NW-1
	NW-1	NW-4	NW-2	NW-3	NW-3	NW-2	NW-4	NW-1	NW-4	NW-3

NFC CENTRAL-NC

	NC-1		NC-2		NC-3		NC-4		NC-5	
	H	A	H	A	H	A	H	A	H	A
	AE-2	AE-1	AE-1	AE-2	AE-2	AE-1	AE-1	AE-2	AW-5	AE-5
	AE-4	AE-3	AE-3	AE-4	AE-4	AE-3	AE-3	AE-4	NE-5	NE-5
	NE-1	NE-4	NE-2	NE-3	NE-3	NE-2	NE-4	NE-1	NW-1	NW-2
	NW-4	NW-1	NW-3	NW-2	NW-2	NW-3	NW-1	NW-4	NW-3	NW-4

NFC WEST-NW

	NW-1		NW-2		NW-3		NW-4	
	H	A	H	A	H	A	H	A
	AW-2	AW-1	AW-1	AW-2	AW-2	AW-1	AW-1	AW-2
	AW-4	AW-3	AW-3	AW-4	AW-4	AW-3	AW-3	AW-4
	NE-4	NE-1	NE-3	NE-2	NE-2	NE-3	NE-1	NE-4
	NE-5	NC-4	NC-2	NE-5	NE-5	NC-2	NC-4	NE-5
	NC-1	NC-5	NC-5	NC-3	NC-3	NC-5	NC-5	NC-1

Five-Team Division (Top Four Teams Only)

In the AFC West, the schedules for the top four teams have identical structure and include home and away games against the other four teams in the division. Each of the top four teams plays two games against AFC Central teams and two against the AFC East. Also, they play the four teams in the NFC West as part of their three-year cycle of interconference games. In 1986, they will play teams from the NFC East and, in 1987, the NFC Central. Below is the schedule structure for the Denver Broncos.

DENVER BRONCOS (AFC West)

Kansas City Chiefs	AFC West	Home
Kansas City Chiefs	AFC West	Away
Los Angeles Raiders	AFC West	Home
Los Angeles Raiders	AFC West	Away
San Diego Chargers	AFC West	Home
San Diego Chargers	AFC West	Away
Seattle Seahawks	AFC West	Home
Seattle Seahawks	AFC West	Away
Miami Dolphins	AFC East	Home
Indianapolis Colts	AFC East	Away
Houston Oilers	AFC Central	Home
Pittsburgh Steelers	AFC Central	Away
Atlanta Falcons	NFC West	Away
Los Angeles Rams	NFC West	Away
New Orleans Saints	NFC West	Home
San Francisco 49ers	NFC West	Home

Fifth-Placed Teams

In the AFC, the two fifth-placed teams will each play eight games against teams from their own divisions and will always play single games against the four AFC Central teams. In the NFC, the two fifth-placed teams each play eight games within their own divisions and will always play single games against the four NFC West teams. Each of the four fifth-placed teams is guaranteed home and away games against the fifth-placed team in its own conference, and single games against the two fifth-placed teams from the rival conference. The schedule structures for all four teams are set out as follows.

Buffalo (AFC East)

AFC East		8 games
AFC Central		4 games
San Diego	(AFC)	Home
San Diego	(AFC)	Away
Minnesota	(NFC)	Home
Philadelphia	(NFC)	Away

San Diego (AFC West)

AFC West		8 games
AFC Central		4 games
Buffalo	(AFC)	Home
Buffalo	(AFC)	Away
Minnesota	(NFC)	Away
Philadelphia	(NFC)	Home

Philadelphia (NFC East)

NFC East		8 games
NFC West		4 games
Minnesota	(NFC)	Home
Minnesota	(NFC)	Away
San Diego	(AFC)	Away
Buffalo	(AFC)	Home

Minnesota (NFC Central)

NFC Central		8 games
NFC West		4 games
Philadelphia	(NFC)	Home
Philadelphia	(NFC)	Away
San Diego	(AFC)	Home
Buffalo	(AFC)	Away

THE PLAYOFFS

On completion of the regular season, each conference holds an elimination competition known as the Playoffs. The teams involved are the three division winners and two Wild Card teams, namely those two, other than the division winners, who have the best won-lost-tied records. The two wild card teams play each other to decide which one advances to join the three division winners in the Divisional Playoffs (conference semi-final games). The results of the 1984 American Football Conference playoffs are set out as follows:

Wild Card Game
Los Angeles Raiders 7 at Seattle 13

Divisional Playoffs
Seattle 10 at Miami 31
Pittsburgh 24 at Denver 17

AFC Conference Championship Game
Pittsburgh 28 at Miami 45
Miami advanced to Super Bowl XIX as AFC Champions.

Home-Field Advantage in the Playoffs
For the Wild Card game, the team with the better regular season record is given the home-field advantage. Again, in the Divisional Playoffs, the home-field advantage goes to the team with the better regular season record except in so far as the Wild Card winner can never play at home. For the AFC playoffs then, the pecking order was as follows:

	W	L	T
Miami*	14	2	0
Denver*	13	3	0
Pittsburgh*	9	7	0
Seattle†	12	4	0
L.A. Raiders†	11	5	0

* Division champions
† Wild Card teams

TIE-BREAKING PROCEDURES

To separate tied teams, the following criteria are applied:

Teams in the same division
A: *Two teams*
1. Head-to-head (best record in games played between the two teams)
2. Best record in games played within the division
3. Best record in games played within the conference
4. Best record in common games
5. Best net points scored in division games (just like goal difference in soccer)
6. Best net points in all games

B: *Three or More Teams* (if two teams remain tied after all other teams are eliminated, the tie-breaking procedure reverts to A:1.)
1. Head-to-head (best record in games played between the teams)
2. Best record in games played within the division
3. Best record in games played within the conference
4. Best record in common games
5. Best net points in division games
6. Best net points in all games

Tie-Breaker for the Wild Card places
(a) If the teams are from the same division, the division tie-breaker is applied.
(b) If the teams are from different divisions, the following procedure is adopted:
C: *Two Teams*
1. Head-to-head (if they have played each other)
2. Best record in games played within the conference
3. Best record in common games (minimum of four)
4. Best average net points in conference games
5. Best net points in all games

D: *Three or More Teams* (If two teams remain tied after all other teams are eliminated, the tie-breaking procedure reverts to A:1, or C:1, whichever is applicable)
1. Head-to-head sweep (this applies only if one team has either beaten or lost to all the others)
2. Best record in games played within the conference
3. Best record in common games (minimum of four)
4. Best average net points in conference games
5. Best net points in all games

In the 1984 season the formula was put to use only once, to establish which one of the New York Giants, St Louis or Dallas would be the second-ranking NFC wild card team (all three had 9-7-0 records). It was decided by application of criterion B:1, i.e. best record in games played between the three teams. The Giants were 3-1, St Louis 2-2 and Dallas 1-3. The Giants thus became the second-ranking NFC wild card team and played away against the Los Angeles Rams in the NFC wild card game.

THE SUPER BOWL

Though the obvious comparison is with the FA Cup Final, the Super Bowl is more sensibly seen as the culmination of an end-of-season elimination competition, involving the champions of six mini leagues together with the wild card teams, the latter being considered, perhaps, as potential giant killers. (Only one team, the Oakland Raiders, has won the Super Bowl Championship starting from the wild card position.) Unlike for the FA Cup Final, the Super Bowl venue changes from year to year and, since the site is chosen some three years in advance, it is possible for one team to be playing 'at home'. Surprisingly, this has never occurred, though both the Los Angeles Rams and the San Francisco 49ers were less than one hour's drive from home when they played in Super Bowls XIV and XIX respectively. In selecting the venue, great importance is placed on the likelihood of good weather. Consequently, with the exception of the Pontiac Silverdome (this is a domed stadium), all past Super Bowl stadia have been in the 'sunshine belt', stretching from Florida to California. Super Bowl XX will be played in the New Orleans Superdome and XXI at the Rose Bowl in Pasadena, California.

THE PRO BOWL

This annual game between the two representative teams from each conference is a pleasant way to end the season. Everyone flies off to Hawaii to give the fans out there a treat. The teams are selected by a ballot of head coaches and players in each conference. Each team has two equal votes – the head coach's and a consensus of the players' selections. Coaches and players vote only for players in their own conference and may not vote for players from their own teams. In the 1985 game, the AFC edged closer to the NFC in the series, winning 22-14.

Chicago's Pro Bowl inside linebacker, Mike Singletary

AFC-NFC Pro Bowl Results – NFC leads series 9-6					
YEAR	**DATE**	**WINNER**	**LOSER**	**SITE**	**ATTENDANCE**
1985	Jan. 27	AFC 22	NFC 14	Honolulu	50,385
1984	Jan. 29	NFC 45	AFC 3	Honolulu	50,445
1983	Feb. 6	NFC 20	AFC 19	Honolulu	47,201
1982	Jan. 31	AFC 16	NFC 13	Honolulu	49,521
1981	Feb. 1	NFC 21	AFC 7	Honolulu	47,879
1980	Jan. 27	NFC 37	AFC 27	Honolulu	48,060
1979	Jan. 29	NFC 13	AFC 7	Los Angeles	46,281
1978	Jan. 23	NFC 14	AFC 13	Tampa	51,337
1977	Jan. 17	AFC 24	NFC 14	Seattle	64,151
1976	Jan. 26	NFC 23	AFC 20	New Orleans	30,546
1975	Jan. 20	NFC 17	AFC 10	Miami	26,484
1974	Jan. 20	AFC 15	NFC 13	Kansas City	66,918
1973	Jan. 21	AFC 33	NFC 28	Dallas	37,091
1972	Jan. 23	AFC 26	NFC 13	Los Angeles	53,647
1971	Jan. 24	NFC 27	AFC 6	Los Angeles	48,222

PRO BOWL ROSTERS
(Original selections – starters in Capitals)

OFFENSE	American Football Conference		National Football Conference	
Wide Receivers	MARK DUPER	Miami	ROY GREEN	St Louis
	JOHN STALLWORTH	Pittsburgh	JAMES LOFTON	Green Bay
	Steve Largent	Seattle	Art Monk	Washington
	Mark Clayton	Miami	Mike Quick	Philadelphia
Tight Ends	OZZIE NEWSOME	Cleveland	PAUL COFFMAN	Green Bay
	Todd Christensen	L.A. Raiders	Doug Cosbie	Dallas
Tackles	ANTHONY MUNOZ	Cincinnati	JOE JACOBY	Washington
	BRIAN HOLLOWAY	New England	MIKE KENN	Atlanta
	Henry Lawrence	L.A. Raiders	Keith Fahnhorst	San Francisco
Guards	JOHN HANNAH	New England	RUSS GRIMM	Washington
	ED NEWMAN	Miami	RANDY CROSS	San Francisco
	Mike Munchak	Houston	Kent Hill	L.A. Rams
Centers	DWIGHT STEPHENSON	Miami	FRED QUILLAN	San Francisco
	Mike Webster	Pittsburgh	Doug Smith	L.A. Rams
Quarterbacks	DAN MARINO	Miami	JOE MONTANA	San Francisco
	Dave Krieg	Seattle	Neil Lomax	St Louis
Running Backs	MARCUS ALLEN	L.A. Raiders	ERIC DICKERSON	L.A. Rams
	FREEMAN McNEIL	N.Y. Jets	WALTER PAYTON	Chicago
	Earnest Jackson	San Diego	James Wilder	Tampa Bay
	Sammy Winder	Denver	Wendell Tyler	San Francisco

DEFENSE				
Defensive Ends	MARK GASTINEAU	N.Y. Jets	LEE ROY SELMON	Tampa Bay
	HOWIE LONG	L.A. Raiders	RICHARD DENT	Chicago
	Art Still	Kansas City	Bruce Clark	New Orleans
Nose Tackles	JOE NASH	Seattle	DAN HAMPTON	Chicago
	Bob Baumhower	Miami	Randy White	Dallas
Outside Linebackers	ROD MARTIN	L.A. Raiders	LAWRENCE TAYLOR	N.Y. Giants
	MIKE MERRIWEATHER	Pittsburgh	RICKEY JACKSON	New Orleans
	Andre Tippett	New England	Keena Turner	San Francisco
Inside Linebackers	STEVE NELSON	New England	MIKE SINGLETARY	Chicago
	ROBIN COLE	Pittsburgh	E.J. JUNIOR	St Louis
	A.J. Duhe	Miami	Harry Carson	N.Y. Giants
Cornerbacks	MIKE HAYNES	L.A. Raiders	MARK HAYNES	N.Y. Giants
	LESTER HAYES	L.A. Raiders	DARRELL GREEN	Washington
	Dave Brown	Seattle	Ronnie Lott	San Francisco
Safeties	KENNY EASLEY	Seattle	TODD BELL	Chicago
	VANN McELROY	L.A. Raiders	DWIGHT HICKS	San Francisco
	Deron Cherry	Kansas City	Carlton Williamson	San Francisco

SPECIAL TEAMS

Placekicker	Norm Johnson	Seattle	Jan Stenerud	Minnesota
Punter	Reggie Roby	Miami	Brian Hansen	New Orleans
Kick Returner	Louis Lipps	Pittsburgh	Henry Ellard	L.A. Rams
Special-team Specialist	Fredd Young	Seattle	Bill Bates	Dallas
Coach	Chuck Noll	Pittsburgh	Mike Ditka	Chicago

THE ALL-PRO TEAM

The major periodicals and news services (AP and UPI) each produce what they consider to be the best team selected from the whole NFL. Not everyone would agree with me, but here is my dream team.

Tackle Mike Kenn (#78) 'holds' off Joe Klecko (#71) while Neil Lomax passes in the 1985 Pro Bowl

Mike Webster (#52) and Dan Marino (#13), 1985 Pro Bowl

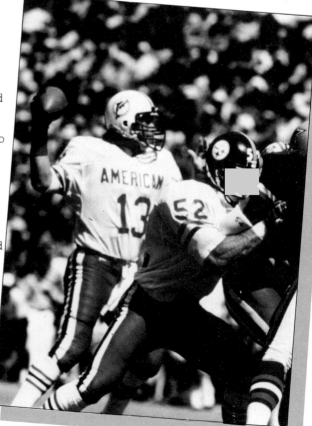

Wide Receivers	James Lofton	Green Bay
	Art Monk	Washington
Tight End	Kellen Winslow	San Diego
Tackles	Joe Jacoby	Washington
	Anthony Munoz	Cincinnati
Guards	John Hannah	New England
	Kent Hill	L.A. Rams
Center	Dwight Stephenson	Miami
Quarterback	Joe Montana	San Francisco
Running Backs	Eric Dickerson	L.A. Rams
	Walter Payton	Chicago
Defensive Ends	Mark Gastineau	N.Y. Jets
	Howie Long	L.A. Raiders
Defensive Tackles	Dan Hampton	Chicago
	Randy White	Dallas
Outside Linebackers	Lawrence Taylor	N.Y. Giants
	Andre Tippett	New England
Inside Linebackers	Mike Singletary	Chicago
	E.J. Junior	St. Louis
Safeties	Kenny Easley	Seattle
	Todd Bell	Chicago
Cornerbacks	Lester Hayes	L.A. Raiders
	Mike Haynes	L.A. Raiders
Placekicker	Jan Stenerud	Minnesota
Punter	Reggie Roby	Miami
Punt Returner	Henry Ellard	L.A. Rams
Kickoff Returner	Carl Roaches	Houston
Special-team Specialist	Bill Bates	Dallas
Head Coach	Chuck Knox	Seattle

CHAPTER FOUR

ALL-TIME RECORDS

CHAMPIONS 1921-1984

National Football League 1921-1969
(Until 1933 based solely on regular season play)

1921	Chicago Staleys
1922	Canton Bulldogs
1923	Canton Bulldogs
1924	Cleveland Bulldogs
1925	Chicago Cardinals
1926	Frankford Yellowjackets
1927	New York Giants
1928	Providence Steamroller
1929	Green Bay Packers
1930	Green Bay Packers
1931	Green Bay Packers
1932	Chicago Bears 9 – Portsmouth Spartans 0 (Championship Playoff)
1933	Chicago Bears 23 – New York Giants 21
1934	New York Giants 30 – Chicago Bears 13
1935	Detroit Lions 26 – New York Giants 7
1936	Green Bay Packers 21 – Boston Redskins 6
1937	Washington Redskins 28 – Chicago Bears 21
1938	New York Giants 23 – Green Bay Packers 17
1939	Green Bay Packers 27 – New York Giants 0
1940	Chicago Bears 73 – Washington Redskins 0
1941	Chicago Bears 37 – New York Giants 9
1942	Washington Redskins 14 – Chicago Bears 6
1943	Chicago Bears 41 – Washington Redskins 21
1944	Green Bay Packers 14 – New York Giants 7
1945	Cleveland Rams 15 – Washington Redskins 14
1946	Chicago Bears 24 – New York Giants 14
1947	Chicago Cardinals 28 – Philadelphia Eagles 21
1948	Philadelphia Eagles 7 – Chicago Cardinals 0
1949	Philadelphia Eagles 14 – Los Angeles Rams 0
1950	Cleveland Browns 30 – Los Angeles Rams 28
1951	Los Angeles Rams 24 – Cleveland Browns 17
1952	Detroit Lions 17 – Cleveland Browns 7
1953	Detroit Lions 17 – Cleveland Browns 16
1954	Cleveland Browns 56 – Detroit Lions 10
1955	Cleveland Browns 38 – Los Angeles Rams 14
1956	New York Giants 47 – Chicago Bears 7
1957	Detroit Lions 59 – Cleveland Browns 14
1958	Baltimore Colts 23 – New York Giants 17
1959	Baltimore Colts 31 – New York Giants 16

1960	Philadelphia Eagles 17 – Green Bay Packers 13
1961	Green Bay Packers 37 – New York Giants 0
1962	Green Bay Packers 16 – New York Giants 7
1963	Chicago Bears 14 – New York Giants 10
1964	Cleveland Browns 27 – Baltimore Colts 0
1965	Green Bay Packers 23 – Cleveland Browns 12
1966	Green Bay Packers 34 – Dallas Cowboys 27
1967	Green Bay Packers 21 – Dallas Cowboys 17
1968	Baltimore Colts 34 – Cleveland Browns 0
1969	Minnesota Vikings 27 – Cleveland Browns 7

American Football League 1960-1969

1960	Houston Oilers 24 – Los Angeles Chargers 16
1961	Houston Oilers 10 – San Diego Chargers 3
1962	Dallas Texans 20 – Houston Oilers 17
1963	San Diego Chargers 51 – Boston Patriots 10
1964	Buffalo Bills 20 – San Diego Chargers 7
1965	Buffalo Bills 23 – San Diego Chargers 0
1966	Kansas City Chiefs 31 – Buffalo Bills 7
1967	Oakland Raiders 40 – Houston Oilers 7
1968	New York Jets 27 – Oakland Raiders 23
1969	Kansas City Chiefs 17 – Oakland Raiders 7

Conference Champions 1970-1984

NFC

1970	Dallas Cowboys 17 – San Francisco 49ers 10
1971	Dallas Cowboys 14 – San Francisco 49ers 3
1972	Washington Redskins 26 – Dallas Cowboys 3
1973	Minnesota Vikings 27 – Dallas Cowboys 10
1974	Minnesota Vikings 14 – Los Angeles Rams 10
1975	Dallas Cowboys 37 – Los Angeles Rams 7
1976	Minnesota Vikings 24 – Los Angeles Rams 13
1977	Dallas Cowboys 23 – Minnesota Vikings 6
1978	Dallas Cowboys 28 – Los Angeles Rams 0
1979	Los Angeles Rams 9 – Tampa Bay Buccaneers 0
1980	Philadelphia Eagles 20 – Dallas Cowboys 7
1981	San Francisco 49ers 28 – Dallas Cowboys 27
1982	Washington Redskins 31 – Dallas Cowboys 17
1983	Washington Redskins 24 – San Francisco 49ers 21
1984	San Francisco 49ers 23 – Chicago Bears 0

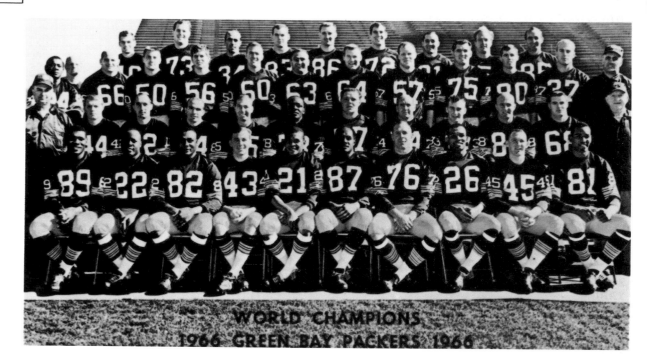

**WORLD CHAMPIONS
1966 GREEN BAY PACKERS 1966**

The World Champion 1966 Green Bay Packers

AFC

1970	Baltimore Colts 27 – Oakland Raiders 17
1971	Miami Dolphins 21 – Baltimore Colts 0
1972	Miami Dolphins 21 – Pittsburgh Steelers 17
1973	Miami Dolphins 27 – Oakland Raiders 10
1974	Pittsburgh Steelers 24 – Oakland Raiders 13
1975	Pittsburgh Steelers 16 – Oakland Raiders 10
1976	Oakland Raiders 24 – Pittsburgh Steelers 7
1977	Denver Broncos 20 – Oakland Raiders 17
1978	Pittsburgh Steelers 34 – Houston Oilers 5
1979	Pittsburgh Steelers 27 – Houston Oilers 13
1980	Oakland Raiders 34 – San Diego Chargers 27
1981	Cincinnati Bengals 27 – San Diego Chargers 7
1982	Miami Dolphins 14 – New York Jets 0
1983	Los Angeles Raiders 30 – Seattle Seahawks 14
1984	Miami Dolphins 45 – Pittsburgh Steelers 28

Super Bowl 1966-1984

Season	SB	Winner		Loser		Stadium	Attendance
1966	I	Green Bay	35	Kansas City	10	Los Angeles Coliseum	61,946
1967	II	Green Bay	33	Oakland	14	Miami Orange Bowl	75,546
1968	III	N.Y. Jets	16	Baltimore	7	Miami Orange Bowl	75,389
1969	IV	Kansas City	23	Minnesota	7	New Orleans Tulane Stadium	80,562
1970	V	Baltimore	16	Dallas	13	Miami Orange Bowl	79,204
1971	VI	Dallas	24	Miami	3	New Orleans Tulane Stadium	81,023
1972	VII	Miami	14	Washington	7	Los Angeles Coliseum	90,182
1973	VIII	Miami	24	Minnesota	7	Houston Rice Stadium	71,882
1974	IX	Pittsburgh	16	Minnesota	6	New Orleans Tulane Stadium	80,997
1975	X	Pittsburgh	21	Dallas	17	Miami Orange Bowl	80,107
1976	XI	Oakland	32	Minnesota	14	Pasadena Rose Bowl	103,438
1977	XII	Dallas	27	Denver	10	New Orleans Superdome	75,583
1978	XIII	Pittsburgh	35	Dallas	31	Miami Orange Bowl	79,484
1979	XIV	Pittsburgh	31	L.A. Rams	19	Pasadena Rose Bowl	103,985
1980	XV	Oakland	27	Philadelphia	10	New Orleans Superdome	76,135
1981	XVI	San Francisco	26	Cincinnati	21	Pontiac Silverdome	81,270
1982	XVII	Washington	27	Miami	17	Pasadena Rose Bowl	103,667
1983	XVIII	L.A. Raiders	38	Washington	9	Tampa Stadium	72,920
1984	XIX	San Francisco	38	Miami	16	Stanford Stadium	84,059

ALL-TIME INDIVIDUAL RECORDS
(Regular Season)

Career Best

SEASONS PLAYED	26	George Blanda
GAMES PLAYED	340	George Blanda
POINTS	2,002	George Blanda (9-TD, 943-EP, 335-FG)
EXTRA POINTS	943	George Blanda
FIELD GOALS	358	Jan Stenerud
TOUCHDOWNS		
Rushing and Pass Receiving	126	Jim Brown (106-R, 20-PR)
Rushing	106	Jim Brown
Pass Receiving	99	Don Hutson
Passes Thrown	342	Fran Tarkenton
By Interception Return	9	Ken Houston
By Punt Return	8	Jack Christiansen
By Kickoff Return	6	Ollie Matson
		Gale Sayers
		Travis Williams
By Fumble Recovery Return	4	Bill Thompson
YARDAGE		
Rushing	13,309	Walter Payton
Pass Receiving	11,834	Don Maynard
Passing	47,003	Fran Tarkenton
HOW MANY TIMES		
Pass Receptions	657	Charlie Joiner
Passes Completed	3,686	Fran Tarkenton
Interceptions	81	Paul Krause
100-Yard Rushing Games	63	Walter Payton
1,000-Yard Rushing Seasons	8	Franco Harris
		Walter Payton

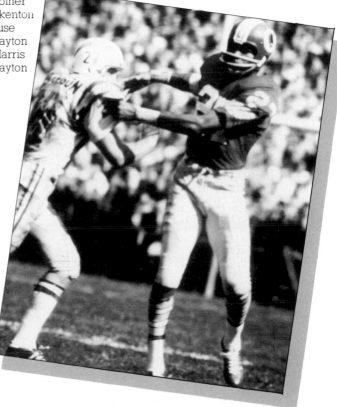

Ken Houston returned the most interceptions for touchdowns

◀ *Fran Tarkenton, the all-time passing leader in most categories*

MOST SEASONS LEADING LEAGUE

Points	5	Don Hutson, Green Bay 1940-44
		Gino Cappelletti, Boston 1961, 1963-66
Extra Points	8	George Blanda, Chicago Bears 1956, Houston 1961-62,
		Oakland 1967-69, 1972, 1974
Field Goals	5	Lou Groza, Cleveland Browns 1950, 1952-54, 1957
Touchdowns	8	Don Hutson, Green Bay 1935-38, 1941-44
Touchdowns, Rushing	5	Jim Brown, Cleveland Browns 1957-59, 1963, 1965
Touchdowns, Pass Receiving	9	Don Hutson, Green Bay 1935-38, 1940-44
Touchdowns, Passes Thrown	4	Johnny Unitas, Baltimore 1957-60
		Len Dawson, Dallas Texans 1962, Kansas City 1963, 1965-66
Yards, Rushing	8	Jim Brown, Cleveland Browns 1957-61, 1963-65
Yards, Pass Receiving	7	Don Hutson, Green Bay 1936, 1938-39, 1941-44
Yards, Passing	5	Sonny Jurgensen, Philadelphia 1961-62,
		Washington 1966-67, 1969
Pass Receptions	8	Don Hutson, Green Bay 1936-37, 1939, 1941-45
Passes Completed	5	Sammy Baugh, Washington 1937, 1943, 1945, 1947-48

Season Best

POINTS	176	Paul Hornung, Green Bay (15-TD, 41-EP, 15-FG)
EXTRA POINTS	66	Uwe von Schamann, Miami 1984
FIELD GOALS	34	Jim Turner, N.Y. Jets 1968
TOUCHDOWNS		
Rushing and Pass Receiving	24	John Riggins, Washington 1983 (24-R)
Rushing	24	John Riggins, Washington 1983
Pass Receiving	18	Mark Clayton, Miami 1984
Passes Thrown	48	Dan Marino, Miami 1984
By Interception Return	4	Ken Houston, Houston 1971
		Jim Kearney, Kansas City 1972
By Punt Return	4	Jack Christiansen, Detroit 1951
		Rick Upchurch, Denver 1976
By Kickoff Return	4	Travis Williams, Green Bay 1967
		Cecil Turner, Chicago 1970
By Fumble Recovery Return	2	By many players
YARDAGE		
Rushing	2,105	Eric Dickerson, L.A. Rams 1984
Pass Receiving	1,746	Charley Hennigan, Houston 1961
Passing	5,084	Dan Marino, Miami 1984
HOW MANY TIMES		
Pass Receptions	106	Art Monk, Washington 1984
Passes Completed	362	Dan Marino, Miami 1984
Interceptions	14	Dick 'Night Train' Lane, L.A. Rams 1952

Game Best

POINTS	40	Ernie Nevers (6-TD, 4-EP), Chicago Cardinals v
		Chicago Bears 1929
EXTRA POINTS	9	Pat Harder, Chicago Cardinals v N.Y. Giants 1948
		Bob Waterfield, L.A. Rams v Baltimore 1950
		Charley Gogolak, Washington v N.Y. Giants 1966
FIELD GOALS	7	Jim Bakken, St Louis v Pittsburgh 1967
TOUCHDOWNS		
Rushing and Pass Receiving	6	Ernie Nevers (6-R), Chicago Cardinals v Chicago Bears 1929
		Dub Jones (4-R, 2-PR), Cleveland v Chicago Bears 1951
		Gale Sayers (4-R, 1-PR, 1-K Ret), Chicago Bears
		v San Francisco 1965
Rushing	6	Ernie Nevers, Chicago Cardinals v Chicago Bears 1929
Pass Receiving	5	Bob Shaw, Chicago Cardinals v Baltimore 1950
		Kellen Winslow, San Diego v Oakland 1981

Passes Thrown	7	Sid Luckman, Chicago Bears v N.Y. Giants 1943
		Adrian Burk, Philadelphia v Washington 1954
		George Blanda, Houston v N.Y. Titans 1961
		Y.A. Tittle, N.Y. Giants v Washington 1962
		Joe Kapp, Minnesota v Baltimore 1969

YARDAGE

Rushing	275	Walter Payton, Chicago Bears v Minnesota 1977
Pass Receiving	303	Jim Benton, Cleveland Rams v Detroit 1945
Passing	554	Norm Van Brocklin, L.A. Rams v N.Y. Yanks 1951

HOW MANY TIMES

Rushing Attempts	43	Butch Woolfolk, N.Y. Giants v Philadelphia 1983
		James Wilder, Tampa Bay v Green Bay 1984
Pass Receptions	18	Tom Fears, L.A. Rams v Green Bay 1950
Passes Completed	42	Richard Todd, N.Y. Jets v San Francisco 1980
Interceptions	4	By many players

LONGEST

Touchdown Rushing	99 yds	Tony Dorsett, Dallas v Minnesota 1982
Touchdown Pass Receiving	99 yds	Andy Farkas (from Filchock) Washington v Pittsburgh 1939
		Bobby Mitchell (from Izo) Washington v Cleveland 1963
		Pat Studstill (from Sweetan) Detroit v Baltimore 1966
		Gerry Allen (from Jurgensen) Washington v Chicago 1968
		Cliff Branch (from Plunkett) L.A. Raiders v Washington 1983
Field Goal	63 yds	Tom Dempsey, New Orleans v Detroit 1970
Punt Return (All TDs)	98 yds	Gil LeFebvre, Cincinnati v Brooklyn 1933
		Charlie West, Minnesota v Washington 1968
		Dennis Morgan, Dallas v St Louis 1974
Kickoff Return (All TDs)	106 yds	Al Carmichael, Green Bay v Chicago Bears 1956
		Noland Smith, Kansas City v Denver 1067
		Roy Green, St Louis v Dallas 1979
Interception Return (All TDs)	102 yds	Bob Smith, Detroit v Chicago Bears 1949
		Erich Barnes, N.Y. Giants v Dallas 1961
		Gary Barbaro, Kansas City v Seattle 1977
		Louis Breeden, Cincinnati v San Diego 1981
Fumble Recovery Return (TD)	104 yds	Jack Tatum, Oakland v Green Bay 1972

TEAM RECORDS

MOST CHAMPIONSHIPS	11	Green Bay, 1929-31, 1936, 1939, 1944, 1961-62, 1965-67
	8	Chicago Bears, 1921, 1932-33, 1940-41, 1943, 1946, 1963
	4	N.Y. Giants, 1927, 1934, 1938, 1956
		Detroit, 1935, 1952-53, 1957
		Cleveland Browns, 1950, 1954-55, 1964
		Baltimore, 1958-59, 1968, 1970
		Pittsburgh, 1974-75, 1978-79
MOST CONSECUTIVE GAMES WON (inc. playoffs)	18	Chicago Bears, 1933-34 and 1941-42; Miami, 1972-73
MOST CONSECUTIVE GAMES WON (exc. playoffs)	17	Chicago Bears, 1933-34
MOST CONSECUTIVE GAMES LOST	26	Tampa Bay, 1976-77
MOST POINTS IN A SEASON	541	Washington, 1983
FEWEST POINTS IN A SEASON	37	Cincinnati-St Louis, 1934
MOST POINTS IN A GAME	72	Washington v N.Y. Giants, 1966
MOST POINTS (BOTH TEAMS) IN A GAME	113	Washington v N.Y. Giants, 1966
FEWEST POINTS (BOTH TEAMS) IN A GAME	0	Many teams; last time N.Y. Giants v Detroit 1943

ALL-TIME TOP TWENTY
(1984 Active players in capitals)

All-Time Leading Rushers

		Yrs.	Att.	Yards	Ave.	TDs
1.	WALTER PAYTON	10	3,047	13,309	4.4	89
2.	Jim Brown	9	2,359	12,312	5.2	106
3.	FRANCO HARRIS	13	2,949	12,120	4.1	91
4.	O.J. Simpson	11	2,404	11,236	4.7	61
5.	JOHN RIGGINS	13	2,740	10,675	3.9	96
6.	TONY DORSETT	8	2,136	9,525	4.5	59
7.	EARL CAMPBELL	7	2,029	8,764	4.3	73
8.	Jim Taylor	10	1,941	8,597	4.4	83
9.	Joe Perry	14	1,737	8,378	4.8	53
10.	Larry Csonka	11	1,891	8,081	4.3	64
11.	OTTIS ANDERSON	6	1,690	7,364	4.4	40
12.	Leroy Kelly	10	1,727	7,274	4.2	74
13.	John Henry Johnson	13	1,571	6,803	4.3	48
14.	CHUCK MUNCIE	9	1,561	6,702	4.3	71
15.	Mark van Eeghen	10	1,652	6,650	4.0	37
16.	Lawrence McCutcheon	10	1,521	6,578	4.3	26
17.	MIKE PRUITT	9	1,593	6,540	4.1	47
18.	WILBERT MONTGOMERY	8	1,465	6,538	4.5	45
19.	Lydell Mitchell	9	1,675	6,534	3.9	30
20.	Floyd Little	9	1,641	6,323	3.8	43

All-Time Leading Receivers

		Yrs.	No.	Yards	Ave.	TDs
1.	CHARLIE JOINER	16	657	10,774	16.4	56
2.	Charley Taylor	13	649	9,110	14.0	79
3.	Don Maynard	15	633	11,834	18.7	88
4.	Raymond Berry	13	631	9,275	14.7	68
5.	HAROLD CARMICHAEL	14	590	8,985	15.2	79
6.	Fred Biletnikoff	14	589	8,974	15.2	76
7.	Harold Jackson	15	579	10,372	17.9	76
8.	Lionel Taylor	10	567	7,195	12.7	45
9.	STEVE LARGENT	9	545	8,772	16.1	72
10.	Lance Alworth	11	542	10,266	18.9	85
11.	Bobby Mitchell	11	521	7,954	15.3	65
12.	Billy Howton	12	503	8,459	16.8	61
13.	CLIFF BRANCH	13	501	8,685	17.3	67
14.	Tommy McDonald	12	495	8,410	17.0	84
15.	Ahmad Rashad	10	495	6,831	13.8	44
16.	Drew Pearson	11	489	7,822	16.0	48
17.	Don Hutson	11	488	7,991	16.4	99
18.	Jackie Smith	16	480	7,918	16.5	40
19.	Art Powell	10	479	8,046	16.8	81
20.	Boyd Dowler	12	474	7,270	15.4	40

All-Time Leading Scorers

		Yrs.	TDs	EPs	FGs	Total
1.	George Blanda	26	9	943	335	2,002
2.	JAN STENERUD	18	0	539	358	1,613
3.	Jim Turner	16	1	521	304	1,439
4.	Jim Bakken	17	0	534	282	1,380
5.	Fred Cox	15	0	519	282	1,365
6.	Lou Groza	17	1	641	234	1,349
7.	MARK MOSELEY	14	0	426	266	1,224
8.	Gino Cappelletti*	11	42	350	176	1,130

Tom Fears caught a league record 18 passes in one game in 1950

9.	Don Cockroft	13	0	432	216	1,080
10.	Garo Yepremian	14	0	444	210	1,074
11.	Bruce Gossett	11	0	374	219	1,031
12.	Sam Baker	15	2	428	179	977
13.	Lou Michaels**	13	1	386	187	955
14.	Roy Gerela	11	0	351	184	903
15.	Bobby Walston	12	46	365	80	881
16.	Pete Gogolak	10	0	344	173	863
17.	Errol Mann	11	0	315	177	846
18.	RAY WERSCHING	12	0	319	171	832
19.	Don Hutson	11	105	172	7	823
20.	PAT LEAHY	11	0	306	158	780

 * Includes four two-point conversions
 ** Includes a safety recorded in 1965 when Michaels played as a defensive end.

All-Time Passer Ratings

(Minimum 1,500 attempts)

Lance Alworth has the highest career average per catch among the all-time top twenty receivers

		Yrs.	Att.	Comp.	Yards	TDs	Int.	Rating
1.	JOE MONTANA	6	2,077	1,324	15,609	106	54	92.7
2.	Roger Staubach	11	2,958	1,685	22,700	153	109	83.5
3.	Sonny Jurgensen	18	4,262	2,433	32,224	255	189	82.8
4.	DANNY WHITE	9	1,943	1,155	14,754	109	90	82.7
5.	Len Dawson	19	3,741	2,136	28,711	239	183	82.6
6.	KEN ANDERSON	14	4,420	2,627	32,497	194	158	81.9
7.	DAN FOUTS	12	4,380	2,585	33,854	201	185	81.3
8.	Fran Tarkenton	18	6,467	3,686	47,003	342	266	80.5
9.	Bart Starr	16	3,149	1,808	24,718	152	138	80.3
10.	JOE THEISMANN	11	3,301	1,877	23,432	152	122	79.0
11.	Johnny Unitas	18	5,186	2,830	40,239	290	253	78.2
	Bert Jones	10	2,551	1,430	18,190	124	101	78.2
13.	Otto Graham	6	1,565	872	13,499	88	94	78.1
14.	Frank Ryan	13	2,133	1,090	16,042	149	111	77.7
15.	Bob Griese	14	3,429	1,926	25,092	192	172	77.3
16.	STEVE BARTKOWSKI	10	3,219	1,802	22,732	149	140	75.6
17.	Norm Van Brocklin	12	2,895	1,553	23,611	173	178	75.3
18.	Sid Luckman	12	1,744	904	14,686	137	132	75.0
	Brian Sipe	10	3,439	1,944	23,713	154	149	75.0
	KEN STABLER	15	3,793	2,270	27,938	194	222	75.0

PASSES COMPLETED	No.	YARDS PASSING	Yards	TOUCHDOWN PASSES	No.
1. Fran Tarkenton	3,686	1. Fran Tarkenton	47,003	1. Fran Tarkenton	342
2. Johnny Unitas	2,830	2. Johnny Unitas	40,239	2. Johnny Unitas	290
3. KEN ANDERSON	2,627	3. JIM HART	34,665	3. Sonny Jurgensen	255
4. JIM HART	2,593	4. DAN FOUTS	33,854	4. John Hadl	244
5. DAN FOUTS	2,585	5. John Hadl	33,503	5. Len Dawson	239
6. John Brodie	2,469	6. KEN ANDERSON	32,497	6. George Blanda	236
7. Sonny Jurgensen	2,433	7. Sonny Jurgensen	32,224	7. John Brodie	214
8. Roman Gabriel	2,366	8. John Brodie	31,548	8. Terry Bradshaw	212
9. John Hadl	2,363	9. Norm Snead	30,797	Y.A. Tittle	212
10. Norm Snead	2,276	10. Roman Gabriel	29,444	10. JIM HART	209
11. KEN STABLER	2,270	11. Len Dawson	28,711	11. DAN FOUTS	201
12. JOE FERGUSON	2,188	12. Y.A. Tittle	28,339	Roman Gabriel	201
13. Len Dawson	2,136	13. Terry Bradshaw	27,989	13. Norm Snead	196
14. Y.A. Tittle	2,118	14. KEN STABLER	27,938	Bobby Layne	196
15. Craig Morton	2,053	15. Craig Morton	27,908	15. KEN ANDERSON	194
16. Terry Bradshaw	2,025	16. Joe Namath	27,663	KEN STABLER	194
17. ARCHIE MANNING	2,011	17. JOE FERGUSON	27,590	17. Bob Griese	192
18. Brian Sipe	1,944	18. George Blanda	26,920	18. Sammy Baugh	187
19. Bob Griese	1,926	19. Bobby Layne	26,768	19. Craig Morton	183
20. George Blanda	1,911	20. Bob Griese	25,092	20. JOE FERGUSON	181

INDEX OF RETIRED PLAYERS LISTED IN ALL-TIME STATISTICS

KRAUSE Paul, Washington (1964-67), Minnesota (1968-79)

LANE Dick 'Night Train', L.A. Rams (1952-53), Chicago Cardinals (1954-59), Detroit (1960-65)

LAYNE Bobby, Chicago Bears (1948), N.Y. Giants (1949), Detroit (1950-58), Pittsburgh (1958-62)

LeFEBVRE Gil, Cincinnati Reds (1933)

LITTLE Floyd, Denver (1967-75)

LUCKMAN Sid, Chicago Bears (1939-50)

MANN Errol, Green Bay (1968), Detroit (1969-76), Oakland (1976-78)

MATSON Ollie, Chicago Cardinals (1952 and 1954-58), L.A. Rams (1959-62), Detroit (1963), Philadelphia (1964)

MAYNARD Don, N.Y. Jets (1960-72), St Louis (1973)

McCUTCHEON Lawrence, L.A. Rams (1972-79), Denver (1980), Seattle (1980), Buffalo (1981)

McDONALD Tommy, Philadelphia (1957-63), Dallas (1964), L.A. Rams (1965-66)

MICHAELS Lou, L.A. Rams (1958-60), Pittsburgh (1961-63), Baltimore (1964-69), Green Bay (1971)

MITCHELL Bobby, Cleveland (1958-61), Washington (1962-68)

MITCHELL Lydell, Baltimore (1972-77), San Diego (1978-79)

MORGAN Dennis, Dallas (1974), Philadelphia (1975)

MORRALL Earl, San Francisco (1956), Pittsburgh (1957-58), Detroit (1958-64), N.Y. Giants (1965-67), Baltimore (1968-71), Miami (1972-76)

MORTON Craig, Dallas (1965-74), N.Y. Giants (1974-76), Denver (1977-82)

NAMATH Joe, N.Y. Jets (1965-76), L.A. Rams (1977)

NEVERS Ernie, Duluth Eskimos (1926-27), Chicago Cardinals (1929-31)

PERRY Joe, San Francisco (1948-60 and 1963), Baltimore (1961-62)

POWELL Art, Philadelphia (1959), N.Y. Titans (1960-62), Oakland (1963-66), Buffalo (1967)

RASHAD Ahmad, St Louis (1972-73), Buffalo (1974-75), Minnesota (1976-82)

RYAN Frank, L.A. Rams (1958-61), Cleveland (1962-68), Washington (1969-70)

SAYERS Gale, Chicago (1965-71)

SHAW Bob, L.A. Rams (1945-49), Chicago Cardinals (1950)

SIMPSON O.J., Buffalo (1969-77), San Francisco (1978-79)

SIPE Brian, Cleveland (1974-83)

SMITH Bob, Detroit (1949-54)

SMITH Jackie, St Louis (1963-77), Dallas (1978)

SMITH Noland, Kansas City (1967-69), San Francisco (1969)

SNEAD Norm, Washington (1961-63), Philadelphia (1964-70), Minnesota (1971), N.Y. Giants (1972-74 and 1976), San Francisco (1974-75)

STABLER Ken, L.A. Raiders (1970-79), Houston (1980-81), New Orleans (1982-84)

STARR Bart, Green Bay (1956-71)

STAUBACH Roger, Dallas (1969-79)

STUDSTILL Pat, Detroit (1961-67), L.A. Rams (1968-71)

SWEETAN Karl, Detroit (1966-67), New Orleans (1968), L.A. Rams (1969-70)

TARKENTON Fran, Minnesota (1961-66 and 1972-78), N.Y. Giants (1967-71)

TATUM Jack, Oakland (1971-79), Houston (1980)

TAYLOR Charley, Washington (1964-77)

TAYLOR Jim, Green Bay (1958-66), New Orleans (1967)

TAYLOR Lionel, Chicago Bears (1959), Denver (1960-66), Houston (1967-68)

THOMPSON Bill, Denver (1969-81)

TITTLE Y.A., Baltimore (1948-50), San Francisco (1951-60), N.Y. Giants (1961-64)

TURNER Cecil, Chicago (1968-73)

TURNER Jim, N.Y. Jets (1964-70), Denver (1971-79)

UNITAS Johnny, Baltimore (1956-72), San Diego (1973)

VAN BROCKLIN Norm, L.A. Rams (1949-57), Philadelphia (1958-60)

WALSTON Bobby, Philadelphia (1951-62)

WATERFIELD Bob, Cleveland Rams (1945), L.A. Rams (1946-52)

WEST Charlie, Minnesota (1968-73), Detroit (1974-77), Denver (1978-79)

WILLIAMS Travis, Green Bay (1967-70), L.A. Rams (1971)

YEPREMIAN Garo, Detroit (1966-67), Miami (1970-78), New Orleans (1979), Tampa Bay (1980-81)

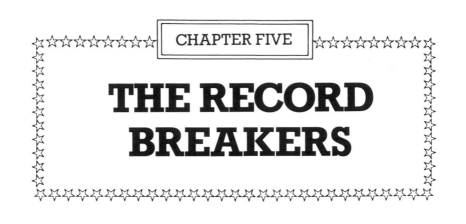

CHAPTER FIVE

THE RECORD BREAKERS

Coming into the season, one NFL career record was going to be broken. Of that there was little doubt. Both Franco Harris and Walter Payton were poised to go beyond Jim Brown's career rushing yardage total of 12,312. Adrift by only 362 yards, Harris needed just three good games whilst his Chicago rival, the younger of the two, required 687 yards and would have to bide his time. What couldn't be predicted was Harris's inability to reach contractual agreement with his team, the Pittsburgh Steelers. He was subsequently released. An injury to Seattle's Curt Warner on Week One gave Harris an unexpected chance to rejoin the race but, playing with a new club and, more importantly, in a different offensive system, he was unable to regain his momentum and, sadly, his challenge never materialised. Payton meanwhile swept on, overtaking Harris's new total of 12,032 on Week Four, and relegating Brown into second place on Week Six.

At that time the Rams' Eric Dickerson had rushed for 605 yards on the year but, four weeks later, he was up to 1,171 yards and was gathering pace. In order to exceed O.J. Simpson's single-season rushing record of 2,003 yards, he needed to average 139 yards over the remaining six games. As it turned out, he took only five but, for the moment, his goal was one which just might be achieved – attentions were focussed elsewhere.

Over in Miami, the prolific Dan Marino was enjoying what can only be described as a turkey shoot. As everyone knows, the turkey is not the most elusive of targets and doesn't fire back. At the halfway stage, Marino was on schedule for throwing 48 touchdown passes in the season. And that's exactly what he did, eclipsing the old record by twelve. Of course, someone has to catch the passes and, in Mark Duper, the Dolphins had the man for that. But it was the other half of the partnership

nicknamed the 'Mark Brothers', Mark Clayton, who stole the limelight and ended the campaign in possession of the single-season record for touchdown receptions with eighteen.

Around the league, it seemed, the quarterback had simply to put the ball up – someone would catch it. And that was happening with regular frequency in Washington, where wide receiver Art Monk was netting them in. With a late-season flurry, which saw him catch eleven, six, seven and eleven again, he took his total to 106 receptions, five more than the previous best by Charley Hennigan.

San Diego's Charlie Joiner has been catching passes in the NFL for as long as most people can remember, and it was a fitting tribute to a career which is not yet over, that he became the NFL all-time leader, now with 657 receptions to his credit.

Another veteran, Minnesota's Jan Stenerud, breaks the all-time record every time he kicks a field goal. With 20 in 1984, he built his total up to 358 and still counting. For accuracy in this department, kicking field goals, Kansas City's Nick Lowery rose to the top with a new NFL career-best percentage of 74.7. Miami's Uwe von Schamann had a poor year when it came to three-pointers but he was on target a single-season record 66 times with his extra point attempts. San Francisco's Ray Wersching didn't kick as many PATs but tied the existing single-season record by converting 56 without a failure. Houston's John James has to catch the ball before he puts in the boot. As a punter he entered the record book with a career total of 1,083 – and that adds up to a lot of nervous encounters.

Not only for productivity but also for sheer resilience, you have to admire Tampa Bay's James Wilder. He established a new single-season record for rushing attempts, with 407, after equalling Butch Woolfolk's single-game record of 43 on the way. In addition, as a demonstration of his versatility, his combined total of rushing attempts and pass receptions exceeded by 50 the previous single-season best of 442.

Pittsburgh's Louis Lipps was drafted primarily as a wide receiver but turned out to be a brilliant punt returner. On 53 attempts he gained 656 yards, beating the previous best by a rookie, Neal Colzie's 655 in 1975. For good measure he returned one 76 yards for a touchdown. Houston quarterback Warren Moon spent six years learning his trade in the Canadian Football League but was still formally an NFL first-year man in 1984. To him went the first-year records for most passing attempts (450), completions (259) and yards (3,338).

WALTER PAYTON

In the 1984 regular season, the remarkable Walter Payton established or equalled a total of six NFL records. The career rushing yardage record was one of three he took from Jim Brown. The others were those for 100-yard rushing games and total offensive yardage, which now stand at 63 and 17,304 yards respectively. Franco Harris did not escape attention and though he retains a share of the record

for 1,000-yard rushing seasons (eight), his records for most career rushing attempts and career attempts at advancing the ball went to Payton, with new highs of 3,047 and 3,456 respectively. Payton is reported to have given himself two more years to raise his career rushing total to 15,000 yards. At his current rate of progress, he'll have to slow down.

Career Rushing Statistics

Year	Att	Yds	Ave	Long	TD
1975	196	679	3.5	54t	7
1976	311	1,390	4.5	60	13
1977	339	1,852	5.5	73	14
1978	333	1,395	4.2	76	11
1979	369	1,610	4.4	43t	14
1980	317	1,460	4.6	69t	6
1981	339	1,222	3.6	39	6
1982*	148	596	4.0	26	1
1983	314	1,421	4.5	49t	6
1984	381	1,684	4.4	72t	11
Totals	**3,047**	**13,309**	**4.4**	**76**	**89**

* Season shortened to nine games because of the players' strike

Chicago's Walter Payton (#34) on his record-breaking day

ERIC DICKERSON

Needing just 212 yards, with two weeks remaining in the regular season, Eric Dickerson could have coasted to the single-season rushing record. Indeed, the final week was all set up for it – the Rams would be playing away to the 49ers, the game was to be televised nationwide and O.J. Simpson would be in the TV commentators' booth. That's how it was supposed to be. But he hadn't come so close to the record by hanging around and, on his twenty-seventh carry on Week Fifteen, he took his total for the game to a career-best 215 yards, and his total for the season to 2,007 yards. The record-breaking last nine yards came on a play known in the Rams' playbook as '47-gap'. With his twelfth 100-yard rushing game of the season, Dickerson went beyond the existing record of eleven, held jointly by Simpson and Earl Campbell. Walter Payton doesn't exactly need to worry yet, but he will be aware that, over a ten-year career, Dickerson's yardage from his first two years in the NFL projects to almost 20,000.

Game by Game – 1984						
Date	Opponent	Att	Yds	Ave	Long	TD
3/9	Dallas	21	138	6.6	27	1
9/9	Cleveland	27	102	3.8	18	0
16/9	at Pittsburgh	23	49	2.1	10	0
23/9	at Cincinnati	22	89	4.0	14	1
30/9	N.Y. Giants	22	120	5.5	32	0
7/10	Atlanta	19	107	5.6	47t	2
14/10	at N. Orleans	20	175	8.8	66	0
22/10	at Atlanta	24	125	6.0	33	1
28/10	S. Francisco	13	38	2.9	15	0
4/11	at St Louis	21	208	9.9	49	2
11/11	Chicago	28	149	5.3	19	0
18/11	at Green Bay	25	132	5.3	10	3
25/11	at Tampa Bay	28	191	6.8	51	1
2/12	N. Orleans	33	149	4.5	21	2
9/12	Houston	27	215	8.0	33	1
14/12	at S. Francisco	26	98	3.8	22	1
Totals		379	2,105	5.6	66	14

DAN MARINO

On Week Three of the 1983 season, the Raiders were leading Miami by the score of 27-0 in the fourth quarter, when Don Shula decided to give rookie quarterback Dan Marino his first taste of real NFL action. And the lad was quite impressive, passing for two late touchdowns. On Week Fourteen of the 1984 season, again the Raiders beat Miami but, this time, the victory came only after a titanic struggle against Marino who, with a sense of timing, threw four touchdown passes, the first of which took him beyond the single-season record of 36. By the end of the regular season he had raised his record total to an astonishing 48 and, in addition, set new single-season records for passing yardage (5,084), completions (362), 300-yard passing games (9) and 400-yard passing games (4). Passing into double-coverage doesn't bother a quarterback who has the quickest release since the retired Joe Namath, and even exceeds the consistency of his current rival, San Diego's Dan Fouts. Namath is now in the Pro Football Hall of Fame; Fouts seems certain to join him, and you have the feeling that there may be a place reserved for Marino.

Dan Marino (#13)

Game by Game – 1984							
Date	Opponent	Att	Comp	Yds	Long	Int	TD
2/9	at Washington	28	21	311	74t	0	5
9/9	N. England	27	16	234	38t	2	2
17/9	at Buffalo	35	26	296	23	1	3
23/9	Indianapolis	29	14	257	80t	0	2
30/9	at St Louis	36	24	429	51	0	3
7/10	at Pittsburgh	24	16	226	34t	1	2
14/10	Houston	32	25	321	32t	0	3
21/10	at N. England	39	24	316	28	1	4
28/10	Buffalo	28	19	282	65t	3	3
4/11	at N.Y. Jets	42	23	422	54	2	2
11/11	Philadelphia	34	20	246	21	1	1
18/11	at San Diego	41	28	338	32	1	2
26/11	N.Y. Jets	31	19	192	24	0	4
2/12	L.A. Raiders	57	35	470	64t	2	4
9/12	at Indianapolis	41	29	404	42	1	4
17/12	Dallas	40	23	340	63t	2	4
Totals		**564**	**362**	**5,084**	**80t**	**17**	**48**

◄ Eric Dickerson (#29), new holder of the single-season rushing record

MARK CLAYTON

It always pays to read the fine print, especially in NFL club media guidebooks. The Dolphins' 1984 publication reported that the 1983 rookie, Mark Clayton, had averaged 9.6 yards when setting a club single-season record by returning punts for 392 yards, and had caught six passes at the average of 19 yards per reception. Also, coach Shula had mentioned, in one of many preseason interviews, '. . . and Mark Clayton will be given more playing time at wide receiver.' From his good punt returning, he had to be elusive and fast. And a 19-yard receiving average is excellent. It also turned out to be a very accurate measure of his abilities as a starting wide receiver. He maintained that 19-yard average over 73 receptions in 1984. With 18 touchdown receptions in a single season, he exceeded the previous best of 17, a figure which is shared by Don Hutson, Elroy 'Crazylegs' Hirsch and Bill Groman.

Mark Clayton (#83) in the clear for his 18th touchdown of the season

Game by Game – 1984						
Date	Opponent	No	Yds	Ave	Long	TD
2/9 at Washington		3	31	10.3	20	1
9/9 N. England		5	75	15.0	38t	2
17/9 at Buffalo		2	34	17.0	22	1
23/9 Indianapolis*		–	–	–	–	–
30/9 at St Louis		5	143	28.6	42	1
7/10 at Pittsburgh		5	110	22.0	33	0
14/10 Houston		4	61	15.3	27t	1
21/10 at N. England		7	99	14.1	20	1
28/10 Buffalo		3	106	35.3	65t	2
4/11 at N.Y. Jets		2	61	30.5	47t	1
11/11 Philadelphia		4	75	18.8	20	0
18/11 at San Diego		6	71	11.8	23	1
26/11 N.Y. Jets		5	69	13.8	24	1
2/12 L.A. Raiders		9	177	19.7	64t	2
9/12 at Indianapolis		9	127	14.1	32	1
17/12 Dallas		4	150	37.5	63t	3
Totals		**73**	**1,389**	**19.0**	**65t**	**18**

* Injured

Art Monk (#81) breaking the all-time single-season record against St Louis

ART MONK

With wide receivers 'Downtown' Charlie Brown and Alvin Garrett injured for much of the 1984 season, Redskins fans were treated to a new sight. They had become used to the graceful, flowing moves of wide receiver Art Monk, but now they saw a fierce competitor, often making his clutch receptions in the teeth of trouble. Someone had to do it – there was nobody else. In the Week Eleven game against Detroit, his first reception gave him a personal best 59 for the season and he just kept on going. For most of the time, his approach to Charley Hennigan's 20-year-old record of 101 receptions went unnoticed. But, by the final weekend, Payton, Dickerson and the like had achieved their goals, and the cameras focussed on Monk, literally, in the Redskins' final game. At stake was the NFC Eastern Division Championship, and Monk used the occasion to parade his talent eleven times for receptions which brought him the new single-season record by the margin of five.

Game by Game – 1984

Date	Opponent	No	Yds	Ave	Long	TD
2/9	Miami	3	54	18.0	24	0
10/9	at S. Francisco	10	200	20.0	32	0
16/9	N.Y. Giants	8	78	9.8	18	0
23/9	at N. England	5	37	7.4	15	0
30/9	Philadelphia	5	80	16.0	51t	1
7/10	at Indianapolis	8	141	17.6	48t	3
14/10	Dallas	4	67	16.8	35	0
21/10	at St Louis	6	87	14.5	25	0
28/10	at N.Y. Giants	4	104	26.0	72	0
5/11	Atlanta	5	45	9.0	12	0
11/11	Detroit	5	34	6.8	9	0
18/11	at Philadelphia	8	80	10.0	16	0
25/11	Buffalo	11	104	9.5	17	1
29/11	at Minnesota	6	45	7.5	10	0
9/12	at Dallas	7	80	11.4	30	0
16/12	St Louis	11	136	12.4	36	2
Totals		**106**	**1,372**	**12.9**	**72**	**7**

CHARLIE JOINER

Coming into the season, Charlie Joiner needed 54 receptions to surpass Charley Taylor's career record of 649. It seemed to be asking a lot of a player who would be 37 years old in October. But the total duly arrived, without fuss, on Week Thirteen against Pittsburgh, when all but one of his six receptions of the game came in the final quarter. Typical of the man, he was more concerned about the possible touchdown pass he had dropped, early in the second quarter. With one major goal achieved, he can now set his sights on the NFL career record for receiving yardage. He already has 10,774 and needs another 1,061 to surpass the retired Don Maynard.

Career Pass Receiving Statistics

Year	Team	No	Yds	Ave	Long	TD
1969	Houston	7	77	11.0	21	0
1970	Houston	28	416	14.9	87t	3
1971	Houston	31	681	22.0	55	7
1972	Hou/Cin	24	439	18.3	82	2
1973	Cincinnati	13	214	16.5	26	0
1974	Cincinnati	24	390	16.3	55	1
1975	Cincinnati	37	726	19.6	51	5
1976	San Diego	50	1,056	21.1	81t	7
1977	San Diego	35	542	15.5	32t	6
1978	San Diego	33	607	18.4	46	1
1979	San Diego	72	1,008	14.0	39	4
1980	San Diego	71	1,132	15.9	51	4
1981	San Diego	70	1,188	17.0	57	7
1982*	San Diego	36	545	15.1	43	0
1983	San Diego	65	960	14.8	33t	3
1984	San Diego	61	793	13.0	41	6
Totals		**657**	**10,774**	**16.4**	**87t**	**56**

* Season shortened to nine games because of the players' strike.

Charlie Joiner (#18) evades Pittsburgh's David Little (#50) on his big day

JAN STENERUD

After being released by the Green Bay Packers, at the age of forty, Jan Stenerud may well have considered retirement. Already, he held the NFL career record for most successful field goal attempts, with 338. He wore a Super Bowl Championship ring from his days with Kansas City, he had played in three AFC-NFC Pro Bowls and had been voted to many All-Pro squads. Yet, when the opportunity to play for Minnesota arose, before the 1984 season, he grabbed it with both hands. Extending his own NFL field goal record was just part of the story. He kicked three field goals of over 50 yards, including a 53-yarder to beat Tampa Bay with just three seconds remaining, and kicked five field goals in Minnesota's 29-28 victory over Detroit. The best field goal percentage in the league was good enough to take him to a fourth Pro Bowl.

Jan Stenerud

Career Field Goal Statistics

Year		FGA	FGM	%
1967	Kansas City	36	21	.583
1968	Kansas City	40	30	.750
1969	Kansas City	35	27	.771
1970	Kansas City	42	30	.714
1971	Kansas City	44	26	.591
1972	Kansas City	36	21	.583
1973	Kansas City	38	24	.632
1974	Kansas City	24	17	.708
1975	Kansas City	32	22	.688
1976	Kansas City	38	21	.553
1977	Kansas City	18	8	.444
1978	Kansas City	30	20	.667
1979	Kansas City	23	12	.522
1980	Green Bay*	5	3	.600
1981	Green Bay	24	22	.917
1982	Green Bay**	18	13	.722
1983	Green Bay	26	21	.808
1984	Minnesota	23	20	.870
Totals		**532**	**358**	**.673**

* Stenerud played only four games
** Season shortened to nine games because of the players' strike

AMERICAN FOOTBALL CONFERENCE

TEAM RANKINGS

| | OFFENSE | | | | | | DEFENSE | | | | | |
	Total Yds.	Rushing	Passing	Points For	%Intercepted	%Sacked	Total Yds.	Rushing	Passing	Points Against	%Interceptions	%Sacks
Buffalo	13	13	13	=11	10	9	10	12	9	14	12	14
Cincinnati	3	=2	6	8	8	7	6	5	8	8	5	10
Cleveland	12	9	10	=11	9	12	1	8	1	4	6	4
Denver	10	4	12	7	5	4	12	2	13	1	4	6
Houston	11	10	9	13	2	8	14	14	4	13	14	12
Indianapolis	14	6	14	14	12	14	9	10	11	12	10	9
Kansas City	8	14	3	10	6	3	11	9	12	7	3	8
L.A. Raiders	6	8	5	5	14	11	2	7	2	2	8	1
Miami	1	7	1	1	3	1	7	13	6	5	7	11
New England	5	5	8	6	1	13	5	6	5	9	11	2
N.Y. Jets	7	1	11	9	7	10	8	11	10	10	13	7
Pittsburgh	4	=2	7	4	13	5	3	1	7	6	2	5
San Diego	2	11	2	3	4	2	13	4	14	11	9	13
Seattle	9	12	4	2	11	6	4	3	3	3	1	3

AFC PASSERS

	Att	Comp	% Comp	Yards	Ave Gain	TD	% TD	Long	Int	% Int	Rating Points
Marino, Dan, *Mia.*	564	362	64.2	5084	9.01	48	8.5	t80	17	3.0	108.9
Eason, Tony, *N.E.*	431	259	60.1	3228	7.49	23	5.3	t76	8	1.9	93.4
Fouts, Dan, *S.D.*	507	317	62.5	3740	7.38	19	3.7	t61	17	3.4	83.4
Krieg, Dave, *Sea.*	480	276	57.5	3671	7.65	32	6.7	t80	24	5.0	83.3
Anderson, Ken, *Cin.*	275	175	63.6	2107	7.66	10	3.6	t80	12	4.4	81.0
Kenney, Bill, *K.C.*	282	151	53.5	2098	7.44	15	5.3	t65	10	3.5	80.7
Moon, Warren, *Hou.*	450	259	57.6	3338	7.42	12	2.7	76	14	3.1	76.9
Elway, John, *Den.*	380	214	56.3	2598	6.84	18	4.7	73	15	3.9	76.8
Malone, Mark, *Pitt.*	272	147	54.0	2137	7.86	16	5.9	t61	17	6.3	73.4
Ryan, Pat, *Jets*	285	156	54.7	1939	6.80	14	4.9	t44	14	4.9	72.0
Wilson, Marc, *Raiders*	282	153	54.3	2151	7.63	15	5.3	92	17	6.0	71.7
McDonald, Paul, *Clev.*	493	271	55.0	3472	7.04	14	2.8	64	23	4.7	67.3
Ferguson, Joe, *Buff.*	344	191	55.5	1991	5.79	12	3.5	t68	17	4.9	63.5
Blackledge, Todd, *K.C.*	294	147	50.0	1707	5.81	6	2.0	t46	11	3.7	59.2

t = Touchdown
Leader based on rating points, minimum 230 attempts

AFC RECEIVERS

	No	Yards	Ave	Long	TD
Newsome, Ozzie, *Clev.*	89	1001	11.2	52	5
Stallworth, John, *Pitt.*	80	1395	17.4	51	11
Christensen, Todd, *Raiders*	80	1007	12.6	38	7
Largent, Steve, *Sea.*	74	1164	15.7	65	12
Clayton, Mark, *Mia.*	73	1389	19.0	t65	18
Duper, Mark, *Mia.*	71	1306	18.4	t80	8
Watson, Steve, *Den.*	69	1170	17.0	73	7
Smith, Tim, *Hou.*	69	1141	16.5	t75	4
Franklin, Byron, *Buff.*	69	862	12.5	t64	4
Shuler, Mickey, *Jets*	68	782	11.5	49	6
Ramsey, Derrick, *N.E.*	66	792	12,0	34	7
Collinsworth, Cris, *Cin.*	64	989	15.5	t57	6
Allen, Marcus, *Raiders*	64	758	11.8	92	5
Marshall, Henry, *K.C.*	62	912	14.7	37	4
Joiner, Charlie, *S.D.*	61	793	13.0	41	6
Nathan, Tony, *Mia.*	61	579	9.5	26	2
Carson, Carlos, *K.C.*	57	1078	18.9	57	4
Holohan, Pete, *S.D.*	56	734	13.1	51	1
Winslow, Kellen, *S.D.*	55	663	12.1	33	2
Chandler, Wes, *S.D.*	52	708	13.6	t63	6
Harris, M.L., *Cin.*	48	759	15.8	t80	2
Starring, Stephen, *N.E.*	46	657	14.3	t65	4
Lipps, Louis, *Pitt.*	45	860	19.1	t80	9
Barnwell, Malcolm, *Raiders*	45	851	18.9	t51	2
Winder, Sammy, *Den.*	44	288	6.5	21	2
Butler, Raymond, *Ind.*	43	664	15.4	t74	6
Moore, Nat, *Mia.*	43	573	13.3	t37	6
Johnson, Butch, *Den.*	42	587	14.0	49	6
Walker, Wesley, *Jets*	41	623	15.2	t44	7
Williams, Jamie, *Hou.*	41	545	13.3	32	3
Sievers, Eric, *S.D.*	41	438	10.7	32	3
Dressel, Chris, *Hou.*	40	378	9.5	42	2
Porter, Tracy, *Ind.*	39	590	15.1	t63	2
Dawson, Lin, *N.E.*	39	427	10.9	27	4
Jackson, Earnest, *S.D.*	39	222	5.7	21	1
Morgan, Stanley, *N.E.*	38	709	18.7	t76	5
Erenberg, Rich, *Pitt.*	38	358	9.4	25	1
Brown, Theotis, *K.C.*	38	236	6.2	17	0
Turner, Daryl, *Sea.*	35	715	20.4	t80	10
Brennan, Brian, *Clev.*	35	455	13.0	52	3
Jennings, Stanford, *Cin.*	35	346	9.9	43	3
Johnson, Dan, *Mia.*	34	426	12.5	42	3
Bell, Greg, *Buff.*	34	277	8.1	37	1
Brooks, James, *Cin.*	34	268	7.9	t27	2
Young, Charle, *Sea.*	33	337	10.2	31	1
Hunter, Tony, *Buff.*	33	331	10.0	30	2
Moore, Booker, *Buff.*	33	172	5.2	14.0	0
Jones, 'Lam', *Jets*	32	470	14.7	37	1
Doornink, Dan, *Sea.*	31	365	11.8	32	2
Moriarty, Larry, *Hou.*	31	206	6.6	24	1
Paige, Stephone, *K.C.*	30	541	18.0	t65	4
Dennard, Preston, *Buff.*	30	417	13.9	t68	7
Alexander, Charles, *Cin.*	29	203	7.0	22	0
Hardy, Bruce, *Mia.*	28	257	9.2	19	5
Scott, Willie, *K.C.*	28	253	9.0	27	3
Branch, Cliff, *Raiders*	27	401	14.9	47	0
Willhite, Gerald, *Den.*	27	298	11.0	63	0

t = Touchdown

Tony Eason (#11) might have won the AFC passing title in another year

AFC RUSHERS

	Att	Yards	Ave	Long	TD
Jackson, Earnest, *S.D.*	296	1179	4.0	t32	8
Allen, Marcus, *Raiders*	275	1168	4.2	t52	13
Winder, Sammy, *Den.*	296	1153	3.9	24	4
Bell, Greg, *Buff.*	262	1100	4.2	t85	7
McNeil, Freeman, *Jets*	229	1070	4.7	53	5
Pollard, Frank, *Pitt.*	213	851	4.0	52	6
James, Craig, *N.E.*	160	790	4.9	73	1
Moriarty, Larry, *Hou.*	189	785	4.2	t51	6
McMillan, Randy, *Ind.*	163	705	4.3	t31	5
Heard, Herman, *K.C.*	165	684	4.1	t69	4
Green, Boyce, *Clev.*	202	673	3.3	29	0
Kinnebrew, Larry, *Cin.*	154	623	4.0	23	9
Abercrombie, Walter, *Pitt.*	145	610	4.2	31	1
Bennett, Woody, *Mia.*	144	606	4.2	23	7
Nathan, Tony, *Mia.*	118	558	4.7	22	1
Tatupu, Mosi, *N.E.*	133	553	4.2	t20	4
Collins, Anthony, *N.E.*	138	550	4.0	21	5
Hector, Johnny, *Jets*	124	531	4.3	64	1
Dickey, Curtis, *Ind.*	131	523	4.0	30	3
Pruitt, Mike, *Clev.*	163	506	3.1	14	6
Carter, Joe, *Mia.*	100	495	5.0	35	1
Alexander, Charles, *Cin.*	132	479	3.6	22	2
Byner, Earnest, *Clev.*	72	426	5.9	54	2
Erenberg, Rich, *Pitt.*	115	405	3.5	t31	2
Brooks, James, *Cin.*	103	396	3.8	33	2
Jennings, Stanford, *Cin.*	79	379	4.8	t20	2
Hawkins, Frank, *Raiders*	108	376	3.5	17	3
Willhite, Gerald, *Den.*	77	371	4.8	52	2
Brown, Theotis, *K.C.*	97	337	3.5	25	4
Hughes, David, *Sea.*	94	327	3.5	14	1
Lane, Eric, *Sea.*	80	299	3.7	t40	4
Middleton, Frank, *Ind.*	92	275	3.0	20	1
Edwards, Stan, *Hou.*	60	267	4.5	20	1
King, Kenny, *Raiders*	67	254	3.8	18	0
Elway, John, *Den.*	56	237	4.2	21	1
McGee, Buford, *S.D.*	67	226	3.4	30	4
Jackson, Billy, *K.C.*	50	225	4.5	16	1
Doornink, Dan, *Sea.*	57	215	3.8	25	0
Moon, Warren, *Hou.*	58	211	3.6	31	1
Parros, Rick, *Den.*	46	208	4.5	25	2
Johnson, Pete, *S.D.-Mia.*	87	205	2.4	9	12
Morris, Randall, *Sea.*	58	189	3,3	16	0
Krieg, Dave, *Sea.*	46	186	4.0	t37	3
Neal, 'Speedy', *Buff.*	49	175	3.6	10	1
Harris, Franco, *Sea.*	68	170	2.5	16	0
Lacy, Kenneth, *K.C.*	46	165	3.6	t24	2
Eason, Tony, *N.E.*	40	154	3.9	t25	5
Dixon, Zachary, *Sea.*	52	149	2.9	17	2
Pagel, Mike, *Ind.*	26	149	5.7	23	1
Barber, Marion, *Jets*	31	148	4.8	18	2
Schlichter, Art, *Ind.*	19	145	7.6	22	1
Minter, Cedric, *Jets*	34	136	4.0	14	1
Paige, Tony, *Jets*	35	130	3.7	24	7
Moore, Alvin, *Ind.*	38	127	3.3	18	2
James, Lionel, *S.D.*	35	115	4.6	20	0
Wonsley, George, *Ind.*	37	111	3.0	13	0
Blackledge, Todd, *K.C.*	18	102	5.7	26	1

t = Touchdown

Marcus Allen scored 13 rushing touchdowns

AFC KICKERS

	XP	XPA	FG	FGA	PTS
Anderson, Gary, *Pitt.*	45	45	24	32	117
Johnson, Norm, *Sea.*	50	51	20	24	110
Franklin, Tony, *N.E.*	42	42	22	28	108
Lowery, Nick, *K.C.*	35	35	23	33	104
Breech, Jim, *Cin.*	37	37	22	31	103
Karlis, Rich, *Den.*	38	41	21	28	101
Bahr, Chris, *Raiders*	40	42	20	27	100
Bahr, Matt, *Clev.*	25	25	24	32	97
von Schamann, Uwe, *Mia.*	66	70	9	19	93
Benirschke, Rolf, *S.D.*	41	41	17	26	92
Leahy, Pat, *Jets*	38	39	17	24	89
Allegre, Raul, *Ind.*	14	14	11	18	47
Cooper, Joe, *Hou.*	13	13	11	13	46
Danelo, Joe, *Buff.*	17	17	8	16	41
Kempf, Florian, *Hou.*	14	14	4	6	26
Nelson, Chuck, *Buff.*	14	14	3	5	23
Biasucci, Dean, *Ind.*	13	14	3	5	22
Ricardo, Benny, *S.D.*	5	6	3	3	14
Cox, Steve, *Clev.*	0	0	1	3	3

AFC KICKOFF RETURNERS

	No	Yards	Ave	Long	TD
Humphery, Bobby, *Jets*	22	675	30.7	t97	1
Williams, Dokie, *Raiders*	24	621	25.9	62	0
Anderson, Larry, *Ind.*	22	525	23.9	69	0
Springs, Kirk, *Jets*	23	521	22.7	73	0
Roaches, Carl, *Hou.*	30	679	22.6	49	0
James, Lionel, *S.D.*	43	959	22.3	55	0
Collins, Anthony, *N.E.*	25	544	21.8	46	0
Montgomery, Cleotha, *Raiders*	26	555	21.3	42	0
Walker, Fulton, *Mia.*	29	617	21.3	41	0
Williams, Van, *Buff.*	39	820	21.0	65	0
Jennings, Stanford, *Cin.*	22	452	20.5	46	0
Erenberg, Rich, *Pitt.*	28	575	20.5	47	0
Smith, Phil, *Ind.*	32	651	20.3	t96	1
Paige, Stephone, *K.C.*	27	544	20.1	45	0
Williams, Jon, *N.E.*	23	461	20.0	29	0
Byner, Earnest, *Clev.*	22	415	18.9	28	0
Dixon, Zachary, *Sea.*	25	446	17.8	36	0
Wilson, Don, *Buff.*	34	576	16.9	36	0
(Non-Qualifiers)					
Lang, Gene, *Den.*	19	404	21.3	38	0
Smith, J.T., *K.C.*	19	391	20.6	39	0
Martin, Mike, *Cin.*	19	386	20.3	44	0
Spencer, Todd, *Pitt.*	18	373	20.7	40	0
Davis, Bruce, *Clev.*	18	369	20.5	40	0
Hughes, David, *Sea.*	17	348	20.5	38	0
Walls, Herkie, *Hou.*	15	289	19.3	29	0
McGee, Buford, *S.D.*	14	315	22.5	35	0
Allen, Patrick, *Hou.*	11	210	19.1	23	0
Bird, Steve, *St.L-S.D.*	11	205	18.6	28	0
Minter, Cedric, *Jets*	10	224	22.4	52	0
Heflin, Vince, *Mia.*	9	130	14.4	26	0

t = Touchdown
Leader based on average return, minimum 20 returns

AFC PUNTERS

	No	Yards	Long	Ave	Total Punts	TB	Blk	Opp Ret	Ret Yds	In 20	Net Ave
Arnold, Jim, *K.C.*	98	4397	63	44.9	98	13	0	60	461	22	37.5
Roby, Reggie, *Mia.*	51	2281	69	44.7	51	10	0	17	138	15	38.1
Stark, Rohn, *Ind.*	98	4383	72	44.7	98	7	0	62	600	21	37.2
Cox, Steve, *Clev.*	74	3213	69	43.4	76	8	2	43	489	16	33.7
Prestridge, Luke, *N.E.*	44	1884	89	42.8	44	5	0	21	228	8	35.4
McInally, Pat, *Cin.*	67	2832	61	42.3	67	8	0	38	310	19	35.3
Camarillo, Rich, *N.E.*	48	2020	61	42.1	48	7	0	24	214	12	34.7
Buford, Maury, *S.D.*	66	2773	60	42.0	66	3	0	43	399	11	35.1
Kidd, John, *Buff.*	88	3696	63	42.0	90	8	2	52	597	16	32.7
Guy, Ray, *Raiders*	91	3809	63	41.9	91	12	0	34	345	25	35.4
Colquitt, Craig, *Pitt.*	70	2883	62	41.2	70	5	0	37	351	21	34.7
Norman, Chris, *Den.*	96	3850	83	40.1	96	6	0	44	335	16	35.4
Ramsey, Chuck, *Jets*	74	2935	64	39.7	75	8	1	37	242	19	33.8
James, John, *Hou.*	88	3482	55	39.6	88	5	0	60	618	20	31.4
West, Jeff, *Sea.*	95	3567	60	37.5	95	10	0	32	205	24	33.3

Leader based on gross average, minimum 40 punts.

AFC PUNT RETURNERS

	No	FC	Yards	Ave	Long	TD
Martin, Mike, *Cin.*	24	5	376	15.7	55	0
Lipps, Louis, *Pitt.*	53	2	656	12.4	t76	1
Willhite, Gerald, *Den.*	20	9	200	10.0	35	0
Fryar, Irving, *N.E.*	36	10	347	9.6	55	0
Wilson, Don, *Buff.*	33	8	297	9.0	t65	1
Pruitt, Greg, *Raiders*	53	16	473	8.9	38	0
Springs, Kirk, *Jets*	28	10	247	8.8	33	0
Smith, J.T., *K.C.*	39	14	332	8.5	27	0
Walker, Fulton, *Mia.*	21	14	169	8.0	33	0
Brennan, Brian, *Clev.*	25	10	199	8.0	19	0
James, Lionel, *S.D.*	30	9	208	6.9	t58	1
Anderson, Larry, *Ind.*	27	7	182	6.7	19	0
Roaches, Carl, *Hou.*	26	8	152	5.8	18	0

t = Touchdown
Leader based on average return, minimum 20 returns

AFC INTERCEPTORS

	No	Yards	Ave	Long	TD
Easley, Ken, *Sea.*	10	126	12.6	t58	2
Brown, Dave, *Sea.*	8	179	22.4	t90	2
Cherry, Deron, *K.C.*	7	140	20.0	67	0
Shell, Donnie, *Pitt.*	7	61	8.7	t52	1
Haynes, Mike, *Raiders*	6	220	36.7	t97	1
Blackwood, Glenn, *Mia.*	6	169	28.2	50	0
Washington, Sam, *Pitt.*	6	138	23.0	t69	2
Ross, Kevin, *K.C.*	6	124	20.7	t71	1
Foley, Steve, *Den.*	6	97	16.2	t40	1
Harden, Mike, *Den.*	6	79	13.2	t45	1
Harris, John, *Sea.*	6	79	13.2	29	0
Daniel, Eugene, *Ind.*	6	25	4.2	18	0
Romes, Charles, *Buff.*	5	130	26.0	55	0
Gross, Al, *Clev.*	5	103	20.6	47	0
Woodruff, Dwayne, *Pitt.*	5	56	11.2	t42	1
Dixon, Hanford, *Clev.*	5	31	6.2	18	0
Byrd, Gill, *S.D.*	4	157	39.3	t99	2

Simpson, Keith, *Sea.*	4	138	34.5	t76	2
Judson, William, *Mia.*	4	121	30.3	t60	1
Breeden, Louis, *Cin.*	4	96	24.0	70	0
Jackson, Terry, *Sea.*	4	78	19.5	t62	1
Wilson, Steve, *Den.*	4	59	14.8	22	0
Lewis, Albert, *K.C.*	4	57	14.3	31	0
Tullis, Willie, *Hou.*	4	48	12.0	22	0
McElroy, Vann, *Raiders*	4	42	10.5	31	0
Jackson, Robert, *Cin.*	4	32	8.0	t28	1
Kemp, Bobby, *Cin.*	4	27	6.8	14	0
Carter, Russell, *Jets*	4	26	6.5	19	0
Clayborn, Ray, *N.E.*	3	102	34.0	85	0
Hinkle, Bryan, *Pitt.*	3	77	25.7	43	0
Randle, Tate, *Ind.*	3	66	22.0	54	0
Taylor, Terry, *Sea.*	3	63	21.0	37	0
Lowe, Woodrow, *S.D.*	3	61	20.3	t32	1
Williams, Eric, *Pitt.*	3	49	16.3	44	0
Horton, Ray, *Cin.*	3	48	16.0	t48	1
Freeman, Steve, *Buff.*	3	45	15.0	45	0
McNeal, Don, *Mia.*	3	41	13.7	30	1
Smith, Billy Ray, *S.D.*	3	41	13.7	21	0
Blackwood, Lyle, *Mia.*	3	29	9.7	15	0
Lankford, Paul, *Mia.*	3	25	8.3	22	0
Hartwig, Carter, *Hou.*	3	23	7.7	19	0
Lippett, Ronnie, *N.E.*	3	23	7.7	13	0
Krauss, Barry, *Ind.*	3	20	6.7	18	0
Smith, Dennis, *Den.*	3	13	4.3	10	0
Carpenter, Brian, *Wash.-Buff.*	3	11	3.7	11	0
Burroughs, Jim, *Ind.*	3	9	3.0	6	0
Mecklenburg, Karl, *Den.*	2	105	52.5	63	0
Robbins, Randy, *Den.*	2	62	31.0	t62	1
Radecic, Scott, *K.C.*	2	54	27.0	35	1
Ray, Darrol, *Jets*	2	54	27.0	28	0
King, Linden, *S.D.*	2	52	26.0	37	0
Simmons, John, *Cin.*	2	43	21.5	t43	1
Turner, John, *S.D.*	2	43	21.5	43	0
Marion, Fred, *N.E.*	2	39	19.5	26	0
McAlister, Ken, *K.C.*	2	33	16.5	22	0
Williams, Reggie, *Cin.*	2	33	16.5	33	0
Martin, Rod, *Raiders*	2	31	15.5	17	1
Young, Andre, *S.D.*	2	31	15.5	31	0
Busick, Steve, *Den.*	2	21	10.5	16	0
Burruss, Lloyd, *K.C.*	2	16	8.0	16	0
Lynn, Johnny, *Jets*	2	16	8.0	16	0

t = Touchdown

Mike Martin, the AFC leading punt returner

BUFFALO BILLS AFC East

Address One Bills Drive, Orchard Park, New York 14127.
Stadium Rich Stadium, Orchard Park.
  Capacity 80,290 *Playing Surface* AstroTurf.
Team Colours Royal Blue, Scarlet Red and White.
Head Coach Kay Stephenson – third year.
Championships Division 1980; AFL 1964,'65.
History AFL 1960-69, AFC 1970-

Offense

The departure of veteran quarterback Joe Ferguson, who has been traded to Detroit, leaves the way open for either Matt Kofler or Joe Dufek to make a name for himself. Dufek must come into the season as the favourite, having started the final three games of 1984. However, neither man is likely to produce the kind of dominance required in this position and it seems as if it will remain a problem area for the Bills. Whichever man gets the nod will hope to be better protected by an offensive line which, in 1984, gave up 60 sacks (only New England conceded more in the AFC). Surprisingly, starting right guard Jon Borchardt has been traded to Seattle and it seems likely that seventh-year man Tim Vogler will step up to replace him. However, there will be competition from draftee Mark Traynowicz who, though a center in college, is considered sufficiently versatile to be converted to guard or tackle in the pros. The line is further strengthened by the return of former starting tackle Justin Cross, who missed the final half of 1984 with an ankle injury. Rookie running back Greg Bell was a revelation, rushing for 1,100 yards and leading the club in scoring (he had eight touchdowns). The signs are, however, that he will remain a lone spearhead unless rookie running back Jacque Robinson can repeat the dazzling form he showed on occasions for the University of Washington. (He rushed 20 times for 142 yards and two touchdowns in the Huskies' 1982 Rose Bowl victory over Iowa.) The tight end position is in the cultivated hands of Tony Hunter who caught 33 passes despite missing eight games last year. The Bills must be praying, however, that veteran wide receiver Jerry Butler has shrugged off the injuries which have restricted him to just 16 games in the last three campaigns, and that last season's second-round pick, Eric Richardson, will be fit to make his pro debut after a year on injured reserve. In their absence, the pairing of Byron Franklin and ex-Ram Preston Dennard was adequate but never presented a deep threat.

Defense

The arrival of defensive end Bruce Smith, the first pick overall in this year's draft, could give the Bills a top class three-man line, providing both defensive end Ben Williams and nose tackle Fred Smerlas can reproduce the form which took them to the Pro Bowl in the early 1980s. In total, the defense managed just 26 quarterback sacks last year (only the Vikings had fewer in the entire league). Smerlas was the sharp point of what used to be known and feared as the 'Bermuda Triangle', a graveyard for opposing running backs. Of that threesome, linebacker Shane Nelson went in 1982, but the third component, linebacker Jim Haslett remains. A re-enthused Haslett and the continued improvement of Eugene Marve must bolster up a defense which, in 1984, ranked only 19th in the league against the rush. The return of outside linebacker Lucius Sanford will solidify defense against the pass. The secondary suffered the loss of several injured players, notably cornerbacks Rodney Bellinger and the former Dallas number one pick, Rod Hill. Safety Jeff Nixon, it seems, will always be injury-prone and team doctors are concerned about Matt Vanden Boom. Cornerback Charles Romes, on the other hand, is a solid rock and forms the basis of a rebuilding programme which has started with the drafting of cornerback Derrick Burroughs in the first round.

Special Teams

The one bright spot in an undistinguished special teams performance was the punt returning of rookie free agent Don Wilson, who ranked seventh in the league with a 9.0-yard average. He returned one 65 yards for a touchdown. Elsewhere, there could be changes. Kicker Chuck Nelson, who replaced Joe Danelo late in the season, may not be the answer, and rookie punter John Kidd lacks big-league technique at present but may be given another chance.

1985 DRAFT

Round	Name	Pos.	Ht.	Wt.	College
1.	Smith, Bruce	DE	6-3	290	Virginia Tech.
1.	Burroughs, Derrick	DB	6-1	175	Memphis State
2.	Traynowicz, Mark	T	6-5	270	Nebraska
2.	Burkett, Chris	WR	6-4	195	Jackson State
3.	Reich, Frank	QB	6-3	208	Maryland
3.	Garner, Hal	LB	6-5	217	Utah State
4.	Reed, Andre	WR	6-1	185	Kutztown State
4.	Hellestrae, Dale	T	6-5	270	Southern Methodist
5.	Teal, Jimmy	WR	5-10	170	Texas A&M
6.	Hamby, Mike	DT	6-4	265	Utah State
7.	Pitts, Ron	DB	5-10	175	UCLA
8.	Robinson, Jacque	RB	5-11	215	Washington
9.	Jones, Glenn	DB	5-10	170	Norfolk State
10.	Babyar, Chris	G	6-3	265	Illinois
11.	Seawright, James	LB	6-1	215	South Carolina
12.	Woodside, Paul	K	5-10	170	West Virginia

Veteran nose tackle
Fred Smerlas

1985 SCHEDULE

September

8	SAN DIEGO	4:00
15	at New York Jets	1:00
22	NEW ENGLAND	1:00
29	MINNESOTA	1:00

October

6	at Indianapolis	1:00
13	at New England	1:00
20	INDIANAPOLIS	1:00
27	at Philadelphia	1:00

November

3	CINCINNATI	1:00
10	HOUSTON	1:00
17	at Cleveland	1:00
24	MIAMI	1:00

December

1	at San Diego	4:00
8	NEW YORK JETS	1:00
15	at Pittsburgh	1:00
22	at Miami	1:00

VETERAN ROSTER

No.	Name	Pos.	Ht.	Wt.	NFL Year	College
75	Acker, Bill	NT	6-3	255	6	Texas
50	Azelby, Joe	LB	6-1	225	2	Harvard
84	Barnett, Buster	TE	6-5	235	5	Jackson State
43	Bayless, Martin	S	6-2	195	2	Bowling Green
28	Bell, Greg	RB	5-10	210	2	Notre Dame
36	Bellinger, Rodney	CB	5-8	181	2	Miami
86	Brammer, Mark	TE	6-3	235	6	Michigan State
81	Brookins, Mitchell	WR	5-11	196	2	Illinois
80	Butler, Jerry	WR	6-0	178	7	Clemson
30	Carpenter, Brian	CB	5-10	167	4	Michigan
63	Cross, Justin	T	6-6	265	4	Western Colorado
59	David, Stan	LB	6-3	210	2	Texas Tech
89	Dawkins, Julius	WR	6-1	196	3	Pittsburgh
83	Dennard, Preston	WR	6-1	183	8	New Mexico
70	Devlin, Joe	T	6-5	250	9	Iowa
19	Dufek, Joe	QB	6-4	215	3	Yale
85	Franklin, Byron	WR	6-1	179	5	Auburn
22	Freeman, Steve	S	5-11	185	11	Mississippi State
53	Grant, Will	C	6-4	248	8	Kentucky
55	Haslett, Jim	LB	6-3	232	7	Indiana, Pa.
	Hill, Rod	CB	6-0	182	4	Kentucky State
92	Howell, LeRoy	DE	6-4	235	1	Appalachian State
87	Hunter, Tony	TE	6-3	237	3	Notre Dame
91	Johnson, Ken	DE	6-5	253	7	Knoxville
48	Johnson, Lawrence	CB	5-11	204	6	Wisconsin
72	Jones, Ken	T	6-5	256	10	Arkansas State
52	Keating, Chris	LB	6-2	223	7	Maine
4	Kidd, John	P	6-3	201	2	Northwestern
10	Kofler, Matt	QB	6-3	192	4	San Diego State
42	Kush, Rod	S	6-0	188	6	Nebraska-Omaha
61	Lynch, Tom	G	6-5	250	9	Boston College
54	Marve, Eugene	LB	6-2	230	4	Saginaw Valley
95	McNanie, Sean	DE	6-5	252	2	San Diego State
29	Mistler, John	WR	6-2	186	5	Arizona State
34	Moore, Booker	RB	5-11	224	4	Penn State
88	Mosley, Mike	WR	6-2	192	4	Texas A&M
41	Neal, Speedy	RB	6-2	254	2	Miami
13	Nelson, Chuck	K	5-11	175	2	Washington
38	Nixon, Jeff	S	6-3	190	6	Richmond
49	Norris, Ulysses	TE	6-4	232	7	Georgia
74	Payne, Jimmy	DE	6-3	264	1	Georgia
58	Potter, Steve	LB	6-3	235	5	Virginia
79	Prater, Dean	DE	6-5	245	3	Oklahoma State
82	Richardson, Eric	WR	6-1	183	2	San Jose State
40	Riddick, Robb	RB	6-0	195	4	Millersville, Pa.
51	Ritcher, Jim	G	6-3	251	6	North Carolina State
26	Romes, Charles	CB	6-1	190	9	North Carolina Central
57	Sanford, Lucius	LB	6-2	216	8	Georgia Tech
76	Smerlas, Fred	NT	6-3	270	7	Boston College
56	Talley, Darryl	LB	6-3	231	3	West Virginia
	Taylor, Roger	T	6-6	275	2	Oklahoma State
39	Vanden Boom, Matt	S	6-3	201	1	Wisconsin
65	Vogler, Tim	C	6-3	245	7	Ohio State
60	Wenglikowski, Al	LB	6-1	220	2	Pittsburgh
27	White, Craig	WR	6-1	194	2	Missouri
77	Williams, Ben	DE	6-3	245	10	Mississippi
23	Williams, Van	RB	6-0	208	3	Carson-Newman
21	Wilson, Don	S	6-2	190	2	North Carolina State

AFC EASTERN DIVISION

INDIANAPOLIS COLTS AFC East

Address P.O. Box 20000, Indianapolis, Indiana 46220.
Stadium Hoosier Dome, Indianapolis.
  Capacity 61,000 *Playing Surface* AstroTurf.
Team Colours Royal Blue, White and Silver.
Head Coach Rod Dowhower – first year.
Championships Division 1970,'75,'76,'77; Conference 1970;
  NFL 1958,'59,'68; Super Bowl 1970.
History NFL 1953-69, AFC 1970-
  (Until 1984, they were known as the Baltimore Colts. A
  team of the same name played in the AAFC, from 1947
  to 1949, and in the NFL in 1950, at the end of which they
  went out of business.)

Offense

Rookie head coach Rod Dowhower, formerly the offensive coordinator of the St Louis Cardinals, is looking to give the Colts their first winning season since 1977, when they won the division title with a 10-4 record. The offensive unit, which suffered injuries to key players, is coming off a disappointing season at the end of which they ranked last in the NFL in both total yards and points scored. It would appear that third-year man Art Schlichter, who replaced Mike Pagel for the final five games of 1984, will start at quarterback. Pagel is brave but, it is fair to say, has limitations, whereas Schlichter has a touch of class. There are no problems at running back if Curtis Dickey and Randy McMillan stay healthy. Dickey is a genuine game-breaker and McMillan is a more-than-reliable fullback. Beyond these two, however, the Colts are a little thin. Potentially, the starting offensive line is very good. Chris Hinton made the 1984 Pro Bowl in his rookie year as a guard and was just as good at tackle last year before suffering a season-ending injury on Week Six. He'll be back to team up with last year's number one pick, right guard Ron Solt, who lived up to expectations. Center Ray Donaldson is a steadying influence on the youngsters, right tackle Jim Mills and left guard Ben Utt. There is talk of tackle Karl Baldischwiler returning after a year's retirement – and that would be a real bonus in a unit which, last year, gave up a club record 58 quarterback sacks. The starting wide receivers, Ray Butler and Tracy Porter,

maintain a respectable average and yet do not strike terror in the opposition. With this in mind, the Colts used two late draft options to acquire James Harbour and Ricky Nichols, both of whom are said to be really quick. The output from the tight end position is modest at best – Dave Young and Tim Sherwin caught just 25 passes between them last year.

Defense

Colts fans can anticipate the 1985 season with some optimism. The defensive line seems settled for years to come, with ends Blaise Winter and Donnell Thompson flanking nose tackle Leo Wisniewski. Behind them, the linebacking squad is joined by yet another high draft pick, Duane Bickett, who was selected fifth overall. He should fit in well alongside Barry Krauss, a first-rounder in 1979, Johnie Cooks, another first-rounder who led the team in sacks last year, and Vernon Maxwell who has emerged as a fearsome blitzer. Both Cliff Odom and Greg Bracelin are experienced competitors who have started in the past and provide excellent reserve strength. Last year, the Colts were unable to sign cornerback Leonard Coleman, who could have provided the basis for the reconstruction of a pass defense which went on to rank a lowly 22nd in the league and was consistently beaten by the bomb. To make matters worse, both cornerback Jim Burroughs and strong safety Larry Anderson were sidelined with injuries, exposing inexperienced reserves. Helped by the presence of the indestructible veteran free safety, Nesby Glasgow, draftees Don Anderson and Anthony Young could go some way towards solving the problems.

Special Teams

There are no worries about the kicking game in which both placekicker Raul Allegre and punter Rohn Stark maintain a consistently high standard. So far, after two years, Allegre has been successful with seven out of eleven field goal attempts from over 50 yards. For the third consecutive season, Stark's gross punting average was over 44 yards and he is noticeably improving his hang time. Larry Anderson, the former Pittsburgh Steeler, ranked third in the NFL, returning kicks at an average of 23.9 yards, and the opposition can not afford to kick in the direction of Anderson's partner, Phil Smith, who returned one 96 yards for a touchdown against St Louis.

1985 DRAFT

Round	Name	Pos.	Ht.	Wt.	College
1.	Bickett, Duane	LB	6-4	232	Southern California
2.	Anderson, Don	DB	5-10	185	Purdue
3.	Young, Anthony	DB	5-11	187	Temple
4.	Broughton, Willie	DE	6-4	245	Miami
5.	Caron, Roger	T	6-4	270	Harvard
7.	Harbour, James	WR	6-0	190	Mississippi
8.	Nichols, Ricky	WR	5-9	175	East Carolina
9.	Boyer, Mark	TE	6-3	233	Southern California
10.	Pinesett, Andre	DT	6-2	245	Cal State-Fullerton
12.	Burnette, Dave	T	6-6	255	Central Arkansas

Rohn Stark, one of the league's
best punters

1985 SCHEDULE

September

8	at Pittsburgh	1:00
15	at Miami	4:00
22	DETROIT	1:00
29	at New York Jets	4:00

October

6	BUFFALO	1:00
13	DENVER	1:00
20	at Buffalo	1:00
27	GREEN BAY	1:00

November

3	NEW YORK JETS	4:00
10	at New England	1:00
17	MIAMI	1:00
24	at Kansas City	4:00

December

1	NEW ENGLAND	1:00
8	at Chicago	1:00
15	at Tampa Bay	1:00
22	HOUSTON	4:00

VETERAN ROSTER

No.	Name	Pos.	Ht.	Wt.	NFL Year	College
2	Allegre, Raul	K	5-9	165	3	Texas
30	Anderson, Larry	S	6-1	192	8	Louisiana Tech
61	Bailey, Don	C	6-3	250	2	Miami
	Beach, Pat	TE	6-4	243	4	Washington State
48	Bell, Mark	TE	6-4	240	6	Colorado State
5	Biasucci, Dean	K	6-0	195	2	West Carolina
85	Bouza, Matt	WR	6-3	211	4	California
52	Bracelin, Greg	LB	6-2	213	6	California
45	Burroughs, Jim	CB	6-1	198	4	Michigan State
80	Butler, Raymond	WR	6-3	206	6	Southern California
72	Call, Kevin	T	6-7	289	2	Colorado State
98	Cooks, Johnie	LB	6-4	234	4	Mississippi
38	Daniel, Eugene	CB	6-0	181	2	Louisiana State
27	Davis, Preston	CB			2	
33	Dickey, Curtis	RB	6-1	214	6	Texas A&M
53	Donaldson, Ray	C	6-3	269	6	Georgia
79	Ekern, Andy	T	6-6	263	2	Missouri
65	Gardner, Ellis	G	6-4	263	3	Georgia Tech
25	Glasgow, Nesby	S	5-10	187	7	Washington
58	Hathaway, Steve	LB	6-4	220	2	West Virginia
88	Henry, Bernard	WR	6-0	179	4	Arizona State
75	Hinton, Chris	T	6-4	280	3	Northwestern
57	Humiston, Mike	LB	6-3	238	4	Weber State
51	Jones, Ricky	LB	6-2	227	9	Tuskegee
29	Kafentzis, Mark	S	5-10	185	4	Hawaii
63	Kirchner, Mark	T	6-3	261	3	Baylor
55	Krauss, Barry	LB	6-3	247	7	Alabama
56	Maxwell, Vernon	LB	6-2	219	3	Arizona State
32	McMillan, Randy	RB	6-1	220	5	Pittsburgh
	Metcalf, Bo	CB	6-2	193	2	Baylor
43	Middleton, Frank	RB	5-11	205	2	Florida A&M
76	Mills, Jim	T	6-9	271	3	Hawaii
23	Moore, Alvin	RB	6-0	194	3	Arizona State
93	Odom, Clifton	LB	6-2	233	5	Texas-Arlington
90	Padjen, Gary	LB	6-2	251	4	Arizona State
18	Pagel, Mike	QB	6-2	201	4	Arizona State
78	Parker, Steve	DE	6-4	250	3	Eastern Illinois
71	Petersen, Ted	T	6-5	245	8	Eastern Illinois
87	Porter, Tracy	WR	6-1	196	5	Louisiana State
21	Radachowsky, George	S	5-11	178	2	Boston College
35	Randle, Tate	CB	6-0	202	4	Texas Tech
10	Schlichter, Art	QB	6-3	208	3	Ohio State
95	Scott, Chris	DT	6-5	245	2	Purdue
83	Sherwin, Tim	TE	6-6	238	5	Boston College
91	Smith, Byron	DE	6-4	245	2	California
86	Smith, Phil	WR	6-3	188	3	San Diego State
66	Solt, Ron	G	6-3	265	2	Maryland
3	Stark, Rohn	P	6-3	199	4	Florida State
99	Thompson, Donnell	DE	6-4	263	5	North Carolina
64	Utt, Ben	T	6-5	267	4	Georgia Tech
	Virkus, Scott	DE	6-5	248	3	San Francisco C.C.
92	White, Brad	NT	6-2	255	5	Tennessee
39	Williams, Newton	RB	5-10	204	4	Arizona State
40	Williams, Vaughn	S	6-2	195	2	Stanford
96	Winter, Blaise	DE	6-3	262	2	Syracuse
69	Wisniewski, Leo	NT	6-1	264	4	Penn State
34	Wonsley, George	RB	6-0	205	2	Mississippi State
81	Young, Dave	TE	6-5	240	4	Purdue

MIAMI DOLPHINS AFC East

Address 4770, Biscayne Boulevard, Suite 1440, Miami, Florida 33137.

Stadium Orange Bowl, Miami.
Capacity 75,206 *Playing Surface* Grass.

Team Colours Aqua, Coral and White.

Head Coach Don Shula – sixteenth year.

Championships Division 1971,'72,'73,'74,'79,'81,'83,'84; Conference 1971,'72,'73,'82,'84' Super Bowl 1972,'73.

History AFL 1966-69, AFC 1970-

Offense

Quarterback Dan Marino enters 1985 with the reputation for being the most prolific passer in the history of the game. He set single-season records for yardage (5,084), touchdowns (48), pass completions (362), 300-yard games (9) and 400-yard games (4). Riding his success, the Dolphins established NFL club records for touchdowns (70) and yardage (6,936). And they could be even more effective this coming season. Dwight Stephenson has assumed the mantle of the league's best center and accompanied right guard Ed Newman to the 1985 Pro Bowl. Tackle Jon Giesler is a fixture on the left as is guard Roy Foster (both are former number one picks). Collectively, the line allowed only fourteen quarterback sacks. Moreover, for most of the campaign, they were without right tackle Eric Laakso, who returns to challenge Cleveland Green for the starting spot. Head coach Don Shula rarely needs to look to his running backs for offense but Woody Bennett and Tony Nathan are on hand to keep the wheels turning – they averaged 4.2 and 4.7 yards per carry, respectively. In addition, rookie Joe Carter showed great promise before going into a late-season slump. And then there is the powerful fullback, Pete Johnson, on hand for short-yardage. It doesn't stop there, with Andra Franklin, a former Pro Bowler, returning from injury. Even so, Shula wasted no time drafting Florida's Lorenzo Hampton in the first round. The two 'Mark Brothers', wide receivers Clayton and Duper, murdered the opposition, gaining a combined yardage total of 2,695 and scoring 26 touchdowns on 144 receptions. The veteran Nat Moore has had

a new lease of life and many teams would like to have Jimmy Cefalo, who had a 76-yard touchdown reception in Super Bowl XVII. When Marino found the time to look for his tight ends, the trio of Dan Johnson, Bruce Hardy and Joe Rose, held on to 74 passes and scored ten touchdowns. Not very long ago, the whole package would have sounded like a fairy tale – it is still hard to believe.

Defense

Surprisingly, defense is a different story, despite close attention over the years from the highly respected defensive coordinator, Bill Arnsparger, and more recently, Chuck Studley. Against Washington in Super Bowl XVII, they were beaten by John Riggins' rushing, and again in January they had no answer to the combination of San Francisco's Wendell Tyler, Roger Craig and Joe Montana. In 1984 they sought to solve a problem at linebacker by drafting Jackie Shipp and Jay Brophy in the first two rounds. This year, they went for defensive tackle George Little and linebacker Alex Moyer in rounds two and three. Last season's plans for rebuilding were frustrated by injuries to three linebackers, Pro Bowler A.J. Duhe, Earnest Rhone and reserve Rodell Thomas. Rhone will be back but doubts remain over Duhe, who has had his third major knee operation, and Thomas, who is troubled with a neck injury. Defense against the pass is less of a worry. Defensive left end Doug Betters and outside linebacker Charles Bowser led the team in sacks with 14 and 10 respectively. The defensive secondary contains one of the NFL's better pairings at cornerback in Don McNeal and William Judson whilst strong safety Glenn Blackwood led the team with six pass interceptions. Glenn's brother, Lyle, at free safety, may be past his best and could be replaced by the versatile Paul Lankford.

Special Teams

Kicker Uwe von Schamann's longest field goal on the year was a 37-yarder and draftee Fuad Reveiz will be given every chance to stake his claim. There were no problems in the punting department where Reggie Roby had an NFL-best net punting average of 38.1 yards. The latter adds up to good distance, excellent hang time and good coverage by the tacklers. It's hardly a special team statistic but, for the ninth consecutive season and the eleventh time in all, Miami led the NFL in fewest yards penalised – and that's good discipline.

1985 DRAFT

Round	Name	Pos.	Ht.	Wt.	College
1.	Hampton, Lorenzo	RB	5-10	205	Florida
3.	Little, George	DT	6-3	255	Iowa
3.	Moyer, Alex	LB	6-1	220	Northwestern
4.	Smith, Mike	DB	5-11	170	Texas-El Paso
4.	Dellenbach, Jeff	T	6-6	295	Wisconsin
6.	Shorthose, George	WR	6-0	200	Missouri
6.	Davenport, Ron	RB	6-1	220	Louisville
7.	Reveiz, Fuad	K	5-10	220	Tennessee
8.	Sharp, Dan	TE	6-1	230	Texas Christian
9.	Hinds, Adam	DB	6-3	205	Oklahoma State
10.	Pendleton, Mike	DB	6-0	175	Indiana
11.	Jones, Mike	RB	5-10	188	Tulane
12.	Noble, Ray	DB	6-0	170	California

Pro Bowl guard Ed Newman

1985 SCHEDULE

September

8 at Houston	1:00
15 INDIANAPOLIS	4:00
22 KANSAS CITY	4:00
29 at Denver	4:00

October

6 PITTSBURGH	1:00
14 at New York Jets	9:00
20 TAMPA BAY	4:00
27 at Detroit	1:00

November

3 at New England	1:00
10 NEW YORK JETS	4:00
17 at Indianapolis	1:00
24 at Buffalo	1:00

December

2 CHICAGO	9:00
8 at Green Bay	1:00
16 NEW ENGLAND	9:00
22 BUFFALO	1:00

VETERAN ROSTER

No.	Name	Pos.	Ht.	Wt.	NFL Year	College
70	Barnett, Bill	DE	6-4	250	6	Nebraska
73	Baumhower, Bob	DT	6-5	265	9	Alabama
34	Bennett, Woody	RB	6-2	222	7	Miami
78	Benson, Charles	DE	6-3	267	3	Baylor
75	Betters, Doug	DE	6-7	260	8	Nevada-Reno
47	Blackwood, Glenn	S	6-0	188	7	Texas
42	Blackwood, Lyle	S	6-1	195	13	Texas Christian
58	Bokamper, Kim	DE	6-6	250	9	San Jose State
56	Bowser, Charles	LB	6-3	232	4	Duke
53	Brophy, Jay	LB	6-3	227	2	Miami
43	Brown, Bud	S	6-0	187	2	Southern Mississippi
51	Brown, Mark	LB	6-2	218	3	Purdue
59	Brudzinski, Bob	LB	6-4	229	9	Ohio State
23	Carter, Joe	RB	5-11	198	3	Alabama
81	Cefalo, Jimmy	WR	5-11	188	7	Penn State
71	Charles, Mike	DE	6-4	283	3	Syracuse
	Clark, Bryan	QB	6-2	196	3	Michigan State
76	Clark, Steve	G	6-4	255	4	Utah
83	Clayton, Mark	WR	5-9	172	3	Louisville
77	Duhe, A.J.	LB	6-4	240	9	Louisiana State
85	Duper, Mark	WR	5-9	193	4	Northwestern Louisiana
61	Foster, Roy	G	6-4	272	4	Southern California
37	Franklin, Andra	RB	5-10	228	5	Nebraska
79	Giesler, Jon	T	6-5	260	7	Michigan
74	Green, Cleveland	T	6-3	262	7	Southern University
84	Hardy, Bruce	TE	6-4	232	8	Arizona State
88	Heflin, Vince	WR	6-2	185	4	Central State, Ohio
53	Hester, Ron	LB	6-1	226	3	Florida State
31	Hill, Eddie	RB	6-2	206	7	Memphis State
11	Jensen, Jim	WR-QB	6-4	215	5	Boston University
87	Johnson, Dan	TE	6-3	240	3	Iowa State
46	Johnson, Pete	RB	6-0	272	9	Ohio State
49	Judson, William	CB	6-1	187	4	South Carolina State
40	Kozlowski, Mike	S	6-0	198	6	Colorado
68	Laakso, Eric	T	6-4	265	8	Tulane
44	Lankford, Paul	CB	6-1	182	4	Penn State
72	Lee, Ronnie	T	6-3	260	7	Baylor
13	Marino, Dan	QB	6-3	214	3	Pittsburgh
28	McNeal, Don	CB	5-11	192	5	Alabama
89	Moore, Nat	WR	5-9	188	12	Florida
22	Nathan, Tony	RB	6-0	206	7	Alabama
64	Newman, Ed	G	6-2	255	13	Duke
55	Rhone, Earnest	LB	6-2	224	10	Henderson State
4	Roby, Reggie	P	6-2	243	3	Iowa
80	Rose, Joe	TE	6-3	230	6	California
50	Shipp, Jackie	LB	6-3	235	2	Oklahoma
45	Sowell, Robert	CB-S	5-11	175	3	Howard
57	Stephenson, Dwight	C	6-2	255	6	Alabama
10	Strock, Don	QB	6-5	220	12	Virginia Tech.
54	Thomas, Rodell	LB	6-2	225	5	Alabama State
60	Toews, Jeff	G	6-3	255	7	Washington
32	Vigorito, Tom	RB	5-10	190	4	Virginia
5	Von Schamann, Uwe	K	6-0	188	7	Oklahoma
41	Walker, Fulton	CB	5-10	196	5	West Virginia

NEW ENGLAND PATRIOTS AFC East

Address Sullivan Stadium, Route 1, Foxboro, Mass. 02035.
Stadium Sullivan Stadium, Foxboro.
   Capacity 61,150 *Playing Surface* Super Turf.
Team Colours Red, White and Blue.
Head Coach Raymond Berry – second year.
Championships Division 1978.
History AFL 1960-69, AFC 1970-
   (Until 1971, they were known as the Boston Patriots.)

Offense

It always seems that the Patriots are just one or two good players away from being a playoff team and, once again, this is the case. In 1984, they were 8-4 after Week Twelve and well placed for a wild card spot. And then they came up against Dallas, on a Thanksgiving Day which quarterback Tony Eason would rather forget. He was sacked a Patriots club record ten times as his offensive line could find no answer to the Cowboys' blitz. One week before that game, center Pete Brock was injured and it may well have been his absence which led to the Patriots conceding a total of 29 sacks in the last four games. Other than this weakness, which could be corrected by Brock's return and the drafting of Trevor Matich in round one, the line is adequate. Both left tackle Brian Holloway and left guard John Hannah are Pro Bowlers. It is an understatement that Eason emerged as a bright young prospect – he showed great poise throwing 23 touchdown passes and only eight interceptions. Equally encouraging was the late-season form of running back Craig James, who rushed for 712 yards at an average of 5.1 yards per carry, over the last eight games. The Patriots could well revert to the more traditional two-running back formation to exploit the talents of Mosi Tatupu and the former Pro Bowler, Anthony Collins, the latter who rushed for 1,049 yards in 1983 and may be given the chance to re-establish himself under head coach Raymond Berry. Wide receiver Irving Fryar's impact on the NFL was muted by a succession of minor injuries but look out, he's going to be a good one. The veteran Stanley Morgan, too, retains his blazing speed having recovered from the hamstring problems he suffered in the early going. There's more – Stephen Starring led the club wide receivers with 46 receptions for 657 yards and Darryal Wilson, who has yet to make his debut after two years on injured reserve, could well be the fastest of the lot. The former Raider, tight end Derrick Ramsey, broke the club single-season pass receiving record with 66, whilst his partner, Lin Dawson, chipped in with a valuable 39.

Defense

The strength of a defense which, last year, rated ninth in the NFL in yardage conceded, lies at linebacker. Andre Tippett came second in the NFL with 18.5 sacks and, together with Steve Nelson, went to the Pro Bowl. In the absence of the injured Clayton Weishuhn and Johnny Rembert, Larry McGrew and Don Blackmon played well. Last year's second-round pick, Ed Williams, is maturing steadily. The defensive line will be strengthened by the return of nose tackle Lester Williams who, too, was missing for the second half of last year. It seems that defensive end Ken Sims may not develop as a pass rusher and, for this department, the Patriots drafted Garin Veris and Ben Thomas in the search for a successor to Julius Adams, who is now 37 years old. The defensive secondary contains former first-round picks in safeties Rick Sanford and Roland James, and right cornerback Ray Clayborn. However, the unit can hardly be described as 'ball-hawking' – they intercepted just 17 passes last year. Ernest Gibson and Ronnie Lippett will compete for the starting spot on the left corner, whilst draftees Jim Bowman and Audrey McMillan will make their bid for playing time at safety.

Special Teams

Barefoot kicker Tony Franklin has rediscovered his form after arriving from Philadelphia. He was successful on 22 of 28 field goal attempts, including six out of nine from over 40 yards. Punter Rich Camarillo shook off the effects of a hamstring injury to displace Luke Prestridge, who was subsequently released. Perhaps it was a bit risky using Irving Fryar as a punt returner but this natural athlete showed that he had a good pair of hands and put his speed to great use. Tony Collins kept his hand in, returning kickoffs at a respectable 21.8-yard average.

1985 DRAFT

Round	Name	Pos.	Ht.	Wt.	College
1.	Matich, Trevor	C	6-4	260	Brigham Young
2.	Veris, Garin	DE	6-4	255	Stanford
2.	Bowman, Jim	DB	6-1	215	Central Michigan
2.	Thomas, Ben	DE	6-3	275	Auburn
3.	McMillian, Audrey	DB	5-11	185	Houston
4.	Toth, Tom	T	6-5	270	Western Michigan
4.	Phelan, Gerard	WR	6-0	185	Boston College
8.	Hodge, Milford	DT	6-3	255	Washington State
11.	Lewis, Paul	RB	5-8	190	Boston University
12.	Mumford, Tony	RB	6-0	205	Penn State

John Hannah, New England's
All-Pro guard

1985 SCHEDULE

September

8	GREEN BAY	1:00
15	at Chicago	1:00
22	at Buffalo	1:00
29	LOS ANGELES RAIDERS	1:00

October

6	at Cleveland	1:00
13	BUFFALO	1:00
20	NEW YORK JETS	4:00
27	at Tampa Bay	1:00

November

3	MIAMI	1:00
10	INDIANAPOLIS	1:00
17	at Seattle	4:00
24	at New York Jets	1:00

December

1	at Indianapolis	1:00
8	DETROIT	1:00
16	at Miami	9:00
22	CINCINNATI	1:00

VETERAN ROSTER

No.	Name	Pos.	Ht.	Wt.	NFL Year	College
85	Adams, Julius	DE	6-3	270	14	Texas Southern
55	Blackmon, Don	LB	6-3	235	5	Tulsa
58	Brock, Pete	C	6-5	270	10	Colorado
3	Camarillo, Rich	P	5-11	191	5	Washington
26	Clayborn, Ray	CB	6-0	186	9	Texas
33	Collins, Anthony	RB	5-11	203	5	East Carolina
92	Creswell, Smiley	DE	6-4	251	1	Michigan State
91	Crump, George	DE	6-4	260	3	East Carolina
87	Dawson, Lin	TE	6-3	240	5	North Carolina State
47	Dombroski, Paul	S	6-0	185	6	Linfield
11	Eason, Tony	QB	6-4	212	3	Illinois
66	Fairchild, Paul	G	6-3	267	2	Kansas
1	Franklin, Tony	K	5-8	182	7	Texas A&M
80	Fryar, Irving	WR	5-11	198	2	Nebraska
43	Gibson, Ernest	CB	5-10	189	2	Furman
59	Golden, Tim	LB	6-1	220	4	Florida
14	Grogan, Steve	QB	6-4	210	11	Kansas State
68	Haley, Darryl	T	6-4	265	4	Utah
73	Hannah, John	G	6-3	265	13	Alabama
40	Hawthorne, Greg	WR-RB	6-2	225	7	Baylor
60	Henson, Luther	NT	6-0	275	4	Ohio State
76	Holloway, Brian	T	6-7	288	5	Stanford
51	Ingram, Brian	LB	6-4	235	4	Tennessee
32	James, Craig	RB	6-0	215	2	Southern Methodist
38	James, Roland	S	6-2	191	6	Tennessee
83	Jones, Cedric	WR	5-11	184	4	Duke
19	Kerrigan, Mike	QB	6-3	205	3	Northwestern
22	Lee, Keith	CB	5-11	193	5	Colorado State
42	Lippett, Ronnie	CB	5-11	180	3	Miami
31	Marion, Fred	S	6-2	191	4	Miami
50	McGrew, Larry	LB	6-5	233	5	Southern California
23	McSwain, Rod	CB	6-1	198	2	Clemson
67	Moore, Steve	T	6-4	285	3	Tennessee State
86	Morgan, Stanley	WR	5-11	181	9	Tennessee
75	Morriss, Guy	C	6-4	255	13	Texas Christian
57	Nelson, Steve	LB	6-2	230	12	North Dakota State
98	Owens, Dennis	NT	6-1	258	3	North Carolina State
88	Ramsey, Derrick	TE	6-5	235	8	Kentucky
	Ramsey, Tom	QB	6-0	188	1	UCLA
52	Rembert, Johnny	LB	6-3	234	3	Clemson
95	Reynolds, Ed	LB	6-5	230	3	Virginia
41	Robinson, Bo	RB	6-2	235	7	West Texas State
65	Rogers, Doug	DE	6-5	260	4	Stanford
25	Sanford, Rick	S	6-1	192	7	South Carolina
77	Sims, Ken	DE	6-5	271	4	Texas
81	Starring, Stephen	WR	5-10	172	3	McNeese State
30	Tatupu, Mosi	RB	6-0	227	8	Southern California
56	Tippett, Andre	LB	6-3	241	4	Iowa
82	Weathers, Clarence	WR	5-9	170	3	Clemson
24	Weathers, Robert	RB	6-2	222	4	Arizona State
53	Weishuhn, Clayton	LB	6-2	221	4	Angelo State
54	Williams, Ed	LB	6-3	244	2	Texas
44	Williams, Jon	RB	5-9	205	2	Penn State
72	Williams, Lester	NT	6-3	272	4	Miami
90	Williams, Toby	DE	6-3	254	3	Nebraska
48	Wilson, Darryal	WR	6-0	182	3	Tennessee
61	Wooten, Ron	G	6-4	273	4	North Carolina

NEW YORK JETS AFC East

Address 598, Madison Avenue, New York, N.Y. 10022.
Stadium Giants Stadium, East Rutherford, N.J. 07073.
   Capacity 76,891 *Playing Surface* AstroTurf.
Team Colours Kelly Green and White.
Head Coach Joe Walton – third year.
Championships AFL 1968; Super Bowl 1968.
History AFL 1960-69, AFC 1970-
   (Until 1963, they were known as the New York Titans.)

Offense

The Jets are still shaking their heads trying to work out how they failed to reach the playoffs, after opening the season 6-2. One reason might be a Week Eleven injury to veteran quarterback Pat Ryan, who had beaten out the younger Ken O'Brien in the preseason. O'Brien, who started the last five games, was able to generate only one victory. Another reason might be the absence of their outstanding running back, Freeman McNeil, for three of the last six games. He is an essential part of the squad – he makes the offense go. Despite missing McNeil, the Jets ended up fifth in the league in yards rushing with Johnny Hector stepping in to gain 53 yards at a 4.3 average (including a 64-yard run against Cleveland). Rookie Tony Paige carried the ball only 35 times but scored seven touchdowns. Former Pro Bowlers right tackle Marvin Powell and center Joe Fields provide the quality on the offensive line and rookie left guard Jim Sweeney did enough in the last two regular season games to suggest that he will be joining them permanently this year. At wide receiver, stalwarts Wesley Walker and Johnny 'Lam' Jones are fast enough to scare the living daylights out of anybody but, increasingly, are going down with injuries. It was time to introduce a new flier to the 'Big Apple' and he came in the form of Wisconsin's Al Toon who, they say, has everything, good speed, terrific hands and courage. Also, fourth-round draft pick Doug Allen could be a 'steal'. Though on the small side at 5-10 and 170lb, he too has burning speed. Meanwhile, the Jets' leading receiver was tight end Mickey Shuler who, with 68 catches, is coming off his best year as a pro. One of last year's second-round picks, tight end Glenn Dennison, turned out not to be quite the pass receiver the Jets had hoped for but he earned his corn as a blocker.

Defense

Such is the dominance of number 99, the defensive line might just as well be renamed the 'Gastineau Line' – collectively they are no longer the awesome front four which truly earned the nickname of the 'New York Sack Exchange'. Gastineau registered 22 of a disappointing team total of 44 quarterback sacks. For the future, rookie defensive end Ron Faurot showed great promise, starting in nine games. There is the distinct possibility that they will adopt the 3-4 formation popular with the majority of teams. This would require four top-quality linebackers and, in Lance Mehl, they certainly have one. However, the doubts surrounding the fitness of middle linebacker Bob Crable, place a great responsibility on the shoulders of last year's third-round pick, Kyle Clifton, and fourth-rounder Bobby Bell Jr. (His dad was a great player with the Chiefs.) A former Kansas City starter, Charles Jackson, has been acquired for his veteran know-how. No one can expect to lose so many starters from the secondary as did the Jets last year, and still defend effectively against the modern passing offenses. Russell Carter, a first-rounder in 1984, was terrific when fit, and proved his versatility by playing at both cornerback and free safety. He is a real blue-chipper. Harry Hamilton did enough as nickel back and on special team duty to suggest that he has a future in the NFL. They are reinforced by safety Lester Lyles and cornerback Donnie Elder, who were drafted in rounds two and three respectively, but the return of veterans Ken Schroy, Bobby Jackson and Johnny Lynn to full fitness will be welcomed.

Special Teams

This area is a Jets strength. Pay Leahy kicked 17 of 24 field goal attempts while kickoff returner Bobby Humphery led the NFL with an average of 30.7 yards, and included a 97-yard return for a touchdown. Humphery's partner, Kirk Springs, ranked seventh in the NFL returning kickoffs, and ninth in the league returning punts. Veteran punter Chuck Ramsey has been released to be succeeded by last year's rookie, Bret Wright, who spent the year on injured reserve.

1985 DRAFT

Round	Name	Pos.	Ht.	Wt.	College
1.	Toon, Al	WR	6-4	205	Wisconsin
2.	Lyles, Lester	DB	6-1	208	Virginia
3.	Elder, Donnie	DB	5-9	172	Memphis State
4.	Allen, Doug	WR	5-10	170	Arizona State
5.	Benson, Troy	LB	6-1	235	Pittsburgh
5.	Luft, Brian	DT	6-5	270	Southern California
5.	Smith, Tony	WR			San Jose State
6.	Deaton, Jeff	G	6-2	280	Stanford
6.	Miano, Rich	DB	6-0	195	Hawaii
8.	Monger, Matt	LB	6-2	215	Oklahoma State
9.	Waters, Mike	RB	6-2	210	San Diego State
10.	Glenn, Kerry	DB	5-8	170	Minnesota
11.	White, Brad	DE	6-6	240	Texas Tech.
12.	Wallace, Bill	WR	6-1	190	Pittsburgh

*Tight end Mickey Shuler (#82)
enjoyed the best season of his
seven-year career in 1984*

1985 SCHEDULE

September
8	at Los Angeles Raiders	4:00
15	BUFFALO	1:00
22	vs Green Bay (at Milwaukee)	4:00
29	INDIANAPOLIS	4:00

October
6	at Cincinnati	4:00
14	MIAMI	9:00
20	at New England	4:00
27	SEATTLE	1:00

November
3	at Indianapolis	4:00
10	at Miami	4:00
17	TAMPA BAY	1:00
24	NEW ENGLAND	1:00
28	at Detroit	12:30

December
8	at Buffalo	1:00
14	CHICAGO	12:30
22	CLEVELAND	1:00

VETERAN ROSTER

No.	Name	Pos.	Ht.	Wt.	NFL Year	College
60	Alexander, Dan	G	6-4	260	9	Louisiana State
35	Augustyniak, Mike	RB	5-11	226	5	Purdue
17	Avellini, Bob	QB	6-2	210	11	Maryland
95	Baldwin, Tom	DT	6-4	255	2	Tulsa
63	Banker, Ted	G-T	6-2	260	2	Southeastern Missouri
31	Barber, Marion	RB	6-3	224	4	Minnesota
58	Bell, Bobby	LB	6-2	217	2	Missouri
78	Bennett, Barry	DT	6-4	257	8	Concordia, Minnesota
64	Bingham, Guy	C-G	6-3	255	6	Montana
83	Bruckner, Nick	WR	5-11	185	3	Syracuse
51	Buttle, Greg	LB	6-3	232	10	Penn State
27	Carter, Russell	CB	6-2	195	2	Southern Methodist
59	Clifton, Kyle	LB	6-3	230	2	Texas Christian
50	Crable, Bob	LB	6-3	232	4	Notre Dame
88	Davidson, Chy	WR	5-11	175	2	Rhode Island
22	Dennis, Mike	S	5-10	190	6	Wyoming
86	Dennison, Glenn	TE	6-3	225	2	Miami
52	Eliopulos, Jim	LB	6-2	229	2	Wyoming
74	Faurot, Ron	DE	6-7	260	2	Arkansas
65	Fields, Joe	C	6-2	253	10	Widener
38	Floyd, George	S	5-11	190	3	Eastern Kentucky
81	Gaffney, Derrick	WR	6-1	182	8	Florida
99	Gastineau, Mark	DE	6-5	265	7	East Central Oklahoma
94	Guilbeau, Rusty	DE	6-4	260	4	McNeese State
30	Hamilton, Harry	S	5-11	190	2	Penn State
42	Harper, Bruce	RB	5-8	177	9	Kutztown State, Pa.
34	Hector, Johnny	RB	5-11	197	3	Texas A&M
84	Humphery, Bobby	WR	5-10	170	2	New Mexico State
40	Jackson, Bobby	CB	5-10	180	8	Florida State
	Jackson, Charles	LB	6-2	222	8	Washington
80	Jones, Johnny 'Lam'	WR	5-11	180	6	Texas
73	Klecko, Joe	DE-DT	6-3	263	9	Temple
89	Klever, Rocky	TE	6-3	225	3	Montana
5	Leahy, Pat	K	6-0	189	12	St Louis
29	Lynn, Johnny	CB	6-0	198	6	UCLA
93	Lyons, Marty	DT	6-5	265	7	Alabama
68	McElroy, Reggie	T	6-6	270	3	West Texas State
24	McNeil, Freeman	RB	5-11	218	5	UCLA
56	Mehl, Lance	LB	6-3	233	6	Penn State
25	Minter, Cedric	RB	5-10	190	2	Boise State
20	Mullen, Davlin	CB	6-1	177	3	Western Kentucky
7	O'Brien, Ken	QB	6-4	210	3	Cal-Davis
49	Paige, Tony	RB	5-10	225	2	Virginia Tech.
79	Powell, Marvin	T	6-5	260	9	Southern California
28	Ray, Darrol	S	6-1	198	6	Oklahoma
10	Ryan, Pat	QB	6-3	210	8	Tennessee
48	Schroy, Ken	S	6-2	198	9	Maryland
82	Shuler, Mickey	TE	6-3	231	8	Penn State
87	Sohn, Kurt	WR	5-11	180	4	Fordham
21	Springs, Kirk	S-PR	6-0	192	5	Miami, Ohio
53	Sweeney, Jim	C	6-4	260	2	Pittsburgh
70	Waldemore, Stan	G	6-4	269	8	Nebraska
85	Walker, Wesley	WR	6-0	179	9	California
57	Woodring, John	LB	6-2	232	5	Brown

CINCINNATI BENGALS AFC Central

Address 200, Riverfront Stadium, Cincinnati, Ohio 45202.
Stadium Riverfront Stadium, Cincinnati.
  Capacity 59,754 *Playing Surface* AstroTurf.
Team Colours Black, Orange and White.
Head Coach Sam Wyche –second year.
Championships Divison 1970,'73,'81; Conference 1981.
History AFL 1968-69, AFC 1970-

Offense

It speaks volumes for the tenacity of a team when it loses six of its first seven games and then comes back to fall just one victory short of reaching the playoffs. On the other hand, the Bengals won only one game against a team which, overall, had a winning record on the year, and several players will have to reproduce their best form if they are to compete with the improving Steelers. It is still not certain that veteran quarterback and winner of four NFL passing titles, Ken Anderson, will return for a 15th season. An increasing susceptibility to injury may restrict Anderson's scrambling ability but his presence will be vital if the Bengals are going to exploit the talents of an exciting pass receiving corps. Of the reserve quarterbacks, Turk Schonert is coming off shoulder surgery and last year's rookie, 'Boomer' Esiason, still needs to refine his technique. Given adequate service, wide receiver Cris Collinsworth and tight end M.L. Harris are ready and waiting to produce, as are running backs Stanford Jennings and James Brooks who, last year, caught 35 and 34 passes respectively. They are joined by draftee Eddie Brown, who is considered to be one of the best three wide receivers in the rookie crop and, unexpectedly, was still available when it came to the 13th pick of round one. The offensive line is shaping up as one of the league's best. The Bengals have been fortunate in the last two years to draft, firstly, center Dave Rimington and then left guard Brian Blados. Even before their arrival, Anthony Munoz, Max Montoya and Mike Wilson rated highly. They gave up an uncomfortable 45 sacks, but that figure looks less tragic when it is considered that, over the season, they had to protect three different quarterbacks, each with his different style. They had greater success clearing a lane for the running backs, who combined for the sixth-best rushing yardage total in the league. The heavyweight Larry Kinnebrew has emerged as the leading rusher and the fleet-footed James Brooks is expected to be more productive, having taken a year to learn the system after arriving from San Diego. Even so, he will be pushed for a starting spot by last year's rookie, Stanford Jennings, who maintained an average of 4.8 yards over 79 carries.

Defense

The defense ranked above average in the AFC in almost every category but only rarely did they smother the opposition. Defensive ends Eddie Edwards and Ross Browner had nine and eight quarterback sacks respectively out of a team total of 40. They are two of the league's reliable veterans. However, defensive end Pete Koch, one of three first-round picks last year, took some time to learn the trade. Accepting the need for a more effective pass rush, the Bengals drafted defensive end Emanuel King with their second first-round option, and inside linebacker Carl Zander in the second round. King, at 6ft 4in, 246lb, is just the right size for conversion to outside linebacker, as is the Bengals intension, whilst Zander is said to be good against the run. Following the Bengals' inability to sign last year's number one pick, linebacker Ricky Hunley, the veteran Reggie Williams remained the best of the linebacking quartet, with his partner, Glenn Cameron, not far behind. At defensive back there are the makings of a settled unit with safety Bobby Kemp and cornerbacks Louis Breeden and Ray Horton expected to start. Should Bryan Hicks not recover from injury, Robert Jackson would continue at free safety. They are joined by draftees Sean Thomas and Anthony Tuggle.

Special Teams

Both kicker Jim Breech and punter Pat McInally are trusty veterans whilst second-year man Mike Martin was a real find, returning 24 punts at an NFL-best average of 15.7 yards. Martin may take over as the senior kickoff returner releasing Stanford Jennings for duties in the offensive backfield.

1985 DRAFT

Round	Name	Pos.	Ht.	Wt.	College
1.	Brown, Eddie	WR	5-11	180	Miami
1.	King, Emanuel	LB	6-4	246	Alabama
2.	Zander, Carl	LB	6-1	220	Tennessee
3.	Thomas, Sean	DB	5-10	190	Texas Christian
4.	Tuggle, Anthony	DB	6-1	205	Nicholls State
5.	Degrate, Tony	DT	6-2	280	Texas
5.	Davis, Lee	DB	5-11	190	Mississippi
6.	Stokes, Eric	T	6-4	275	Northeastern
6.	Lester, Keith	TE	6-4	240	Murray State
7.	Locklin, Kim	RB	5-11	190	New Mexico State
7.	Walter, Joe	T	6-6	270	Texas State
8.	Strobel, Dave	LB	6-2	230	Iowa
9.	Cruise, Keith	DE	6-3	260	Northwestern
10.	King, Bernard	LB	6-0	222	Syracuse
11.	Stanfield, Harold	TE	6-3	235	Mississippi College
12.	Garza, Louis	T	6-3	310	New Mexico State

Center Dave Rimington

1985 SCHEDULE

September

8	SEATTLE	1:00
15	at St Louis	1:00
22	SAN DIEGO	1:00
30	at Pittsburgh	9:00

October

6	NEW YORK JETS	4:00
13	NEW YORK GIANTS	1:00
20	at Houston	1:00
27	PITTSBURGH	4:00

November

3	at Buffalo	1:00
10	CLEVELAND	1:00
17	at Los Angeles Raiders	4:00
24	at Cleveland	1:00

December

1	HOUSTON	1:00
8	DALLAS	1:00
15	at Washington	1:00
22	at New England	1:00

VETERAN ROSTER

No.	Name	Pos.	Ht.	Wt.	NFL Year	College
40	Alexander, Charles	RB	6-1	226	7	Louisiana State
14	Anderson, Ken	QB	6-3	212	15	Augustana, Ill.
53	Barker, Leo	LB	6-1	221	2	New Mexico State
74	Blados, Brian	G	6-4	308	2	North Carolina
61	Boyarsky, Jerry	NT	6-3	290	5	Pittsburgh
3	Breech, Jim	K	5-6	161	7	California
34	Breeden, Louis	CB	5-11	185	8	North Carolina State
21	Brooks, James	RB	5-9	177	5	Auburn
79	Browner, Ross	DE	6-3	261	8	Notre Dame
50	Cameron, Glenn	LB	6-2	228	11	Florida
76	Collins, Glen	DE	6-6	265	4	Mississippi State
80	Collinsworth, Cris	WR	6-5	192	5	Florida
85	Curtis, Isaac	WR	6-1	192	13	San Diego State
73	Edwards, Eddie	DE	6-5	256	9	Miami
7	Esiason, Boomer	QB	6-4	220	2	Maryland
33	Farley, John	RB	5-10	202	2	Cal. State-Sacramento
58	Frazier, Guy	LB	6-2	221	5	Wyoming
22	Griffin, James	CB-S	6-2	197	3	Middle Tennessee
44	Griffin, Ray	CB	5-10	186	8	Ohio State
83	Harris, M.L.	TE	6-5	238	6	Kansas State
27	Hicks, Bryan	S	6-0	192	5	McNeese State
82	Holman, Rodney	TE	6-3	232	4	Tulane
20	Horton, Ray	CB	5-11	190	3	Washington
37	Jackson, Robert	S	5-10	186	4	Central Michigan
36	Jennings, Stanford	RB-KR	6-1	205	2	Furman
26	Kemp, Bobby	S	6-0	191	5	Cal. State-Fullerton
89	Kern, Don	TE	6-4	225	2	Arizona State
28	Kinnebrew, Larry	RB	6-1	252	3	Tennessee State
71	Koch, Pete	DE	6-6	265	2	Maryland
64	Kozerski, Bruce	C-G	6-4	275	2	Holy Cross
86	Kreider, Steve	WR	6-3	192	7	Lehigh
69	Krumrie, Tim	NT	6-2	262	3	Wisconsin
55	Maidlow, Steve	LB	6-2	234	3	Michigan State
88	Martin, Mike	WR	5-10	186	3	Illinois
87	McInally, Pat	P	6-6	212	10	Harvard
65	Montoya, Max	G	6-5	275	7	UCLA
78	Munoz, Anthony	T	6-6	278	6	Southern California
68	Obrovac, Mike	G	6-6	275	5	Bowling Green
	Peace, Wayne	QB	6-2	218	1	Florida
42	Pickering, Clay	WR	6-5	215	2	Maine
97	Pillman, Brian	LB	5-10	228	2	Miami, Ohio
51	Razzano, Rick	LB	5-11	227	6	Virginia Tech.
75	Reimers, Bruce	T	6-7	280	2	Iowa State
52	Rimington, Dave	C	6-3	288	3	Nebraska
15	Schonert, Turk	QB	6-1	190	6	Stanford
59	Schuh, Jeff	LB	6-2	228	5	Minnesota
25	Simmons, John	CB	5-11	192	5	Southern Methodist
56	Simpkins, Ron	LB	6-1	235	5	Michigan
62	Smith, Gary	G	6-2	265	2	Virginia Tech.
35	Turner, Jimmy	S	6-0	187	3	UCLA
81	Verser, David	WR	6-1	202	5	Kansas
82	Williams, Gary	WR	6-1	205	2	Ohio State
57	Williams, Reggie	LB	6-0	228	10	Dartmouth
77	Wilson, Mike	T	6-5	271	8	Georgia
32	Wilson, Stanley	RB	5-10	210	3	Oklahoma

CLEVELAND BROWNS AFC Central

Address Tower B, Cleveland Stadium, Cleveland, Ohio 44114.

Stadium Cleveland Stadium, Cleveland.
Capacity 80,098 *Playing Surface* Grass.

Team Colours Seal Brown, Orange and White.

Head Coach Marty Schottenheimer – second year.

Championships Divison 1971,'80; AAFC 1946,'47,'48,'49; NFL 1950,'54,'55,'64.

History AAFC 1946-49, NFL 1950-69, AFC 1970-

Offense

The acquisition of rookie quarterback Bernie Kosar (if he can pass his college exams) could ignite the Browns offense which, last year, ranked 24th in the NFL. Firstly though, he'll have to beat out Paul McDonald and Gary Danielson, the latter who was acquired from Detroit. The starting quarterback couldn't have a more reliable target than tight end Ozzie Newsome, who led the AFC with 89 pass receptions, lots of them in heavy traffic. Many experts feel that the younger tight end, Harry Holt, would start elsewhere in the league. At wide receiver, the Browns are not quite up to the standard of earlier years. Rookie Brian Brennan is a disciplined pattern runner, as is Ricky Feacher who was slowed by nagging injuries. Bruce Davis is a speed merchant but is more useful as a shock weapon than as a full-time starter at present. Glen Young has been around the league a bit but may find a permanent spot with the Browns – Young really can move. The offensive line will miss the retired Doug Dieken as they did right tackle Cody Risien, who was out for the whole of 1984 with a knee injury. The effects of many years in the NFL may be telling elsewhere on the line. Between them, guards Robert Jackson and Joe DeLamielleure, and reserve center Tom DeLeone, have 35 years' experience. There are no problems at center, where Mike Baab earned the unqualified praise of Detroit's All-Pro defensive tackle, Doug English, who quipped, 'Baab is as strong as nine acres of Texas onions.' The former great, running back Mike Pruitt, may find it difficult to break back into the starting lineup. The incumbents, Boyce Green and Earnest Byner, have settled in nicely. Byner, a tenth-round draft pick, was a rookie surprise, averaging 5.9 when rushing for a total of 426 yards, 188 of them in one game against Houston. Draftee Greg Allen comes with the reputation of being a big-play specialist, and Kevin Mack, a former USFL player, is a tough inside runner.

Defense

A hard-tackling, uncompromising defense gave up the second-fewest yards in the league last year. A young and improving defensive line of Reggie Camp, Bob Golic and Keith Baldwin, keeps the pressure on while the rest move in for the coup de grâce. They don't often sack the quarterback but play their full part in the AFC's best pass defense. At linebacker, the starting quartet was undisturbed all year and is now particularly strong on the outsides where Chip Banks and Clay Matthews patrol. Somewhat surprisingly for an inside linebacker, Tom Cousineau has emerged as an effective pass rusher, blitzing and stunting. Perhaps because of this, combined with the absence of the injured veteran, Dick Ambrose, the Browns were less effective against the run (they ranked 15th in the NFL). Three top-class players joined the secondary in 1984. First-round pick Don Rogers was a hard-hitting sensation and Frank Minnifield, who came from the USFL, was just the ticket at left cornerback. The third player, second-round pick Chris Rockins, couldn't break into the starting lineup. That says a lot for strong safety Al Gross, originally a ninth-round pick of the Cowboys in 1983, who shared the lead for interceptions with right cornerback Hanford Dixon (each player had five). They are further strengthened by the recovery from injury of safety Mike Whitwell, who was a starter throughout 1983.

Special Teams

Surprisingly, kicker Matt Bahr was more effective from over 40 yards out than he was from between 30 and 39 yards out. Nonetheless, he is a reliable pro, unlikely to make errors. For the really long field goal attempts and for kickoffs, Steve Cox takes over. In 1984, he kicked the second-longest field goal in NFL history (a 60-yarder against Cincinnati on Week Eight). As a punter he achieves great distances but not with the best of hang times, and two were blocked. In the absence of obvious candidates in the kick and punt returning departments, Glen Young might find a roster spot.

1985 DRAFT

Round	Name	Pos.	Ht.	Wt.	College
2.	Allen, Greg	RB	5-11	199	Florida State
6.	Krerowicz, Mark	G	6-2	280	Ohio State
7.	Langhorne, Reginald	WR	6-1	187	Elizabeth City State
8.	Banks, Fred	WR	5-10	173	Liberty Baptist
10.	Williams, Larry	G	6-5	270	Notre Dame
11.	Tucker, Travis	TE	6-2	225	Southern Connecticut
12.	Swanson, Shane	WR		195	Nebraska

Paul McDonald will have to fight for his place in 1985

1985 SCHEDULE

September
8	ST LOUIS	1:00
16	PITTSBURGH	9:00
22	at Dallas	1:00
29	at San Diego	4:00

October
6	NEW ENGLAND	1:00
13	at Houston	1:00
20	LOS ANGELES RAIDERS	1:00
27	WASHINGTON	1:00

November
3	at Pittsburgh	1:00
10	at Cincinnati	1:00
17	BUFFALO	1:00
24	CINCINNATI	1:00

December
1	at New York Giants	1:00
8	at Seattle	4:00
15	HOUSTON	1:00
22	at New York Jets	1:00

VETERAN ROSTER

No.	Name	Pos.	Ht.	Wt.	NFL Year	College
80	Adams, Willis	WR-TE	6-2	200	6	Houston
52	Ambrose, Dick	LB	6-0	228	11	Virginia
53	Anderson, Stuart	LB	6-1	224	4	Virginia
61	Baab, Mike	C-G	6-4	270	4	Texas
9	Bahr, Matt	K	5-10	175	7	Penn State
99	Baldwin, Keith	DE	6-4	250	4	Texas A&M
56	Banks, Chip	LB	6-4	233	4	Southern California
24	Best, Greg	S	5-10	185	3	Kansas State
88	Bolden, Rickey	TE	6-6	250	2	Southern Methodist
47	Braziel, Larry	CB	6-0	184	7	Southern California
86	Brennan, Brian	WR	5-9	178	2	Boston College
49	Burrell, Clinton	S	6-1	192	6	Louisiana State
44	Byner, Earnest	RB	5-10	215	2	East Carolina
96	Camp, Reggie	DE	6-4	264	3	California
75	Contz, Bill	G-C	6-5	260	3	Penn State
50	Cousineau, Tom	LB	6-3	225	4	Ohio State
15	Cox, Steve	P-K	6-4	195	5	Arkansas
	Danielson, Gary	QB	6-2	196	9	Purdue
85	Davis, Bruce	WR	5-8	160	2	Baylor
38	Davis, Johnny	RB	6-1	235	8	Alabama
64	DeLamielleure, Joe	G	6-3	260	13	Michigan State
54	DeLeone, Tom	C	6-2	254	14	Ohio State
29	Dixon, Hanford	CB	5-11	182	5	Southern Mississippi
74	Farren, Paul	T	6-5	251	3	Boston University
83	Feacher, Ricky	WR	5-10	180	10	Mississippi Valley
10	Flick, Tom	QB	6-3	190	4	Washington
94	Franks, Elvis	DE	6-4	265	6	Morgan State
79	Golic, Bob	NT	6-2	260	6	Notre Dame
30	Green, Boyce	RB	5-11	215	3	Carson-Newman
27	Gross, Al	S	6-3	186	3	Arizona
78	Hairston, Carl	DE	6-4	260	10	Maryland E.S.
81	Holt, Harry	TE	6-4	230	3	Arizona
68	Jackson, Robert E.	G	6-5	260	11	Duke
51	Johnson, Eddie	LB	6-1	215	5	Louisville
87	Lewis, Darryl	TE	6-6	226	2	Texas
62	Lilja, George	T-C	6-4	250	4	Michigan
	Mack, Kevin	RB	5-11	198	1	Clemson
59	Marshall, David	LB	6-3	220	2	Eastern Michigan
57	Matthews, Clay	LB	6-2	230	8	Southern California
16	McDonald, Paul	QB	6-2	185	6	Southern California
31	Minnifield, Frank	CB	5-9	180	2	Louisville
82	Newsome, Ozzie	TE	6-2	232	8	Alabama
58	Nicolas, Scott	LB	6-3	226	4	Miami
7	Nugent, Terry	QB	6-4	218	2	Colorado State
	Oatis, Victor	WR	6-0	177	2	Northwestern Louisiana
43	Pruitt, Mike	RB	6-0	225	10	Purdue
72	Puzzuoli, Dave	NT	6-3	260	3	Pittsburgh
63	Risien, Cody	T	6-7	270	8	Texas A&M
37	Rockins, Chris	S	6-0	195	2	Oklahoma
20	Rogers, Don	S	6-1	206	2	UCLA
	Sikora, Robert	T	6-8	285	1	Indiana
	Stracka, Tim	TE	6-3	225	3	Wisconsin
89	Walker, Dwight	WR-PR	5-10	185	4	Nicholls State
55	Weathers, Curtis	LB	6-5	230	7	Mississippi
21	Whitwell, Mike	S	6-0	175	4	Texas A&M
84	Young, Glen	WR	6-2	205	3	Mississippi State

HOUSTON OILERS AFC Central

Address Box 1516, Houston, Texas 77001.
Stadium The Astrodome, Houston.
 Capacity 50,496 *Playing Surface* AstroTurf.
Team Colours Columbia Blue, Scarlet and White.
Head Coach Hugh Campbell – second year.
Championships AFL 1960, '61.
History AFL 1960-69, AFC 1970-

Offense

Quarterback Warren Moon came through his NFL baptism with credit and this, at a time when the Oilers are still in the process of reconstruction. In this, stage one has been completed satisfactorily with the formation of a potentially awesome offensive line. When at full strength, they parade number one picks in Mike Munchak, Bruce Matthews and Dean Steinkuhler. All three of Harvey Salem, ex-Raider Jim Romano and the former Falcon, Pat Howell, were second-rounders and, going back a bit, the veteran Doug France was a first-round pick of the Rams (1975). They like linemen down in Houston – the picked up another good one, center Mike Kelley, in the 1985 draft. Second-year running back Larry Moriarty wasted no time filling the void left by the departed Earl Campbell, who was traded to New Orleans after Week Six. He is joined by Butch Woolfolk, a former first-round pick of the Giants, and Mike Rozier, the 1983 Heisman Trophy winner, who arrives after two USFL seasons, in the most recent of which he was the second-leading rusher. Wide receiver Tim Smith confirmed the form of 1983 with his second consecutive 1,000-yard receiving campaign. His performance looks even better when it is considered that he is almost permanently double-covered. New talent at wide receiver would be welcome but for the moment, such are the team needs elsewhere that improvement will have to come from the existing roster. Herkie Walls certainly has the speed and, like running back Moriarty, may be just waiting for the chance to impress. The medium-range passing threat comes from the double tight end pairing of Jamie Williams and Chris Dressel (strictly, Dressel is an H-back) who between them caught a valuable 81 passes. This is another area which gives head coach Hugh Campbell reason for optimism.

Defense

The Oilers used the draft to fortify a defense which ranked 27th overall in the league and had difficulty stopping the run all year. Both Ray Childress and Richard Byrd can expect to start, with Byrd converting to nose tackle. The other end, veteran Jesse Baker, is a top-class player and, last year, registered 11 of the team's meagre total of 32 sacks. At linebacker, Robert Abraham and Avon Riley should be approaching their best, but neither Robert 'Doctor Doom' Brazile nor Gregg Bingham is ever likely to be as fearsome as they were in the past. With an eye for the future, Tom Briehl and Frank Bush were drafted in rounds four and five respectively. In the meantime, the second-year players, Johnny Meads and John Grimsley, should play a greater part now that they have learned the system. The veteran quality in the secondary lies with free safety Carter Hartwig, who caught three interceptions in a year punctuated with injuries. He'll be back to act as a rallying point for a young and inexperienced group, now strengthened by Richard Johnson, who is regarded as the best cornerback in the 1985 draft. Willie Tullis led with four of the team total of 13 interceptions. He's likely to continue at right cornerback with Johnson displacing Steve Brown.

Special Teams

There will be a real battle for the job of placekicker between Florian Kempf, returning from injury, and the incumbent, Joe Cooper, who was successful on 11 of 13 field goal attempts. Lee Johnson, a fifth-round draftee, was selected as a kicker but is more likely to displace the veteran John James, who is coming to the end of a distinguished career. Johnson's punting average at Brigham Young University was 45.5 yards. Carl Roaches, who doubles as both kickoff and punt returner, had a sub-par year but the NFL's coverage teams cannot afford to be complacent – he's always likely to break for the big return.

1985 DRAFT

Round	Name	Pos.	Ht.	Wt.	College
1.	Childress, Ray	DE	6-6	275	Texas A&M
1.	Johnson, Richard	CB	6-0	190	Wisconsin
2.	Byrd, Richard	DE	6-3	259	Southern Mississippi
3.	Kelley, Mike	C	6-5	265	Notre Dame
4.	Briehl, Tom	LB	6-3	238	Stanford
5.	Bush, Frank	LB	6-1	210	North Carolina State
5.	Johnson, Lee	K	6-1	205	Brigham Young
6.	Krakoski, Joe	LB	6-1	228	Washington
7.	Akiu, Mike	WR	5-8	172	Hawaii
8.	Thomas, Chuck	C	6-2	270	Oklahoma
9.	Tasker, Steve	KR			Northwestern
10.	Golic, Mike	DE	6-4	245	Notre Dame
11.	Drewrey, Willie	KR	5-8	168	West Virginia
12.	VonderHaar, Mark	DT	6-4	255	Minnesota

Keith Bostic, the Oilers' starting strong safety

1985 SCHEDULE

September
8	MIAMI	1:00
15	at Washington	1:00
22	at Pittsburgh	1:00
29	DALLAS	1:00

October
6	at Denver	4:00
13	CLEVELAND	1:00
20	CINCINNATI	1:00
27	at St Louis	1:00

November
3	KANSAS CITY	1:00
10	at Buffalo	1:00
17	PITTSBURGH	1:00
24	SAN DIEGO	1:00

December
1	at Cincinnati	1:00
8	NEW YORK GIANTS	4:00
15	at Cleveland	1:00
22	at Indianapolis	4:00

VETERAN ROSTER

No.	Name	Pos.	Ht.	Wt.	NFL Year	College
56	Abraham, Robert	LB	6-1	215	4	North Carolina State
29	Allen, Patrick	CB	5-10	180	2	Utah State
75	Baker, Jesse	DE	6-5	272	7	Jacksonville State
54	Bingham, Gregg	LB	6-1	225	13	Purdue
25	Bostic, Keith	S	6-1	212	3	Michigan
52	Brazile, Robert	LB	6-4	237	11	Jackson State
24	Brown, Steve	CB	5-11	188	3	Oregon
81	Bryant, Steve	WR	6-2	191	4	Purdue
8	Cooper, Joe	K	5-10	168	2	California
31	Donaldson, Jeff	S	6-0	180	2	Colorado
88	Dressel, Chris	TE	6-4	231	3	Stanford
21	Eason, Bo	S	6-2	205	2	Cal-Davis
32	Edwards, Stan	RB	6-0	210	4	Michigan
78	Foster, Jerome	DE	6-2	258	3	Ohio State
77	France, Doug	T	6-5	266	10	Ohio State
59	Grimsley, John	LB	6-2	225	2	Kentucky
36	Hartwig, Carter	S	6-0	207	7	Southern California
84	Holston, Michael	WR	6-3	188	5	Morgan State
66	Howell, Pat	G	6-6	260	7	Southern California
50	Hunt, Daryl	LB	6-3	235	7	Oklahoma
6	James, John	P	6-3	196	14	Florida
97	Johnson, Mike	DE	6-5	225	2	Illinois
57	Joiner, Tim	LB	6-4	224	3	Louisiana State
38	Joyner, Willie	RB	5-10	200	2	Maryland
4	Kempf, Florian	K	5-9	170	4	Pennsylvania
27	Kennedy, Mike	S	6-0	195	3	Toledo
	Klug, Dave	LB	6-4	230	4	Concordia, Minnesota
10	Luck, Oliver	QB	6-2	193	4	West Virginia
28	Lyday, Allen	S	5-10	180	2	Nebraska
93	Lyles, Robert	LB	6-1	210	2	Texas Christian
74	Matthews, Bruce	T-C	6-4	269	3	Southern California
89	McCloskey, Mike	TE	6-5	240	3	Penn State
26	Meadows, Darryl	S	6-1	199	3	Toledo
91	Meads, Johnny	LB	6-2	220	2	Nicholls State
1	Moon, Warren	QB	6-3	210	2	Washington
76	Moran, Eric	T	6-6	280	3	Washington
30	Moriarty, Larry	RB	6-1	228	3	Notre Dame
80	Mullins, Eric	WR	5-11	175	2	Stanford
63	Munchak, Mike	G	6-3	275	4	Penn State
12	Ransom, Brian	QB	6-3	205	3	Tennessee State
53	Riley, Avon	LB	6-3	225	5	UCLA
85	Roaches, Carl	WR-PR-KR	5-8	170	6	Texas A&M
55	Romano, Jim	C	6-3	255	4	Penn State
	Rozier, Mike	RB	5-10	210	1	Nebraska
73	Salem, Harvey	T	6-6	264	3	California
62	Schuhmacher, John	G	6-3	267	5	Southern California
83	Smith, Tim	WR	6-2	203	6	Nebraska
72	Sochia, Brian	MG	6-3	250	3	Northwest Oklahoma
70	Steinkuhler, Dean	T	6-3	275	2	Nebraska
67	Stensrud, Mike	MG	6-5	285	7	Iowa State
98	Studaway, Mark	DE	6-3	250	2	Tennessee
51	Thompson, Ted	LB	6-1	219	11	Southern Methodist
20	Tullis, Willie	CB	6-0	193	5	Troy State
82	Walls, Herkie	WR	5-8	154	3	Texas
87	Williams, Jamie	TE	6-5	230	2	Nebraska
35	Williams, Richard	RB	6-0	205	3	Memphis State
	Woolfolk, Butch	RB	6-1	207	4	Michigan

PITTSBURGH STEELERS AFC Central

Address Three Rivers Stadium, 300 Stadium Circle, Pittsburgh, Pa. 15212.

Stadium Three Rivers Stadium, Pittsburgh.
Capacity 59,000 *Playing Surface* AstroTurf.

Team Colours Black and Gold.

Head Coach Chuck Noll – seventeenth year.

Championships Division 1972, '74, '75, '76, '77, '78, '79, '83, '84; Conference 1974. '75, '78, '79; Super Bowl 1974, '75, '78, '79.

History NFL 1933-69, AFC 1970-
(Until 1940, they were known as the Pittsburgh Pirates.)

Offense

The Steelers possess a rich blend of veteran experience and raw talent with which to improve on last year's 9-7 record. The rushing partnership of Frank Pollard and Walter Abercrombie is not yet quite up to the standard for which the old Harris-Bleier pairing was renowned. But they were good enough to lift the Steelers to sixth place in the league for rushing offense. Abercrombie's two 100-yard games in the last four weeks of 1984 suggest that he is now on the verge of becoming a genuine 1,000-yard rusher. Mark Malone established himself at quarterback after taking over when David Woodley was injured against Miami on Week Six. Overall, his passer rating of 73.4 was modest but he had no trouble finding his wide receivers, veteran John Stallworth and rookie Louis Lipps. Woodley, who had a passer rating of 79.9, is an excellent reserve. Stallworth had always been a good one, but surprised a lot of people by having his best year, after over a decade in the league, and went to the Pro Bowl for the third time. The sensational Lipps was voted NFL Offensive Rookie of the Year. The output from the tight end position was poor with three players, Chris Kolodziejski, Bennie Cunningham and Darrell Nelson catching a total of just eleven passes between them. In fairness, none of the three played a full season and it is still anticipated that Kolodziejski will confirm his college pedigree (he was a second-round pick). Rookie running back Rich Erenberg chipped in with 38 pass receptions and should develop into a useful dual-purpose player. Injuries led to uncer-tainty for most of the season at offensive tackle but, by playoff time, Pete Rostosky and Tunch Ilkin had settled in. Larry Brown, a veteran of fourteen years in the league, may not return. However, Steve August and draftee Mark Behning provide insurance. Ray Snell is returning to compete with Terry Long and Blake Wingle for the right guard position. There is no doubt about the identity of the player who will snap the ball. That man, the indomitable Mike Webster, returns to extend his sequence of seven Pro Bowl appearances.

Defense

The defense may no longer qualify for the title, 'Steel Curtain', but, name or not, they're still very tough. Overall, they ranked fifth in the NFL and were particularly mean against the run despite the absence of All-Pro inside linebacker Jack Lambert for the major part of the season. Lambert is still troubled with a dislocating big toe and, for this reason, may even retire. Lambert's deputy, David Little, performed admirably but the real success story was the transition of Robin Cole from right outside to the inside position, at which he went to his first Pro Bowl. Mike Merriweather was, at times, awesome, particularly when going after the quarterback – with 15 sacks, he came third in the AFC and joined Cole in the Pro Bowl. The Steelers are one of the clubs who use a variety of substitutions and formations on the defensive line. Goodman and Dunn specialise against the run whilst Ed Nelson and Keith Willis are at their best rushing the passer. Keith Gary does it all. They are strengthened further by first-round pick Darryl Sims, another pass-rushing specialist. A larcenous secondary grabbed 31 pass interceptions on the year with strong safety Donnie Shell and right cornerback Sam Washington leading the way with seven and six respectively. Four interceptions were returned for touchdowns. Playing in reserve, both rookie cornerback Chris Brown and former starter Rick Woods had their moments.

Special Teams

Gary Anderson is one of the league's best kickers and was unlucky not to repeat his 1984 Pro Bowl appearance. However, punter Craig Colquitt will be challenged by draftee Harry Newsome. Punt returner Louis Lipps didn't bother with fair catches, he just took off on 53 rambles at an average of 12.4 yards. It was good enough to land him in the Pro Bowl.

1985 DRAFT

Round	Name	Pos.	Ht.	Wt.	College
1.	Sims, Darryl	DE	6-2	260	Wisconsin
2.	Behning, Mark	T	6-6	290	Nebraska
3.	Hobley, Liffort	DB	5-11	195	Louisiana State
4.	Turk, Dan	C	6-4	260	Wisconsin
5.	Jacobs, Cam	LB	6-1	225	Kentucky
6.	Carr, Gregg	LB	6-1	210	Auburn
7.	Andrews, Alan	TE	6-4	222	Rutgers
8.	Newsome, Harry	P	6-0	185	Wake Forest
9.	Small, Fred	LB	6-0	225	Washington
9.	Harris, Andre	DB	5-10	185	Minnesota
10.	White, Oliver	TE	6-0	225	Kentucky
11.	Matichak, Terry	DB	6-2	195	Missouri
12.	Sanchez, Jeff	DB	5-10	180	Georgia

Pro Bowl linebacker Mike Merriweather (#57)

1985 SCHEDULE

September

8	INDIANAPOLIS	1:00
16	at Cleveland	9:00
22	HOUSTON	1:00
30	CINCINNATI	9:00

October

6	at Miami	1:00
13	at Dallas	1:00
20	ST LOUIS	1:00
27	at Cincinnati	4:00

November

3	CLEVELAND	1:00
10	at Kansas City	1:00
17	at Houston	1:00
24	WASHINGTON	1:00

December

1	DENVER	1:00
8	at San Diego	6:00
15	BUFFALO	1:00
21	at N.Y. Giants	12:30

VETERAN ROSTER

No.	Name	Pos.	Ht.	Wt.	NFL Year	College
34	Abercrombie, Walter	RB	5-10	210	4	Baylor
1	Anderson, Gary	K	5-11	156	4	Syracuse
77	August, Steve	T	6-5	258	9	Tulsa
54	Bingham, Craig	LB	6-2	211	4	Syracuse
71	Boures, Emil	G-C	6-2	261	4	Pittsburgh
23	Brown, Chris	CB	6-0	195	2	Notre Dame
79	Brown, Larry	T	6-4	270	15	Kansas
10	Campbell, Scott	QB	5-11	201	2	Purdue
80	Capers, Wayne	WR	6-2	193	3	Kansas
78	Catano, Mark	DE	6-3	265	2	Valdosta State
33	Clayton, Harvey	CB	5-9	170	3	Florida State
56	Cole, Robin	LB	6-2	220	9	New Mexico
5	Colquitt, Craig	P	6-1	182	7	Tennessee
40	Corley, Anthony	RB	6-0	210	2	Nevada-Reno
89	Cunningham, Bennie	TE	6-5	260	10	Clemson
	Dixon, Tom	C	6-2	250	1	Michigan
67	Dunn, Gary	NT	6-3	260	9	Miami
24	Erenberg, Rich	RB	5-10	200	2	Colgate
92	Gary, Keith	DE	6-3	255	3	Oklahoma
26	Gillespie, Fernandars	RB	5-10	178	2	William Jewell
95	Goodman, John	DE	6-6	250	5	Oklahoma
53	Hinkle, Bryan	LB	6-1	220	4	Oregon
62	Ilkin, Tunch	T	6-3	255	6	Indiana State
29	Johnson, Ron	S	5-11	200	8	Eastern Michigan
90	Kohrs, Bob	LB	6-3	235	5	Arizona State
84	Kolodziejski, Chris	TE	6-3	231	2	Wyoming
58	Lambert, Jack	LB	6-4	220	12	Kent State
83	Lipps, Louis	WR	5-10	190	2	Southern Mississippi
50	Little, David	LB	6-1	220	5	Florida State
74	Long, Terry	G	5-11	272	2	East Carolina
16	Malone, Mark	QB	6-4	223	6	Arizona State
57	Merriweather, Mike	LB	6-2	215	4	Pacific
81	Nelson, Darrell	TE	6-2	235	2	Memphis State
64	Nelson, Edmund	NT	6-3	270	4	Auburn
30	Pollard, Frank	RB	5-10	218	6	Baylor
60	Rasmussen, Randy	C	6-2	253	2	Minnesota
88	Rodgers, John	TE	6-2	220	4	Louisiana Tech.
63	Rostosky, Pete	T	6-4	245	2	Connecticut
59	Seabaugh, Todd	LB	6-4	220	2	San Diego State
31	Shell, Donnie	S	5-11	190	12	South Carolina State
72	Snell, Ray	G	6-4	265	6	Wisconsin
36	Spencer, Todd	RB	6-0	195	2	Southern California
82	Stallworth, John	WR	6-2	191	12	Alabama A&M
85	Sweeney, Calvin	WR	6-2	190	6	Southern California
87	Thompson, Weegie	WR	6-6	210	2	Florida State
38	Veals, Elton	RB	5-11	223	2	Tulane
41	Washington, Sam	CB	5-8	180	4	Mississippi Valley
52	Webster, Mike	C	6-1	250	12	Wisconsin
21	Williams, Eric	S	5-11	183	3	North Carolina State
	Williams, Robert	CB	5-11	202	2	Eastern Illinois
93	Willis, Keith	DE	6-1	251	4	Northeastern
61	Wingle, Blake	G	6-2	267	3	UCLA
73	Wolfley, Craig	G	6-1	265	6	Syracuse
19	Woodley, David	QB	6-2	202	6	Louisiana State
49	Woodruff, Dwayne	CB	5-11	198	7	Louisville
22	Woods, Rick	S	6-0	196	4	Boise State

DENVER BRONCOS AFC West

Address 5700, Logan Street, Denver, Colorado 80216.
Stadium Denver Mile High Stadium.
  Capacity 75,100 *Playing Surface* Grass (Prescription Athletic Turf).
Team Colours Orange, Royal Blue and White.
Head Coach Dan Reeves – fifth year.
Championships Division 1977, '78, '84; Conference 1977.
History AFL 1960-69, AFC 1970-

Offense

John Elway hasn't yet made quite the impact expected of an overall first-round pick but is improving steadily and ominously. When he has been injured or out-of-form, Gary Kubiak has come on and performed well and, though making limited appearances, he had a better passer rating than the illustrious leading man. Wide receiver Butch Johnson seems destined never to be accepted as a regular starter, despite having pulled in many remarkable receptions over the years. Some say that he lacks pace. But that never bothered the likes of the former Raider, Fred Biletnikoff. Nonetheless, the Broncos went for blazing speed when they drafted Vance Johnson. A running back in college, the former Arizona track star will be converted to wide receiver. Operating down the opposite sideline, Steve Watson can be expected to increase his tally of 1,000-yard receiving seasons to four, in his seventh NFL year. Rookie tight end Clarence Kay proved to be a valuable blocker for the running backs but caught only 16 passes. H-back John Sawyer is coming back from injury and there will be extra competition from the enormous Keli McGregor, a local product. Running back Sammy Winder punched out a hard-earned 1,153 yards and went to his first Pro Bowl. Gerald Willhite is coming off a modest season and Rick Parros made little impact, and yet the Broncos' rushing offense was the fourth-best in the AFC. Draftee running back Steve Sewell is very versatile and will fit in well. The offensive line really firmed up in 1984, allowing only 35 quarterback sacks (in 1983, they gave up 55). In addition, they must share the praise for a rushing offense which, though never spectacular, just kept chewing up yardage. With the exception of right guard Paul Howard, the unit is still relatively young and will improve.

Defense

The Broncos' defense bends a lot but doesn't crack very often – they ranked 25th in the league for yardage conceded but only San Francisco gave up fewer points than Denver's 241. Probably because they were so effective against the run (they were 5th in the NFL), teams passed a lot and the Broncos secondary was kept busy, but picked off interceptions when it mattered most. In 1983, teams forgot just how good cornerback Louis Wright was. They went for him and he made six interceptions. Last year, they steered clear and turned on right cornerback Mike Harden – so he grabbed six interceptions. He was matched by free safety Steve Foley, who, with strong safety Dennis Smith, forms one of the league's finest partnerships. In short, it's not wise to be over-ambitious, when passing against the Broncos. The three-man line of Rulon Jones, Barney Chavous and Rubin Carter, stayed intact all year but rookies Andre Townsend and Scott Garnett played well enough on spot duty to show that they are ready to start. Further help comes with the arrival of draftee defensive end Simon Fletcher. Outside linebacker Tom Jackson shows no signs of slowing down after twelve years in the league. He's still a good one but Ken Woodard is expected to challenge for more playing time. There's plenty of talent in the other three starters but room will have to be found for Ricky Hunley, a former first-round pick of the Bengals who came in a trade during last season.

Special Teams

Rich Karlis had his problems, particularly when missing key field goals late in the season. But he came good in the end and retains the coach's confidence. Punter Chris Norman gives the ball a good thump but could improve on his directional control. Gerald Willhite took over punt return duties, after the departure of Zack Thomas, and was a success, finishing fifth in the NFL. Kickoff returning was a problem all year with several people having a go. Willhite had only four returns but averaged 27.3 yards and could have found himself another little diversion from the rigours of rushing with the football.

1985 DRAFT

Round	Name	Pos.	Ht.	Wt.	College
1.	Sewell, Steve	RB	6-3	205	Oklahoma
2.	Johnson, Vance	WR	5-10	175	Arizona
2.	Fletcher, Simon	DE	6-5	240	Houston
4.	McGregor, Keli	TE	6-6	250	Colorado State
5.	Hinson, Billy	G		266	Florida
7.	Cameron, Dallas	NT	6-1	243	Miami
8.	Riley, Eric	DB	5-11	170	Florida State
9.	Smith, Daryl	DB	5-9	185	North Alabama
10.	Funck, Buddy	QB	6-2	200	New Mexico
10.	Anderson, Ron	LB	6-2	215	SMU
11.	Rolle, Gary	WR	5-10	168	Florida
12.	Lynch, Dan	G	6-3	255	Washington State

Denver's rocket-throwing quarterback, John Elway (#7)

1985 SCHEDULE

September

8	at Los Angeles Rams	4:00
15	NEW ORLEANS	4:00
22	at Atlanta	1:00
29	MIAMI	4:00

October

6	HOUSTON	4:00
13	at Indianapolis	1:00
20	SEATTLE	4:00
27	at Kansas City	1:00

November

3	at San Diego	4:00
11	SAN FRANCISCO	9:00
17	SAN DIEGO	4:00
24	at Los Angeles Raiders	4:00

December

1	at Pittsburgh	1:00
8	LOS ANGELES RAIDERS	4:00
14	KANSAS CITY	4:00
20	at Seattle	8:00

VETERAN ROSTER

No.	Name	Pos.	Ht.	Wt.	NFL Year	College
80	Alexander, Ray	WR			2	
54	Bishop, Keith	C-G	6-3	260	5	Baylor
65	Bowyer, Walt	DE	6-4	245	3	Arizona State
26	Brewer, Chris	RB	6-1	192	2	Arizona
64	Bryan, Bill	C	6-2	258	8	Duke
58	Busick, Steve	LB	6-4	227	5	Southern California
68	Carter, Rubin	NT	6-0	256	11	Miami
79	Chavous, Barney	DE	6-3	258	13	South Carolina State
59	Comeaux, Darren	LB	6-1	227	4	Arizona State
63	Cooper, Mark	G	6-5	267	3	Miami
55	Dennison, Rick	LB	6-2	215	4	Colorado State
7	Elway, John	QB	6-4	202	3	Stanford
43	Foley, Steve	S	6-2	190	10	Tulane
62	Freeman, Steve	G	6-2	244	2	Arizona
66	Garnett, Scott	NT	6-2	253	2	Washington
72	Graves, Marsharne	T	6-4	265	2	Arizona
31	Harden, Mike	CB	6-1	192	6	Michigan
74	Hood, Winford	T	6-3	240	2	Georgia
60	Howard, Paul	G	6-3	260	12	Brigham Young
98	Hunley, Ricky	LB	6-1	237	2	Arizona
	Hyde, Glenn	C-G	6-3	252	8	Pittsburgh
28	Jackson, Roger	S	6-0	186	4	Bethune-Cookman
57	Jackson, Tom	LB	5-11	220	13	Louisville
86	Johnson, Butch	WR	6-1	187	10	Cal-Riverside
75	Jones, Rulon	DE	6-6	260	6	Utah State
3	Karlis, Rich	K	6-0	180	4	Cincinnati
88	Kay, Clarence	TE	6-3	225	2	Georgia
8	Kubiak, Gary	QB	6-0	192	3	Texas A&M
33	Lang, Gene	RB	5-10	196	2	Louisiana State
76	Lanier, Ken	T	6-3	269	5	Florida State
22	Lilly, Tony	S	6-0	199	2	Florida
69	Manor, Brison	DE	6-4	235	9	Arkansas
77	Mecklenburg, Karl	LB-NT	6-3	250	3	Minnesota
29	Myers, Wilbur	S	5-11	195	3	Delta State
39	Myles, Jesse	RB	5-10	210	3	Louisiana State
1	Norman, Chris	P	6-3	250	3	South Carolina
24	Parros, Rick	RB	5-11	200	5	Utah State
	Raridon, Scott	T-G	6-3	288	2	Nebraska
48	Robbins, Randy	S	6-1	182	2	Arizona
50	Ryan, Jim	LB	6-1	215	7	William & Mary
84	Sampson, Clinton	WR	5-11	183	3	San Diego State
83	Sawyer, John	TE	6-2	230	10	Southern Mississippi
56	Smith, Aaron	LB	6-2	209	2	Utah State
49	Smith, Dennis	S	6-3	200	5	Southern California
14	Stankavage, Scott	QB	6-1	197	2	North Carolina
70	Studdard, Dave	T	6-4	260	7	Texas
85	Summers, Don	TE	6-4	226	2	Boise State
61	Townsend, Andre	DE	6-2	253	2	Mississippi
81	Watson, Steve	WR	6-4	195	7	Temple
47	Willhite, Gerald	RB	5-10	200	4	San Jose State
45	Wilson, Steve	CB	5-10	195	7	Howard
23	Winder, Sammy	RB	5-11	203	4	Southern Mississippi
52	Woodard, Kenneth	LB	6-1	218	4	Tuskegee
87	Wright, Jim	TE	6-3	240	8	Texas
20	Wright, Louis	CB	6-2	200	11	San Jose State

KANSAS CITY CHIEFS AFC West

Address 1 Arrowhead Drive, Kansas City, Missouri 64129.
Stadium Arrowhead Stadium, Kansas City.
  Capacity 78,067 *Playing Surface* Tartan Turf.
Team Colours Red, Gold and White.
Head Coach John Mackovic – third year.
Championships Division 1971; AFL 1962, '66, '69; Super Bowl 1969.
History AFL 1960-69, AFC 1970-
  (Until 1963, they were known as the Dallas Texans.)

Offense

The Kansas City Chiefs are on the verge of breaking back into contention even in this, the NFL's most competitive division. It's not very often that a club drafting in 15th position gets its man but that's what happened when they were able to pick the North Carolina running back, Ethan Horton. He's an Eric Dickerson type of running back; perhaps not quite as fast but twelve pounds heavier. Rookie Herman Heard did well as the main force coming out of the backfield (684 yards at an average of 4.1) and is sure to derive great benefit from lining up alongside Horton. Theotis Brown, who suffered an off-season heart attack, is unlikely to be back, but happily, he is on the way to full recovery. The Chiefs' passing offense could rival even that of San Diego. Bill Kenney at quarterback is a seasoned pro, and reserve Todd Blackledge didn't make many mistakes when on stand-in duty. There's little doubt, however, that Kenney is the man and, with his battery of receivers, would surprise no-one by reproducing the form of 1983, when he passed for 4,348 yards and 24 touchdowns. The big danger hovers out near the sidelines where Henry Marshall is coming off the best campaign of his nine-year career, and Carlos Carson will be seeking to log his third consecutive 1,000-yard season. Stephone Paige would start with many other NFL teams, as would Anthony Hancock, a former first-round pick. From the tight end position, where former first-round selection Willie Scott has yet to come good, output has been modest, and draftee Jonathan Hayes was a wise choice. He's said to be a little raw but can handle the physical side of things (he is a former linebacker) and has good hands. Despite missing right tackle Dave Lutz for ten games, the line allowed only 33 quarterback sacks. Left guard Brad Budde, center Bob Rush and backup tackle John Alt all are former number one picks who play up to that standard.

Defense

Nose tackle Bill Maas would have been at home in the old (really tough) days of the NFL. Certainly he is a real blue-chipper but, more than that, he'll play with the pain as he showed on returning to action when barely had his broken leg healed. With the opposition now having to double-team Maas, defensive ends Art Still and Mike Bell are given that bit extra freedom to go on the rampage. Last year, they registered 14.5 and 13.5 sacks respectively out of a team-record total of 50. That trio is as good as any other in the league, and better than most. Behind them, there's a fair sprinkling of talent but a few weaknesses do exist. In 1984 the defense ranked 24th overall in the NFL for yardage conceded, and was beaten by the pass rather often. The weaknesses aren't that serious – just about every player was steady, some were superb and most could point to good moments. Inside linebackers Gary Spani and Jerry Blanton prospered from the efforts of Maas up the middle, and rookie second-rounder Scott Radecic did well on spot duty. Ken McAlister slipped a bit, after taking over from Charles Jackson at left outside linebacker. Jeff Paine and Calvin Daniels are the likely starters on the right and left sides respectively. In the secondary, rookie Kevin Ross will be better for having been thrown in at the deep end (he replaced Gary Green who went to the Rams) and, though beaten badly on occasions, pulled in six interceptions, only one fewer than free safety Deron Cherry who again went to the Pro Bowl. Strong safety Lloyd Burruss, a starter in all four of his NFL years, remains as solid as ever.

Special Teams

Kicker Nick Lowery, the NFL's all-time leader in terms of field goal efficiency, will not count 1984 amongst his better years. But his position is secure, as is that of punter Jim Arnold, whose gross average of 44.9 yards was the league's best. J.T. Smith returns most of the punts and shares the kickoff returns with Stephone Paige. For Smith, a big touchdown return is overdue.

1985 DRAFT

Round	Name	Pos.	Ht.	Wt.	College
1.	Horton, Ethan	RB	6-3	231	North Carolina
2.	Hayes, Jonathan	TE	6-4	239	Iowa
4.	Olderman, Bob	G	6-5	268	Virginia
5.	King, Bruce	RB	6-1	210	Purdue
6.	Bostic, Jonathan	DB	5-9	175	Bethune-Cookman
7.	Thomson, Vince	DE	6-4	260	Missouri Western
7.	Heffernan, Dave	G	6-4	250	Miami
8.	Hillary, Ira	WR	5-10	190	South Carolina
9.	Armentrout, Mike	DB	5-10	180	Southwest Missouri
10.	Smith, Jeff	RB	5-9	190	Nebraska
11.	Jackson, Chris	C	6-3	260	Southern Methodist
12.	LeBel, Harper	C	6-4	244	Colorado State

Free safety Deron Cherry went to his second consecutive Pro Bowl last season

1985 SCHEDULE

September
8	at New Orleans	1:00
12	LOS ANGELES RAIDERS	8:00
22	at Miami	4:00
29	SEATTLE	1:00

October
6	at Los Angeles Raiders	4:00
13	at San Diego	4:00
20	LOS ANGELES RAMS	1:00
27	DENVER	1:00

November
3	at Houston	1:00
10	PITTSBURGH	1:00
17	at San Francisco	4:00
24	INDIANAPOLIS	4:00

December
1	at Seattle	4:00
8	ATLANTA	1:00
14	at Denver	4:00
22	SAN DIEGO	1:00

VETERAN ROSTER

No.	Name	Pos.	Ht.	Wt.	NFL Year	College
76	Alt, John	T	6-7	278	2	Iowa
6	Arnold, Jim	P	6-2	212	3	Vanderbilt
87	Arnold, Walt	TE	6-3	234	6	New Mexico
68	Auer, Scott	G	6-4	255	2	Michigan State
77	Baldinger, Rich	T	6-4	280	4	Wake Forest
85	Beckman, Ed	TE	6-4	239	9	Florida State
99	Bell, Mike	DE	6-4	250	6	Colorado State
14	Blackledge, Todd	QB	6-3	225	3	Penn State
57	Blanton, Jerry	LB	6-1	236	7	Kentucky
27	Brown, Theotis	RB	6-3	225	7	UCLA
66	Budde, Brad	G	6-4	260	6	Southern California
34	Burruss, Lloyd	S	6-0	202	5	Maryland
88	Carson, Carlos	WR	5-11	174	6	Louisiana State
20	Cherry, Deron	S	5-11	190	5	Rutgers
65	Condon, Tom	G	6-3	275	12	Boston College
50	Daniels, Calvin	LB	6-3	236	4	North Carolina
73	Dawson, Mike	NT	6-3	254	10	Arizona
38	Gunter, Michael	RB	5-11	205	2	Tulsa
	Hamm, Bob	DE	6-4	248	3	Nevada-Reno
82	Hancock, Anthony	WR	6-0	187	4	Tennessee
44	Heard, Herman	RB	5-10	184	2	Southern Colorado
60	Herkenhoff, Matt	T	6-4	272	10	Minnesota
23	Hill, Greg	CB	6-1	189	3	Oklahoma State
93	Holle, Eric	DE	6-4	250	2	Texas
43	Jackson, Billy	RB	5-10	215	5	Alabama
52	Jolly, Ken	LB	6-2	220	2	Mid-America Nazarene
9	Kenney, Bill	QB	6-4	211	7	Northern Colorado
91	Kremer, Ken	NT	6-4	252	7	Ball State
40	Lacy, Kenneth	RB	6-0	222	2	Tulsa
	Lane, Skip					
29	Lewis, Albert	CB	6-2	190	3	Grambling
71	Lindstrom, Dave	DE	6-6	255	8	Boston University
62	Lingner, Adam	C-G	6-4	240	3	Illinois
8	Lowery, Nick	K	6-4	189	6	Dartmouth
72	Lutz, Dave	T	6-5	280	3	Georgia Tech.
63	Maas, Bill	DT	6-4	265	2	Pittsburgh
89	Marshall, Henry	WR	6-2	220	10	Missouri
94	McAlister, Ken	LB	6-5	220	4	San Francisco
11	Osiecki, Sandy	QB	6-5	202	2	Arizona State
83	Paige, Stephone	WR	6-1	180	3	Fresno State
95	Paine, Jeff	LB	6-2	224	2	Texas A&M
21	Parker, Kerry	CB	6-1	187	2	Grambling
97	Radecic, Scott	LB	6-3	240	2	Penn State
30	Robinson, Mark	S	5-10	206	2	Penn State
31	Ross, Kevin	CB	5-9	180	2	Temple
70	Rourke, Jim	T-G	6-5	263	6	Boston College
53	Rush, Bob	C	6-5	264	8	Memphis State
81	Scott, Willie	TE	6-4	245	5	South Carolina
86	Smith, J.T.	WR	6-2	185	8	North Texas State
59	Spani, Gary	LB	6-2	228	8	Kansas State
67	Still, Art	DE	6-7	245	8	Kentucky
35	Thomas, Ken	RB	5-9	211	3	San Jose State
61	Zamberlin, John	LB	6-2	226	7	Pacific Lutheran

LOS ANGELES RAIDERS AFC West

Address 332, Center Street, El Segundo, California 90245.
Stadium Los Angeles Memorial Coliseum.
  Capacity 92,516 *Playing Surface* Grass.
Team Colours Silver and Black.
Head Coach Tom Flores – seventh year.
Championships Division 1970,'72,'73,'74,'75,'76,'83;
  Conference 1976,'80,'83; AFL 1967; Super Bowl
  1976,'80,'83.
History AFL 1960-69, AFC 1970-
  (Until 1982, they were known as the Oakland Raiders.)

Offense

The Raiders have a few things to sort out in an offensive unit which only rarely put its opponent to the sword in 1984. On the offensive line several players may be feeling the effects of years of effort which consistently produced the traditional Raider dominance. Henry Lawrence, Mickey Marvin, Dave Dalby and the like, will all be back but there is little evidence of new talent emerging. Curt Marsh is still struggling to regain his old form and Don Mosebar has had a recurrence of the back problem which required surgery in 1983. Also, there is uncertainty at quarterback. Marc Wilson was given the chance to establish himself as the starter when Jim Plunkett was injured but he, in turn, was injured and when Plunkett, the old master, came back, he never looked like performing his usual miracle. The Raiders limped quietly out of the playoffs. On the credit side, running back Marcus Allen confirmed his place amongst the league's best dual-purpose backfield players and, after a preseason holdout, tight end Todd Christensen returned with telling effect. Another returning Raider, former All-Pro tight end Dave Casper, who came home after a trip around the league, did enough to show that he could still be a force. Casper's size and savvy will be handy when it comes to blocking on running plays. Here, Kenny King and Frank Hawkins give valuable support to the remarkable Allen. For some time now, the Raiders have been looking for a top-class wide receiver and, in first-round draftee Jesse Hester, they may have found one. Malcolm Barnwell is the accepted club leader in this department and, with the veteran Cliff Branch

beginning to slow a little, Hester and the speedy Dokie Williams will be given every chance to assert themselves.

Defense

The defense will continue to do everything expected of a championship team. A slight weakness against the run will be corrected if inside linebacker Bob Nelson returns from injury. Failing this, neither Brad Van Pelt nor Jack Squirek will let them down. Inside linebacker Matt Millen is a rock upon which many a running back has foundered and Rod Martin remains as one of the league's best outside linebackers on pass coverage. The starting three-man defensive line should remain intact with Pro Bowlers Howie Long and Lyle Alzado at defensive end, and Reggie Kinlaw at nose guard. However, again, they will adopt a variety of formations according to circumstances of down and yards to go. On passing downs, Long moves to defensive tackle where he is joined by Bill Pickel, the latter replacing Kinlaw. Greg Townsend takes over at left defensive end. Pickel plays a key role and, in 1984, led the team with 12.5 sacks. It's just that possible he could take the starting spot from Kinlaw. Sean Jones will play a greater part in relief of Alzado. Cornerbacks Lester Hayes and Mike Haynes, and free safety Vann McElroy, are Pro Bowlers and the fourth starter in the defensive secondary, strong safety Mike Davis, is not far short of that standard. Stacey Toran is a future replacement for Davis. James Davis and Ted Watts, two excellent backups, are joined by third-round draftee Stefon Adams, whom the Raiders hope will make a successful conversion from wide receiver to cornerback.

Special Teams

Chris Bahr, originally a second-round pick of the Bengals in 1976, is a steady placekicker. He's not prolific but rarely misses the ones that matter. Ray Guy, a former Raiders first-round pick, still defies gravity with his punts. Seemingly without nerves, he's a pro's pro. The versatile Dokie Williams was a minor sensation in his first full season returning kickoffs. Averaging 25.9 yards, he came second only to the Jets' Bobby Humphery in the NFL. By contrast, veteran Greg Pruitt had difficulty holding the ball. Pruitt, a former Pro Bowler, originally as a running back and latterly as a punt returner, may give way to Cle Montgomery.

1985 DRAFT

Round	Name	Pos.	Ht.	Wt.	College
1.	Hester, Jesse	WR	5-11	175	Florida State
3.	Moffett, Tim	WR	6-1	181	Mississippi
3.	Adams, Stefon	DB	5-9	190	East Carolina
4.	Kimmel, Jamie	LB	6-3	235	Syracuse
5.	Reeder, Dan	RB	6-0	202	Delaware
6.	Hilger, Rusty	QB	6-2	200	Oklahoma State
7.	Belcher, Kevin	T	6-5	300	Wisconsin
7.	Pattison, Mark	WR	6-1	195	Washington
7.	Clark, Bret	DB	6-2	195	Nebraska
7.	Haden, Nick	C	6-2	250	Penn State
8.	Wingate, Leonard	DT	6-3	260	South Carolina State
9.	Sydnor, Chris	DB	6-0	190	Penn State
10.	McKenzie, Reggie	LB	6-1	235	Tennessee
10.	Myres, Albert	DB	6-0	195	Tulsa
11.	Strachan, Steve	RB	6-0	212	Boston College
12.	Polk, Raymond	DB	5-11	190	Oklahoma State

The AFC's premier dual-purpose running back, Marcus Allen (#32)

1985 SCHEDULE

September
8	NEW YORK JETS	4:00
12	at Kansas City	8:00
22	SAN FRANCISCO	4:00
29	at New England	1:00

October
6	KANSAS CITY	4:00
13	NEW ORLEANS	4:00
20	at Cleveland	1:00
28	SAN DIEGO	9:00

November
3	at Seattle	4:00
10	at San Diego	4:00
17	CINCINNATI	4:00
24	DENVER	4:00

December
1	at Atlanta	4:00
8	at Denver	4:00
15	SEATTLE	4:00
23	at Los Angeles Rams	9:00

VETERAN ROSTER

No.	Name	Pos.	Ht.	Wt.	NFL Year	College
97	Ackerman, Rick	NT	6-4	254	4	Memphis State
59	Adams, Stanley	LB	6-2	215	2	Memphis State
32	Allen, Marcus	RB	6-2	205	4	Southern California
77	Alzado, Lyle	DE	6-3	260	15	Yankton, S.D.
10	Bahr, Chris	K	5-10	175	10	Penn State
56	Barnes, Jeff	LB	6-2	230	9	California
80	Barnwell, Malcolm	WR	5-11	185	5	Virginia Union
21	Branch, Cliff	WR	5-11	170	14	Colorado
66	Bryant, Warren	T	6-7	270	9	Kentucky
54	Byrd, Darryl	LB	6-1	220	3	Illinois
57	Caldwell, Tony	LB	6-1	225	3	Washington
81	Casper, Dave	TE	6-4	241	12	Notre Dame
46	Christensen, Todd	TE	6-3	230	7	Brigham Young
50	Dalby, Dave	C	6-3	250	14	UCLA
79	Davis, Bruce	T	6-6	280	7	UCLA
45	Davis, James	CB	6-0	195	4	Southern University
36	Davis, Mike	S	6-3	205	8	Colorado
8	Guy, Ray	P	6-3	190	13	Southern Mississippi
73	Hannah, Charley	G	6-5	260	9	Alabama
27	Hawkins, Frank	RB	5-9	200	5	Nevada-Reno
37	Hayes, Lester	CB	6-0	200	9	Texas A&M
22	Haynes, Mike	CB	6-2	190	10	Arizona State
11	Humm, David	QB	6-2	190	11	Nebraska
31	Jensen, Derrick	RB-TE	6-1	220	7	Texas-Arlington
99	Jones, Sean	DE	6-7	280	2	Northeastern
74	Jordan, Shelby	T	6-7	285	10	Washington, Mo.
33	King, Kenny	RB	5-11	205	7	Oklahoma
62	Kinlaw, Reggie	NT	6-2	245	6	Oklahoma
70	Lawrence, Henry	T	6-4	270	12	Florida A&M
75	Long, Howie	DE	6-5	270	5	Villanova
60	Marsh, Curt	G	6-5	270	4	Washington
53	Martin, Rod	LB	6-2	220	9	Southern California
65	Marvin, Mickey	G	6-4	265	9	Tennessee
43	McCall, Joe	RB	5-11	195	2	Pittsburgh
90	McCoy, Larry	LB	6-2	235	2	Lamar University
26	McElroy, Vann	S	6-2	190	4	Baylor
23	McKinney, Odis	S	6-2	190	8	Colorado
52	Merrill, Mark	LB	6-3	234	7	Minnesota
55	Millen, Matt	LB	6-2	250	5	Penn State
28	Montgomery, Cleotha	WR	5-8	180	5	Abilene Christian
72	Mosebar, Don	T	6-6	270	3	Southern California
51	Nelson, Bob	LB	6-4	235	9	Nebraska
81	Parker, Andy	TE	6-5	235	2	Utah
71	Pickel, Bill	NT	6-5	260	3	Rutgers
16	Plunkett, Jim	QB	6-2	215	15	Stanford
34	Pruitt, Greg	RB-PR	5-10	190	13	Oklahoma
88	Seale, Sam	WR	5-9	175	2	Western State, Co.
58	Squirek, Jack	LB	6-4	225	4	Illinois
30	Toran, Stacey	S	6-2	200	2	Notre Dame
93	Townsend, Greg	DE	6-3	240	3	Texas Christian
91	Van Pelt, Brad	LB	6-5	235	13	Michigan State
20	Watts, Ted	CB	6-0	195	5	Texas Tech.
67	Wheeler, Dwight	C	6-3	274	7	Tennessee State
85	Williams, Dokie	WR	5-11	180	3	UCLA
38	Willis, Chester	RB	5-11	195	5	Auburn
6	Wilson, Marc	QB	6-6	220	6	Brigham Young

SAN DIEGO CHARGERS AFC West

Address San Diego Jack Murphy Stadium, P.O. Box 20666, San Diego, California 92120.

Stadium San Diego Jack Murphy Stadium.
Capacity 60,100 *Playing Surface* Grass.

Team Colours Royal Blue, Gold and White.

Head Coach Don Coryell – eighth year.

Championships Division 1979,'80,'81; AFL 1963.

History AFL 1960-69, AFC 1970-
(For 1960 only, they were known as the Los Angeles Chargers.)

Offense

First-round draftee Jim Lachey has joined an offensive line which has more than its share of 'old-timers' but can still take good care of its quarterback – they rated equal seventh in the league for fewest sacks allowed. Both right tackle Ed White and left guard Doug Wilkerson will be returning for one more time around. Quarterback Dan Fouts is worth protecting. Back in 1981, he turned in his third consecutive 4,000-yard passing season and, but for the brevity of the 1982 strike-shortened season and injuries which prevented his completing the last two seasons, he would surely have made it six in a row. He enters 1985 with an astonishing NFL-record 40 300-yard passing games to his credit. Ed Luther came in for the last four games of 1984 and did well, but he has departed for the USFL. His replacement as the senior reserve, Mark Herrmann, has yet to reproduce the form of a collegiate career which saw him pass for nine NCAA career records but, after two years with each of Denver and Indianapolis, he may just have found an offensive system more suited to his particular talents. The unavailability of the powerful Chuck Muncie, after just the first week of last season, gave second-year player Earnest Jackson his chance. And he surprised more than a few people by winning the AFC rushing title with 1,179 yards. Buford McGee, who came through a satisfactory rookie year which he will remember for having scored the overtime touchdown which beat Miami, moved ahead in the group of backfield players who relieve Jackson in the one-back formation. Of course, the Chargers will be looking mainly to their squadron of wide receivers to bring the club back into contention. Charlie Joiner may have lost a step or two but still led the team with 61 pass receptions. Wes Chandler slipped a little below his best last year and may have to give way more often for Bobby Duckworth, who caught his 25 passes at the astronomical average of 28.6 yards. It is unlikely that the peerless tight end, Kellen Winslow, will be fit to play before the later part of the season but, in his absence last year, Pete Holohan and Eric Sievers formed an effective partnership and should continue in the same vein.

Defense

Defense has been a San Diego problem for some time and, sad to relate, they made little progress with reconstruction last season. Failure to sign their first-round draftee, defensive back Mossy Cade, was a blow and, equally disheartening, their second-round choice, linebacker Mike Guendling, suffered a career-threatening injury in preseason training. In the immediate future, the existing starters on the defensive line and at linebacker seem likely to be given the opportunity to gel. They have not yet developed a consistent pass rush but, encouragingly, second-year inside linebackers Billy Ray Smith and Mike Green are improving rapidly at the heart of a defensive unit which ranked fourth in the AFC against the run. The Chargers reinforced the part of their squad in most need by using four of their first six draft options and another in round ten to obtain defensive backs. Gill Byrd led the team with four interceptions and will continue to start at left cornerback. However, second-round pick Wayne Davis could displace Bill Kay on the opposite corner. Again, the talented Jeffery Dale who, too, was a second-round pick, will challenge for a starting spot at one of the safety positions currently held down by veterans Ken Greene and Tim Fox.

Special Teams

1983 Pro Bowler Rolf Benirschke is a steady placekicker who can land the odd 50-yard field goal. Punter Maury Buford is in the same category but could do with an extra yard on his 42.0 gross average. Lionel James was drafted as a dual kickoff and punt returner, but was more successful in the former category. His 22.3-yard average was good enough for ninth place in the league. On fewer returns, Buford McGee was equally effective.

1985 DRAFT

Round	Name	Pos.	Ht.	Wt.	College
1.	Lachey, Jim	G	6-6	270	Ohio State
2.	Davis, Wayne	DB	5-11	172	Indiana State
2.	Dale, Jeffery	DB	6-2	210	Louisiana State
3.	Hendy, John	DB	5-11	195	Cal State-Long Beach
4.	Mojsiejenko, Ralf	K-P	6-1	210	Michigan State
6.	Lewis, Terry	DB	5-10	185	Michigan State
7.	Fellows, Mark	LB	6-0	220	Montana State
8.	Adams, Curtis	RB	5-11	190	Central Michigan
9.	Berner, Paul	QB	6-2	210	Pacific
9.	Remsberg, Dan	T	6-5	270	Abilene Christian
10.	King, David	DB	5-8	177	Auburn
11.	Smith, Jeff	NT	6-2	255	Kentucky
12.	Simmons, Tony	DE		240	Tennessee
12.	Pearson, Bret	TE	6-4	230	Wisconsin

Bobby Duckworth (#82) could take over as the Chargers' big-play wide receiver

1985 SCHEDULE

September

8	at Buffalo	4:00
15	SEATTLE	4:00
22	at Cincinnati	1:00
29	CLEVELAND	4:00

October

6	at Seattle	4:00
13	KANSAS CITY	4:00
20	at Minnesota	1:00
28	at Los Angeles Raiders	9:00

November

3	DENVER	4:00
10	LOS ANGELES RAIDERS	4:00
17	at Denver	4:00
24	at Houston	1:00

December

1	BUFFALO	4:00
8	PITTSBURGH	6:00
15	PHILADELPHIA	4:00
22	at Kansas City	1:00

VETERAN ROSTER

No.	Name	Pos.	Ht.	Wt.	NFL Year	College
86	Bendross, Jesse	WR	6-0	192	2	Alabama
6	Benirschke, Rolf	K	6-1	179	9	Cal-Davis
50	Bradley, Carlos	LB	6-0	226	5	Wake Forest
7	Buford, Maury	P	6-0	185	4	Texas Tech.
22	Byrd, Gill	CB	5-11	191	3	San Jose State
89	Chandler, Wes	WR	6-0	183	8	Florida
77	Claphan, Sam	T	6-6	267	5	Oklahoma
82	Duckworth, Bobby	WR	6-3	197	4	Arkansas
84	Egloff, Ron	TE	6-5	227	9	Wisconsin
78	Ehin, Chuck	DE	6-4	254	3	Brigham Young
68	Elko, Bill	NT	6-5	277	3	Louisiana State
76	Ferguson, Keith	DE	6-5	241	5	Ohio State
14	Fouts, Dan	QB	6-3	205	13	Oregon
48	Fox, Tim	S	5-11	186	10	Ohio State
75	Gissinger, Andy	T	6-5	277	4	Syracuse
69	Gofourth, Derrel	G	6-3	260	9	Oklahoma State
58	Green, Mike	LB	6-0	226	3	Oklahoma State
28	Greene, Ken	S	6-3	203	8	Washington State
43	Gregor, Bob	S	6-2	190	5	Washington State
53	Guendling, Mike	LB	6-3	239	2	Northwestern
73	Guthrie, Keith	NT	6-4	264	2	Texas A&M
20	Henderson, Reuben	CB	6-1	188	5	San Diego State
	Herrmann, Mark	QB	6-5	199	5	Purdue
88	Holohan, Pete	TE	6-4	240	5	Notre Dame
41	Jackson, Earnest	RB	5-10	208	3	Texas A&M
26	James, Lionel	RB-KR	5-6	170	2	Auburn
18	Joiner, Charlie	WR	5-11	180	17	Grambling
31	Kay, Bill	DB	6-1	190	5	Purdue
57	King, Linden	LB	6-5	245	8	Colorado State
64	Loewen, Chuck	T	6-4	264	5	South Dakota State
51	Lowe, Woodrow	LB	6-0	226	10	Alabama
11	Luther, Ed	QB	6-3	210	6	San Jose State
62	Macek, Don	C	6-2	260	10	Boston College
12	Mathison, Bruce	QB	6-3	210	3	Nebraska
21	McGee, Buford	RB	6-0	201	2	Mississippi
60	McKnight, Dennis	G	6-3	260	4	Drake
24	McPherson, Miles	CB-S	6-0	191	4	New Haven
	Micho, Bobby	TE	6-3	227	2	Texas
25	Morris, Wayne	RB	6-0	210	10	Southern Methodist
55	Nelson, Derrie	LB	6-1	234	3	Nebraska
56	Osby, Vince	LB	6-0	220	2	Illinois
52	Preston, Ray	LB	6-0	220	10	Syracuse
90	Robinson, Fred	DE	6-4	240	2	Miami
	Salaam, Abdul	NT	6-3	269	10	Kent State
85	Sievers, Eric	TE	6-4	233	5	Maryland
54	Smith, Billy Ray	LB	6-3	239	3	Arkansas
	Smith, Johnny Ray	CB	5-9	185	4	Lamar
33	Smith, Lucious	CB	5-10	190	6	Cal State-Fullerton
32	Thomas, Jewerl	RB	5-10	228	6	San Jose State
59	Thrift, Cliff	LB	6-1	230	7	East Central Oklahoma
27	Turner, John	CB	6-0	200	8	Miami
23	Walters, Danny	CB	6-1	187	3	Arkansas
67	White, Ed	T	6-2	279	17	California
63	Wilkerson, Doug	G	6-3	258	16	North Carolina Central
92	Williams, Eric	LB	6-2	235	9	Southern California
99	Williams, Lee	DE	6-4	260	2	Bethune-Cookman
80	Winslow, Kellen	TE	6-5	251	7	Missouri
49	Young, Andre	S	6-0	203	4	Louisiana Tech.

SEATTLE SEAHAWKS AFC West

Address 5305 Lake Washington Boulevard, Kirkland, Wa. 98033.
Stadium Kingdome, Seattle.
   Capacity 64,757 *Playing Surface* AstroTurf.
Team Colours Blue, Green and Silver.
Head Coach Chuck Knox – third year.
Championships None.
History NFC 1976, AFC 1977-

Offense

The offensive line is not an area of Seahawks strength. Guard Jon Borchardt has been acquired from Buffalo but, with one or two players approaching retirement, it will soon need more attention. Nonetheless, head coach Chuck Knox had sufficient confidence in his veterans to use his first three draft picks for elsewhere in the roster. Guards Reggie McKenzie and Robert Pratt are entering their fourteenth and twelfth NFL years respectively but have every reason for staying on. That reason, of course, is the return of running back Curt Warner, who has made a complete recovery from the knee injury which he sustained on Week One of last season. Warner, whom many experts rate as a better open-field runner than Marcus Allen, will surely ignite a rushing offense which ranked a lowly twelfth in the AFC last year. He is joined by the Seahawks' first pick in the draft, Owen Gill, who was born in England and moved to the USA when he was sixteen. Gill brings his power running to complement the elusiveness of Warner. Last year, Dave Krieg passed for 32 touchdowns, equalling the seventh-best single-season total in NFL history, despite going down under more than his fair share of sacks. He has rapidly become one of the premier NFL quarterbacks. With senior reserve quarterback Jim Zorn unsettled, it made good sense to acquire Jeff Komlo, a former starter with Detroit. Krieg's favourite target, wide receiver Steve Largent, needs only one more 1,000-yard receiving season to tie the NFL career record of seven. He's not the fastest player, even on Seattle's books, but there are few in the league who can match his ability to catch passes under pressure. The other starter, last year's second-round pick, Daryl Turner, exceeded all

expectations. He catches his passes in fine style and though not yet with any subtlety in his moves, he has burning speed. A former starting wide receiver, Paul Jones, should be back after injury and the talent is yet further enriched by the arrival of draftee Danny Greene. Tight end Charle Young may be another Seahawk close to retirement, but he is still good enough to start.

Defense

Against an aggressive, ball-hawking Seahawks defense, not many NFL teams can run or pass with much confidence. It all begins with a howling three-man rush mounted by defensive ends Jacob Green and Jeff Bryant, and nose tackle Joe Nash, the latter who made enormous progress and was a starter in the Pro Bowl. Bryant and Green registered 14.5 and 13 sacks respectively. The linebacking quartet of Bruce Scholtz, Shelton Robinson, Keith Butler and the fearsome Michael Jackson, combine to plug every gap in the middle and cover the outside running lanes with lightning efficiency. The worrying thing (for the opposition) is that the total NFL experience of the front seven players adds up to just 30 seasons – the oldest, Keith Butler, is a mere 29. Only the most accurate passer can hope to avoid interception by a starting four-man defensive secondary which was responsible for 28 of the league-leading, team total of 38. Kenny Easley is the most complete strong safety in the NFL, knocking down running backs or grabbing interceptions. In the latter category, cornerback Dave Brown had the best of his ten superior years as a pro. Free safety John Harris had to 'settle' for six interceptions (he had ten in 1981) and left cornerback Keith Simpson chipped in with his usual four. Ex-Giant Terry Jackson and last year's first-round pick, Terry Taylor, provide excellent support.

Special Teams

Placekicker Norm Johnson is deadly from sensible range (he missed only two field goals from inside 50 yards) and was one of seven Seahawks voted to the Pro Bowl. Jeff West may not hold off the challenge of recent signing Luke Prestridge, who out-punted West by, on average, five yards in 1984. Zachary Dixon and Paul Johns will take care of the kickoff and punt returns respectively, whilst special team tackler Fredd Young can be expected to make his usual contribution to the science of seismology.

1985 DRAFT

Round	Name	Pos.	Ht.	Wt.	College
2.	Gill, Owen	RB	6-0	226	Iowa
3.	Greene, Danny	WR	5-11	190	Washington
4.	Davis, Tony	TE	6-4	237	Missouri
5.	Napolitan, Mark	C	6-2	255	Michigan State
5.	Brown, Arnold	DB			North Carolina Central
5.	Jones, Johnnie	RB	5-9	195	Tennessee
7.	Mattes, Ron	T	6-6	289	Virginia
8.	Lewis, Judious	WR	5-9	167	Arkansas State
9.	Otto, Bob	DE	6-5	245	Idaho State
10.	Conner, John	QB	6-2	210	Arizona
10.	Bowers, James	DB	5-11	190	Memphis State
11.	Cooper, Louis	LB	6-1	225	Western Carolina

Nose tackle Joe Nash who emerged in 1984

1985 SCHEDULE

September

8	at Cincinnati	1:00
15	at San Diego	4:00
23	LOS ANGELES RAMS	9:00
29	at Kansas City	1:00

October

6	SAN DIEGO	4:00
13	ATLANTA	4:00
20	at Denver	4:00
27	at New York Jets	1:00

November

3	LOS ANGELES RAIDERS	4:00
10	at New Orleans	1:00
17	NEW ENGLAND	4:00
25	at San Francisco	9:00

December

1	KANSAS CITY	4:00
8	CLEVELAND	4:00
15	at Los Angeles Raiders	4:00
20	DENVER	8:00

VETERAN ROSTER

No.	Name	Pos.	Ht.	Wt.	NFL Year	College
69	Abramowitz, Sid	T	6-6	279	3	Tulsa
65	Bailey, Edwin	G	6-4	265	5	South Carolina State
	Borchardt, Jon	G	6-5	255	7	Montana State
22	Brown, Dave	CB	6-2	190	11	Michigan
77	Bryant, Jeff	DE	6-5	260	4	Clemson
59	Bush, Blair	C	6-3	252	8	Washington
96	Butler, Chuck	LB	6-0	220	2	Boise State
53	Butler, Keith	LB	6-4	225	8	Memphis State
83	Castor, Chris	WR	6-0	170	3	Duke
78	Cryder, Bob	T	6-4	293	8	Alabama
31	Dixon, Zachary	RB	6-1	204	7	Temple
33	Doornink, Dan	RB	6-3	210	8	Washington State
35	Dufek, Don	S	6-0	195	9	Michigan
45	Easley, Ken	S	6-3	206	5	UCLA
68	Edwards, Randy	DE	6-4	255	2	Alabama
64	Essink, Ron	T	6-6	254	6	Grand Valley State
74	Fanning, Mike	DE-DT	6-6	255	11	Notre Dame
56	Gaines, Greg	LB	6-3	220	4	Tennessee
79	Green, Jacob	DE	6-3	247	6	Texas A&M
44	Harris, John	S	6-2	200	8	Arizona State
63	Hicks, Mark	LB	6-2	225	3	Arizona State
46	Hughes, David	RB	6-0	220	5	Boise State
55	Jackson, Michael	LB	6-1	220	7	Washington
24	Jackson, Terry	CB	5-11	197	8	San Diego State
85	Johns, Paul	WR	5-11	170	5	Tulsa
9	Johnson, Norm	K	6-2	193	4	UCLA
60	Kaiser, John	LB	6-3	221	2	Arizona
62	Kauahi, Kani	C	6-2	260	4	Hawaii
	Komlo, Jeff	QB	6-2	195	7	Delaware
17	Krieg, Dave	QB	6-1	185	6	Milton, Wisconsin
37	Lane, Eric	RB	6-0	195	5	Brigham Young
80	Largent, Steve	WR	5-11	184	10	Tulsa
73	Mangiero, Dino	NT	6-2	264	6	Rutgers
67	McKenzie, Reggie	G	6-5	242	14	Michigan
51	Merriman, Sam	LB	6-3	225	3	Idaho
88	Metzelaars, Pete	TE	6-7	240	4	Wabash
71	Millard, Bryan	T	6-5	282	2	Texas
43	Morris, Randall	RB	6-0	183	2	Tennessee
21	Moyer, Paul	S	6-1	201	3	Arizona
72	Nash, Joe	NT	6-3	250	4	Boston College
52	Norman, Joe	LB	6-1	220	6	Indiana
61	Pratt, Robert	G	6-4	250	12	North Carolina
	Prestridge, Luke	P	6-4	235	7	Baylor
57	Robinson, Shelton	LB	6-2	233	4	North Carolina
84	Scales, Dwight	WR	6-2	182	9	Grambling
58	Scholtz, Bruce	LB	6-6	240	4	Texas
75	Schreiber, Adam	G	6-4	250	2	Texas
42	Simpson, Keith	CB	6-1	195	8	Memphis State
82	Skansi, Paul	WR	5-11	190	3	Washington
20	Taylor, Terry	CB	5-10	175	2	Southern Illinois
86	Tice, Mike	TE	6-7	250	5	Maryland
81	Turner, Daryl	WR	6-3	198	2	Michigan State
89	Walker, Byron	WR	6-4	190	4	Citadel
28	Warner, Curt	RB	5-11	205	3	Penn State
8	West, Jeff	P	6-2	220	10	Cincinnati
54	Williams, Eugene	LB	6-1	220	4	Tulsa
87	Young, Charle	TE	6-4	234	13	Southern California
50	Young, Fredd	LB	6-1	220	2	New Mexico State
10	Zorn, Jim	QB	6-2	200	10	Cal Poly-Pomona

CHAPTER SEVEN

NATIONAL FOOTBALL CONFERENCE

TEAM RANKINGS

	OFFENSE						DEFENSE					
	Total Yds.	Rushing	Passing	Points For	%Intercepted	%Sacked	Total Yds.	Rushing	Passing	Points Against	%Interceptions	%Sacks
Atlanta	10	9	10	12	9	14	9	9	5	12	13	9
Chicago	4	1	13	7	6	7	1	1	2	2	3	1
Dallas	7	12	4	8	10	2	3	11	3	4	1	6
Detroit	8	8	8	11	8	12	11	5	11	13	11	11
Green Bay	3	7	6	4	14	4	10	8	6	5	2	10
L.A. Rams	12	2	14	5	12	6	8	3	12	7	12	12
Minnesota	13	10	11	14	11	13	14	14	14	14	14	14
New Orleans	11	5	12	10	13	8	2	13	1	10	10	2
N.Y. Giants	9	13	3	9	5	11	6	6	9	3	9	8
Philadelphia	14	14	7	13	3	10	7	10	4	8	6	3
St Louis	2	6	1	3	4	5	4	7	7	9	5	5
San Francisco	1	3	2	1	1	1	5	4	10	1	4	7
Tampa Bay	6	11	5	6	7	3	13	12	8	11	7	13
Washington	5	4	9	2	2	9	12	2	13	6	8	4

NFC PASSERS

	Att	Comp	% Comp	Yards	Ave Gain	TD	% TD	Long	Int	% Int	Rating Points
Montana, Joe, *S.F.*	432	279	64.6	3630	8.40	28	6.5	t80	10	2.3	102.9
Lomax, Neil, *St.L.*	560	345	61.6	4614	8.24	28	5.0	t83	16	2.9	92.5
Bartkowski, Steve, *Atl.*	269	181	67.3	2158	8.02	11	4.1	61	10	3.7	89.7
Theismann, Joe, *Wash.*	477	283	59.3	3391	7.11	24	5.0	t80	13	2.7	86.6
Dickey, Lynn, *G.B.*	401	237	59.1	3195	7.97	25	6.2	t79	19	4.7	85.6
Danielson, Gary, *Det.*	410	252	61.5	3076	7.50	17	4.1	t77	15	3.7	83.1
DeBerg, Steve, *T.B.*	509	308	60.5	3554	6.98	19	3.7	55	18	3.5	79.3
Kemp, Jeff, *Rams*	284	143	50.4	2021	7.12	13	4.6	t63	7	2.5	78.7
Simms, Phil, *Giants*	533	286	53.7	4044	7.59	22	4.1	t65	18	3.4	78.1
Jaworski, Ron, *Phil.*	427	234	54.8	2754	6.45	16	3.7	t90	14	3.3	73.5
White, Danny, *Dall.*	233	126	54.1	1580	6.78	11	4.7	t66	11	4.7	71.5
Kramer, Tommy, *Minn.*	236	124	52.5	1678	7.11	9	3.8	t70	10	4.2	70.6
Hogeboom, Gary, *Dall.*	367	195	53.1	2366	6.45	7	1.9	t68	14	3.8	63.7
Todd, Richard, *N.O.*	312	161	51.6	2178	6.98	11	3.5	74	19	6.1	60.6

t = Touchdown
Leader based on rating points, minimum 230 attempts

NFC RECEIVERS

	No	Yards	Ave	Long	TD
Monk, Art, *Wash.*	106	1372	12.9	72	7
Wilder, James, *T.B.*	85	685	8.1	50	0
Green, Roy, *St.L.*	78	1555	19.9	t83	12
Jones, James, *Det.*	77	662	8.6	39	5
House, Kevin, *T.B.*	76	1005	13.2	55	5
Craig, Roger, *S.F.*	71	675	9.5	t64	3
Anderson, Ottis, *St.L.*	70	611	8.7	57	2
Bailey, Stacey, *Atl.*	67	1138	17.0	61	6
Spagnola, John, *Phil.*	65	701	10.8	34	1
Lofton, James, *G.B.*	62	1361	22.0	t79	7
Quick, Mike, *Phil.*	61	1052	17.2	t90	9
Carter, Gerald, *T.B.*	60	816	13.6	t74	5
Cosbie, Doug, *Dall.*	60	789	13.2	36	4
Montgomery, Wilbert, *Phil.*	60	501	8.4	28	0
Hill, Tony, *Dall.*	58	864	14.9	t66	5
Clark, Dwight, *S.F.*	52	880	16.9	t80	6
Tilley, Pat, *St.L.*	52	758	14.6	42	5
Jackson, Alfred, *Atl.*	52	731	14.1	t50	2
Dorsett, Tony, *Dall.*	51	459	9.0	t68	1
Thompson, Leonard, *Det.*	50	773	15.5	t66	6
Johnson, Bob, *Giants*	48	795	16.6	45	7
Mowatt, Zeke, *Giants*	48	698	14.5	34	6
Lewis, Leo, *Minn.*	47	830	17.7	56	4
Springs, Ron, *Dall.*	46	454	9.9	t57	3
Brown, Ted, *Minn.*	46	349	7.6	35	3
Payton, Walter, *Chi.*	45	368	8.2	31	0
Coffman, Paul, *G.B.*	43	562	13.1	t44	9
Muhammad, Calvin, *Wash.*	42	729	17.4	t80	4
Suhey, Matt, *Chi.*	42	312	7.4	23	2
Riggs, Gerald, *Atl.*	42	277	6.6	21	0
Cooper, Earl, *S.F.*	41	459	11.2	26	4
Solomon, Freddie, *S.F.*	40	737	18.4	t64	10
Marsh, Doug, *St.L.*	39	608	15.6	47	5
Jones, Mike, *Minn.*	38	591	15.6	t70	1
Gray, Earnest, *Giants*	38	529	13.9	31	2
Jordan, Steve, *Minn.*	38	414	10.9	26	2
Chadwick, Jeff, *Det.*	37	540	14.6	46	2
Galbreath, Tony, *Giants*	37	357	9.6	37	0
Ellis, Gerry, *G.B.*	36	312	8.7	22	2
Renfro, Mike, *Dall.*	35	583	16.7	t60	2
Gajan, Hokie, *N.O.*	35	288	8.2	51	2
Nichols, Mark, *Det.*	34	744	21.9	t77	1
Ellard, Henry, *Rams*	34	622	18.3	t63	6
Gault, Willie, *Chi.*	34	587	17.3	t61	6
Cox, Arthur, *Atl.*	34	329	9.7	t23	3
Manuel, Lionel, *Giants*	33	619	18.8	53	4
Harris, Duriel, *Clev.-Dall.*	33	521	15.8	43	2
Groth, Jeff, *N.O.*	33	487	14.8	31	0
Wilson, Wayne, *N.O.*	33	314	9.5	t34	3
Haddix, Michael, *Phil.*	33	231	7.0	22	0
Donley, Doug, *Dall.*	32	473	14.8	t49	2
Oliver, Hubert, *Phil.*	32	142	4.4	21	0
Hill, David, *Rams*	31	300	9.7	26	1
Sims, Billy, *Det.*	31	239	7.7	20	0
Woodruff, Tony, *Phil.*	30	484	16.1	38	3
Didier, Clint, *Wash.*	30	350	11.7	44	5

t = Touchdown

James Wilder (#32), Tampa Bay's productive dual-purpose running back

NFC RUSHERS

	Att	Yards	Ave	Long	TD
Dickerson, Eric, *Rams*	379	2105	5.6	66	14
Payton, Walter, *Chi.*	381	1684	4.4	t72	11
Wilder, James, *T.B.*	407	1544	3.8	37	13
Riggs, Gerald, *Atl.*	353	1486	4.2	57	13
Tyler, Wendell, *S.F.*	246	1262	5.1	40	7
Riggins, John, *Wash.*	327	1239	3.8	24	14
Dorsett, Tony, *Dall.*	302	1189	3.9	t31	6
Anderson, Ottis, *St.L.*	289	1174	4.1	24	6
Rogers, George, *N.O.*	239	914	3.8	28	2
Carpenter, Rob, *Giants*	250	795	3.2	22	7
Montgomery, Wilbert, *Phil.*	201	789	3.9	27	2
Anderson, Alfred, *Minn.*	201	773	3.8	23	2
Sims, Billy, *Det.*	130	687	5.3	81	5
Craig, Roger, *S.F.*	155	649	4.2	28	7
Gajan, Hokie, *N.O.*	102	615	6.0	t62	5
Ellis, Gerry, *G.B.*	123	581	4.7	50	4
Ivery, Eddie Lee, *G.B.*	99	552	5.6	49	6
Jones, James, *Det.*	137	532	3.9	34	3
Morris, Joe, *Giants*	133	510	3.8	28	4
Campbell, Earl, *Hou.-N.O.*	146	468	3.2	22	4
Brown, Ted, *Minn.*	98	442	4.5	19	3
Mitchell, Stump, *St.L.*	81	434	5.4	39	9
Suhey, Matt, *Chi.*	124	424	3.4	21	4
Griffin, Keith, *Wash.*	97	408	4.2	31	0
Nelson, Darrin, *Minn.*	80	406	5.1	39	3
Clark, Jessie, *G.B.*	87	375	4.3	t43	4
Jenkins, Ken, *Det.*	78	358	4.6	t25	1
Crutchfield, Dwayne, *Rams*	73	337	4.6	36	1
Theismann, Joe, *Wash.*	62	314	5.1	27	1
Cain, Lynn, *Atl.*	77	276	3.6	t31	3
McMahon, Jim, *Chi.*	39	276	7.1	30	2
Newsome, Tim, *Dall.*	66	268	4.1	30	5
Oliver, Hubert, *Phil.*	72	263	3.7	17	0
Wilson, Wayne, *N.O.*	74	261	3.5	36	1
Redden, Barry, *Rams*	45	247	5.5	35	0
Danielson, Gary, *Det.*	41	218	5.3	40	3
Springs, Ron, *Dall.*	68	197	2.9	16	1
Harmon, Derrick, *S.F.*	39	192	4.9	19	1
Washington, Joe, *Wash.*	56	192	3.4	12	1
Ferrell, Earl, *St.L.*	41	190	4.6	25	1
Thomas, Calvin, *Chi.*	40	186	4.7	37	1
Lomax, Neil, *St.L.*	35	184	5.3	20	3
Crouse, Ray, *G.B.*	53	169	3.2	14	0
Ring, Bill, *S.F.*	38	162	4.3	34	3
Simms, Phil, *Giants*	42	162	3.9	21	0
Kemp, Jeff, *Rams*	34	153	4.5	23	1
Huckleby, Harlan, *G.B.*	35	145	4.1	23	0
Haddix, Michael, *Phil.*	48	130	2.7	21	1
Lisch, Rusty, *Chi.*	18	121	6.7	31	0
Montana, Joe, *S.F.*	39	118	3.0	15	2
Todd, Richard, *N.O.*	28	111	4.0	15	0
Anthony, Tyrone, *N.O.*	20	105	5.3	19	1
Moroski, Mike, *Atl.*	21	98	4.7	17	0
Galbreath, Tony, *Giants*	22	97	4.4	11	0
Rodgers, Del, *G.B.*	25	94	3.8	15	0
Woolfolk, Butch, *Giants*	40	92	2.3	17	1

t = Touchdown

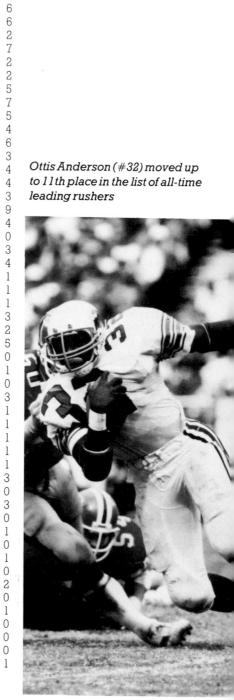

Ottis Anderson (#32) moved up to 11th place in the list of all-time leading rushers

NFC KICKERS

	XP	XPA	FG	FGA	PTS
Wersching, Ray, *S.F.*	56	56	25	35	131
Moseley, Mark, *Wash.*	48	51	24	31	120
O'Donoghue, Neil, *St.L.*	48	51	23	35	117
McFadden, Paul, *Phil.*	26	27	30	37	116
Lansford, Mike, *Rams*	37	38	25	33	112
Septien, Rafael, *Dall.*	33	34	23	29	102
Thomas, Bob, *Chi.*	35	37	22	28	101
Ariri, Obed, *T.B.*	38	40	19	26	95
Andersen, Morten, *N.O.*	34	34	20	27	94
Luckhurst, Mick, *Atl.*	31	31	20	27	91
Murray, Ed, *Det.*	31	31	20	27	91
Stenerud, Jan, *Minn.*	30	31	20	23	90
Haji-Sheikh, Ali, *Giants*	32	35	17	33	83
Del Greco, Al, *G.B.*	34	34	9	12	61
Garcia, Eddie, *G.B.*	14	15	3	9	23

NFC KICKOFF RETURNERS

	No	Yards	Ave	Long	TD
Redden, Barry, *Rams*	23	530	23.0	40	0
Mitchell, Stump, *St.L.*	35	804	23.0	56	0
Nelson, Darrin, *Minn.*	39	891	22.8	47	0
Anthony, Tyrone, *N.O.*	22	490	22.3	64	0
Morton, Michael, *T.B.*	38	835	22.0	43	0
Rodgers, Del, *G.B.*	39	843	21.6	t97	1
Anderson, Alfred, *Minn.*	30	639	21.3	41	0
Hill, Drew, *Rams*	26	543	20.9	40	0
Monroe, Carl, *S.F.*	27	561	20.8	44	0
Nelms, Mike, *Wash.*	42	860	20.5	36	0
Allen, Gary, *Dall.*	33	666	20.2	34	0
McSwain, Chuck, *Dall.*	20	403	20.2	32	0
Hayes, Joe, *Phil.*	22	441	20.0	44	0
Duckett, Kenny, *N.O.*	29	580	20.0	39	0
McConkey, Phil, *Giants*	28	541	19.3	33	0
Cameron, Jack, *Chi.*	26	485	18.7	40	0
Mandley, Pete, *Det.*	22	390	17.7	32	0
(Non-Qualifiers)					
Stamps, Sylvester, *Atl.*	19	452	23.8	50	0
Hall, Alvin, *Det.*	19	385	20.3	46	0
Johnson, Kenny, *Atl.*	19	359	18.9	27	0
Fields, Jitter, *N.O.*	19	356	18.7	31	0
Jenkins, Ken, *Det.*	18	396	22.0	32	0
Thomas, Zack, *Den.-T.B.*	18	351	19.5	33	0
Cooper, Evan, *Phil.*	17	299	17.6	48	0
Bright, Leon, *T.B.*	16	303	18.9	33	0
Pittman, Danny, *St.L.*	14	319	22.8	43	0
Huckleby, Harlan, *G.B.*	14	261	18.6	54	0
Woolfolk, Butch, *Giants*	14	232	16.6	27	0
Harmon, Derrick, *S.F.*	13	357	27.5	51	0
Waters, Andre, *Phil.*	13	319	24.5	t89	1
Harrell, Willard, *St.L.*	13	231	17.8	28	0
Epps, Phillip, *G.B.*	12	232	19.3	47	0
Curran, Willie, *Atl.*	11	219	19.9	42	0
Gentry, Dennis, *Chi.*	11	209	19.0	33	0
Martin, Robbie, *Det.*	10	144	14.4	23	0
Cephous, Frank, *Giants*	9	178	19.8	30	0

t = Touchdown
Leader based on average return, minimum 20 returns

NFC PUNTERS

	No	Yards	Long	Ave	Total Punts	TB	Blk	Opp Ret	Ret Yds	In 20	Net Ave
Hansen, Brian, *N.O.*	69	3020	66	43.8	70	7	1	47	550	9	33.3
Coleman, Greg, *Minn.*	82	3473	62	42.4	82	2	0	49	435	16	36.6
Scribner, Bucky, *G.B.*	85	3596	61	42.3	85	12	0	46	368	18	35.2
Horan, Mike, *Phil.*	92	3880	69	42.2	92	6	0	58	486	21	35.6
Giacomarro, Ralph, *Atl.*	68	2855	58	42.0	70	6	2	42	450	12	32.6
Garcia, Frank, *T.B.*	68	2849	60	41.9	68	9	0	36	310	12	34.7
Runager, Max, *S.F.*	56	2341	59	41.8	57	12	1	26	176	18	33.8
Black, Mike, *Det.*	76	3164	63	41.6	76	8	0	49	516	13	32.7
Finzer, David, *Chi.*	83	3328	87	40.1	85	4	2	41	249	26	35.3
Jennings, Dave, *Giants*	90	3598	54	40.0	93	10	3	50	479	22	31.4
Hayes, Jeff, *Wash.*	72	2834	59	39.4	73	5	1	38	187	11	34.9
Misko, John, *Rams*	74	2866	58	38.7	74	9	0	35	196	21	33.6
Birdsong, Carl, *St.L.*	67	2594	59	38.7	68	8	1	27	239	19	32.3
White, Danny, *Dall.*	82	3151	54	38.4	82	8	0	38	156	21	34.6

Leader based on gross average, minimum 40 punts

NFC PUNT RETURNERS

	No	FC	Yards	Ave	Long	TD
Ellard, Henry, *Rams*	30	3	403	13.4	t83	2
McLemore, Dana, *S.F.*	45	11	521	11.6	t79	1
Mitchell, Stump, *St.L.*	38	3	333	8.8	39	0
Fields, Jitter, *N.O.*	27	6	236	8.7	61	0
Nelms, Mike, *Wash.*	49	1	428	8.7	46	0
Fisher, Jeff, *Chi.*	57	11	492	8.6	28	0
Martin, Robbie, *Det.*	25	8	210	8.4	23	0
Allen, Gary, *Dall.*	54	15	446	8.3	18	0
Nelson, Darrin, *Minn.*	23	9	180	7.8	21	0
Bright, Leon, *T.B.*	23	1	173	7.5	21	0
Epps, Phillip, *G.B.*	29	10	199	6.9	39	0
McConkey, Phil, *Giants*	46	15	306	6.7	31	0
Cooper, Evan, *Phil.*	40	19	250	6.3	16	0
Thomas, Zack, *Den.-T.B.*	21	3	125	6.0	15	0
Flynn, Tom, *G.B.*	15	4	128	8.5	20	0
Johnson, Billy, *Atl.*	15	1	152	10.1	37	0
Johnson, Kenny, *Atl.*	10	1	79	7.9	14	0
Curran, Willie, *Atl.*	9	1	21	2.3	10	0
Harris, Duriel, *Clev.-Dall.*	9	0	73	8.1	13	0
Irvin, LeRoy, *Rams*	9	0	83	9.2	22	0
Seay, Virgil, *Wash.-Atl.*	8	1	10	1.3	7	0
Manuel, Lionel, *Giants*	8	3	62	7.8	22	0
Hall, Alvin, *Det.*	7	1	30	4.3	11	0
Holt, John, *T.B.*	6	3	17	2.8	8	0
Groth, Jeff, *N.O.*	6	12	32	5.3	9	0
McKinnon, Dennis, *Chi.*	5	0	62	12.4	18	0

t = Touchdown
Leader based on average return, minimum 20 returns

NFC INTERCEPTORS

	No	Yards	Ave	Long	TD
Flynn, Tom, *G.B.*	9	106	11.8	31	0
Lewis, Tim, *G.B.*	7	151	21.6	t99	1
Downs, Mike, *Dall.*	7	126	18.0	t27	1
Ellis, Ray, *Phil.*	7	119	17.0	31	0
Dean, Vernon, *Wash.*	7	114	16.3	t36	2

Haynes, Mark, *Giants*	7	90	12.9	22	0
Watkins, Bobby, *Det.*	6	0	0.0	0	0
Irvin, LeRoy, *Rams*	5	166	33.2	t81	2
Cotney, Mark, *T.B.*	5	123	24.6	29	0
Hopkins, Wes, *Phil.*	5	107	21.4	33	0
Fencik, Gary, *Chi.*	5	102	20.4	61	0
Green, Darrell, *Wash.*	5	91	18.2	50	1
Frazier, Leslie, *Chi.*	5	89	17.8	33	0
Thurman, Dennis, *Dall.*	5	81	16.2	43	1
Johnson, Kenny, *Atl.*	5	75	15.0	28	0
Washington, Lionel, *St.L.*	5	42	8.4	18	0
Turner, Keena, *S.F.*	4	51	12.8	21	0
Bell, Todd, *Chi.*	4	46	11.5	t36	1
Smith, Wayne, *St.L.*	4	35	8.8	23	0
Foules, Elbert, *Phil.*	4	27	6.8	20	0
Lott, Ronnie, *S.F.*	4	26	6.5	15	0
Perrin, Benny, *St.L.*	4	22	5.5	22	0
Waymer, Dave, *N.O.*	4	9	2.3	9	0
Green, Gary, *Rams*	3	88	29.3	60	0
Shell, Todd, *S.F.*	3	81	27.0	t53	1
Brantley, Scot, *T.B.*	3	55	18.3	38	0
Cromwell, Nolan, *Rams*	3	54	18.0	t33	1
Hicks, Dwight, *S.F.*	3	42	14.0	29	0
Milot, Rich, *Wash.*	3	42	14.0	27	0
Castille, Jeremiah, *T.B.*	3	38	12.7	30	0
Lee, Mark, *G.B.*	3	33	11.0	14	0
Clinkscale, Dextor, *Dall.*	3	32	10.7	23	0
Anderson, John, *G.B.*	3	24	8.0	22	0
Graham, William, *Det.*	3	22	7.3	15	0
Walls, Everson, *Dall.*	3	12	4.0	12	0
Bess, Rufus, *Minn.*	3	7	2.3	7	0
Williams, Perry, *Giants*	3	7	2.3	7	0
Fellows, Ron, *Dall.*	3	3	1.0	3	0
Hegman, Mike, *Dall.*	3	3	1.0	3	0

t = Touchdown

'Stump' Mitchell (#30), one of the NFL's finest multi-purpose runners

DALLAS COWBOYS NFC East

Address 6116 North Central Expressway, Dallas, Texas 75206.

Stadium Texas Stadium, Irving.
   Capacity 65,101 *Playing Surface* Texas Turf.

Team Colours Royal Blue, Metallic Silver Blue and White.

Head Coach Tom Landry – twenty-sixth year.

Championships Division 1970,'71,'73,'76,'77,'78,'79,'81; Conference 1970,'71,'75,'77,'78; Super Bowl 1971,'77.

History NFL 1960-69, NFC 1970-

Offense

The Cowboys did not reach the 1984 playoffs, and more than one 'expert' took this to indicate that they are entering a period of mediocrity. Another interpretation of their 9-7 season would be that they held tough during a period of transition, despite losing many players through injury. Retirements, too, have been felt as, one by one, household names have been replaced by young men who have yet to earn their spurs. Of the injured veterans, offensive tackle Jim Cooper and guard Howard Richards will return to bolster a line which, despite being down to the walking wounded at times, gave up only 48 quarterback sacks. However, they're still not sure who will be calling the signals behind them. Gary Hogeboom was given every opportunity to take over from former starter Danny White. However, by season's end, White was back at the controls and looked like his old self, even though in defeat, against Washington and Miami. Running back Tony Dorsett is coming off a modest season in which he had only two 100-yard rushing games. Cowboys fans need not worry though; he has lost none of his quickness and may well be inspired by the prospect of becoming the sixth player in league history to rush for over 10,000 yards. He may do it on Week Five against the Giants. Tim Newsome represents the future in the other backfield position but will have to prove his superiority over the reliable Ron Springs. Should the USFL cease to operate, Herschel Walker would come to Dallas as the best fifth-round draftee ever. There have been changes at wide receiver, where the speedy Tony Hill represents the last of the old guard. Mike Renfro came from Houston and showed a surprising turn of foot on occasions and, when the opportunity arose, the Cowboys were quick to acquire another sure-handed veteran, Duriel Harris, formerly of Miami and Cleveland. Track sprinter Mel Lattany will be signed up providing he can hang on to the football. One man sure to do that is tight end Doug Cosbie, the club's leading receiver in 1984. Beyond Cosbie, though, they're a little thin in this department.

Defense

All-Pro defensive tackle Randy White is already one of the game's all-time great players. He is the natural leader of the four-man defensive line and registered a team-best 12.5 sacks. Jim Jeffcoat, who had 11.5 sacks, is now established and has solved a problem at defensive right end. Both John Dutton and Ed 'Too Tall' Jones may have lost a little of their All-Pro best but are good enough to start with any team. First-round draftee Kevin Brooks represents an excellent investment. There are a few problems at linebacker, where the loss of retirees Bob Breunig and last year's first-round draftee, Billy Cannon, will be felt. In time of need, middle linebacker Eugene 'The Hitting Machine' Lockhart came on well but the need for defense against the rush is clear from a ranking of just 24th in the league. Draftee Jesse Penn is said to 'enjoy' physical contact. In the last line of defense, free safety Michael Downs repeated the seven interceptions of his rookie year (1981) as his contribution to a conference-leading team total of 28. Given freedom from injury and assisted by the usual Dallas pass rush, a secondary in which Downs is joined by Ron Fellows, Dextor Clinkscale and the former All-Pro, Everson Walls, has all the talent to develop into one of the league's best.

Special Teams

Placekicker Rafael Septien is deadly from inside 40 yards and can land them from over 50. Danny White is an excellent punter whose 1984 average was lowered only by his deliberate attempts to put the ball out-of-bounds in 'coffin corner'. Responsibility for both kickoff and punt returns falls to Gary Allen. He's steady but needs to break open for the occasional big return which will raise him out of the pack to join the leaders.

1985 DRAFT

Round	Name	Pos.	Ht.	Wt.	College
1.	Brooks, Kevin	DE	6-6	270	Michigan
2.	Penn, Jesse	LB	6-2	225	Virginia Tech.
3.	Ker, Crawford	G	6-3	290	Florida
4.	Lavette, Robert	RB	5-10	190	Georgia Tech.
5.	Walker, Herschel	RB	6-1	220	Georgia
5.	Darwin, Matt	T	6-4	263	Texas A&M
6.	Ploeger, Kurt	DE	6-6	258	Gustavus Adolphus
6.	Moran, Matt	G	6-4	265	Stanford
7.	Powe, Karl	WR	6-1	170	Alabama State
7.	Herrmann, Jim	DE	6-5	260	Brigham Young
8.	Gonzales, Leon	WR	5-10	158	Bethune-Cookman
9.	Strasburger, Scott	LB	6-1	205	Nebraska
10.	Jones, Joe	TE	6-3	240	Virginia Tech.
11.	Dellocono, Neal	LB	6-0	219	UCLA
12.	Jordan, Karl	LB	6-1	244	Vanderbilt

Tight end Doug Cosbie has played in the last two Pro Bowls

1985 SCHEDULE

September

9	WASHINGTON	9:00
15	at Detroit	1:00
22	CLEVELAND	1:00
29	at Houston	1:00

October

6	at New York Giants	8:00
13	PITTSBURGH	1:00
20	at Philadelphia	1:00
27	ATLANTA	1:00

November

4	at St Louis	9:00
10	at Washington	4:00
17	CHICAGO	1:00
24	PHILADELPHIA	4:00
28	ST LOUIS	3:00

December

8	at Cincinnati	1:00
15	NEW YORK GIANTS	1:00
22	at San Francisco	4:00

VETERAN ROSTER

No.	Name	Pos.	Ht.	Wt.	NFL Year	College
36	Albritton, Vince	S	6-1	198	2	Washington
31	Allen, Gary	RB	5-10	183	4	Hawaii
76	Aughtman, Dowe	G	6-2	272	2	Auburn
62	Baldinger, Brian	C-G	6-4	253	4	Duke
40	Bates, Bill	S	6-1	195	3	Tennessee
47	Clinkscale, Dextor	S	5-11	190	5	South Carolina State
61	Cooper, Jim	T	6-5	263	9	Temple
85	Cornwell, Fred	TE	6-5	236	2	Southern California
84	Cosbie, Doug	TE	6-6	232	7	Santa Clara
55	DeOssie, Steve	LB	6-2	250	2	Boston College
51	Dickerson, Anthony	LB	6-2	222	6	Southern Methodist
33	Dorsett, Tony	RB	5-11	192	9	Pittsburgh
26	Downs, Mike	S	6-3	203	5	Rice
78	Dutton, John	DT	6-7	275	12	Nebraska
27	Fellows, Ron	CB	6-0	174	5	Missouri
	Fowler, Todd	RB	6-4	210	1	Stephen F. Austin
28	Granger, Norm	RB	5-9	217	2	Iowa
86	Harris, Duriel	WR	5-11	184	10	New Mexico State
58	Hegman, Mike	LB	6-1	228	10	Tennessee State
80	Hill, Tony	WR	6-2	198	9	Stanford
14	Hogeboom, Gary	QB	6-4	199	6	Central Michigan
21	Howard, Carl	CB	6-2	188	2	Rutgers
79	Hunt, John	G	6-4	262	2	Florida
77	Jeffcoat, Jim	DE	6-5	264	3	Arizona State
72	Jones, Ed	DE	6-9	272	11	Tennessee State
23	Jones, James	RB	5-10	202	5	Mississippi State
73	Kitson, Syd	G	6-4	264	5	Wake Forest
56	Lockhart, Eugene	LB	6-2	228	2	Houston
35	McSwain, Chuck	RB	6-0	191	3	Clemson
30	Newsome, Tim	RB	6-1	231	6	Winston-Salem State
16	Pelluer, Steve	QB	6-4	204	2	Washington
65	Petersen, Kurt	G	6-4	268	6	Missouri
81	Phillips, Kirk	WR	6-1	195	2	Tulsa
75	Pozderac, Phil	T	6-9	270	4	Notre Dame
64	Rafferty, Tom	C-G	6-3	259	10	Penn State
82	Renfro, Mike	WR	6-0	188	8	Texas Christian
70	Richards, Howard	G-T	6-6	258	5	Missouri
50	Rohrer, Jeff	LB	6-3	232	4	Yale
89	Salonen, Brian	TE	6-2	227	2	Montana
66	Schultz, Chris	T	6-8	265	3	Arizona
22	Scott, Victor	CB	5-10	182	2	Colorado
1	Septien, Rafael	K	5-10	180	9	Southwest Louisiana
60	Smerek, Don	DT	6-7	257	4	Nevada-Reno
20	Springs, Ron	RB	6-1	210	7	Ohio State
32	Thurman, Dennis	S	5-11	183	8	Southern California
63	Titensor, Glen	C-G	6-4	260	5	Brigham Young
71	Tuinei, Mark	DT	6-5	270	3	Hawaii
57	Turner, Jimmie	LB			2	
24	Walls, Everson	CB	6-1	194	5	Grambling
5	Warren, John	P	6-0	207	3	Tennessee
11	White, Danny	QB-P	6-2	196	10	Arizona State
54	White, Randy	DT	6-4	263	11	Maryland

NFC EASTERN DIVISION

NEW YORK GIANTS NFC East

Address Giants Stadium, East Rutherford, New Jersey 07073.

Stadium Giants Stadium, East Rutherford.
Capacity 76,891 *Playing Surface* AstroTurf.

Team Colours Blue, Red and White.

Head Coach Bill Parcells – third year.

Championships NFL 1927,'34,'38,'56.

History NFL 1925-69, NFC 1970-

Offense

In a year when the Giants were expected to regroup and consolidate, they went and surprised everyone by missing out that stage and reaching the playoffs. However, they can not yet boast a squad whose talent goes much beyond the starters. This is particularly true of the offensive line where there was no quality reserve support for left guard Billy Ard, whose loss on Week Fourteen was felt in the playoffs. The problems were exacerbated during the close-season, when starting center Kevin Belcher was hurt in a car accident and will not be available for 1985. On the positive side, tackles Karl Nelson and rookie Bill Roberts showed that they could live in the NFL, and the experienced tackle, Gordon King, returns from a lengthy rehabilitation after injury. The line protects one of the NFL's most exciting quarterbacks, Phil Simms, who last year became the eighth man in league history to pass for over 4,000 yards in a season. But numbers alone do not describe this tough competitor, who has come back more than once from career-threatening injury. Now, he's the mature leader with the knack of coaxing the best out of young wide receivers who, otherwise, might never blossom. So rookie wide receivers Bobby Johnson and Lionel Manuel came to play major roles in a passing offense which ranked third in the NFC. With Earnest Gray returning after injury, the explosive Byron Williams in reserve and the potential of draftee Stacy Robinson, the Giants are well-set at wide receiver. At tight end, the late-season form of Zeke Mowatt was a real surprise. Everyone knew he could block but his clutch receiving was phenomenal. Recent signing Don Hasselbeck, for-merly of New England, the Raiders and Minnesota, is an excellent blocker. There could be significant improvement at running back too, with the arrival of ex-USFL Maurice Carthon and first-round draftee George Adams. In Giants history, only twice has a player rushed for over 1,000 yards in a season (Ron Johnson in 1970 and 1972). Carthon would be a good bet to make it three.

Defense

The strength of the Giants defense lies at linebacker, where rookies Gary Reasons and Carl Banks slotted in smoothly alongside All-Pro Harry Carson and All-World Lawrence Taylor. Reasons and Banks kept out some good ones, such as Andy Headen, Byron Hunt and Joe McLaughlin. There's room for optimism elsewhere throughout the defense, with the likes of defensive end Leonard Marshall, a former second-rounder, growing in confidence and Terry Kinard, a former number one pick, playing up to standard as the starting free safety. Of the veterans, All-Pro cornerback Mark Haynes led the club with seven interceptions, and defensive end Casey Merrill confirmed his value as an excellent free agent acquisition (he is a former Green Bay player) by coming on as a third-down pass rusher and recording 8.5 quarterback sacks. There are a few problems to solve, notably at strong safety where the incumbent, Bill Currier, has had back problems and reserve Kenny Hill has been troubled with a persistent injury to his ankle. Third-round draftee Tyrone Davis, a specialist cornerback, would not be an effective replacement and the other draftee defensive backs are unlikely to find a spot on the roster.

Special Teams

Placekicker Ali Haji-Sheikh suffered pro football's traditional second-year blues (it is known also as the sophomore jinx). After being voted a unanimous All-Pro in 1983, his rookie year, he kicked only 8 of 13 field goals in the 30-39 range, 5 of 12 from 40 to 49 and none over 50 yards. Surely, he will improve. Punter Dave Jennings, who also has been an All-Pro, has just had his second modest season in a row but is unlikely to be displaced even though, inevitably, challenged in training camp. Currently, kickoff and punt returning is not an area where the Giants shine, and a performance rating par would be an improvement.

1985 DRAFT

Round	Name	Pos.	Ht.	Wt.	College
1.	Adams, George	RB	6-1	218	Kentucky
2.	Robinson, Stacy	WR	5-10	185	North Dakota State
3.	Davis, Tyrone	DB	5-11	190	Clemson
3.	Johnston, Brian	C	6-3	270	North Carolina
4.	Bavaro, Mark	TE	6-3	238	Notre Dame
5.	Henderson, Tracy	WR	6-0	182	Iowa State
6.	Oliver, Jack	G	6-3	280	Memphis State
6.	Pembrook, Mark	DB	5-11	197	Cal State-Fullerton
8.	Rouson, Lee	RB	6-1	210	Colorado
9.	Wright, Frank	NT	6-2	260	South Carolina
10.	Dubroc, Gregg	LB	6-3	239	Louisiana State
11.	Young, Allen	DB			Virginia Tech.
12.	Welch, Herb	DB	5-11	175	UCLA

The Giants' All-Pro cornerback, Mark Haynes

1985 SCHEDULE

September
8	PHILADELPHIA	1:00
15	at Green Bay	4:00
22	ST LOUIS	1:00
29	at Philadelphia	1:00

October
6	DALLAS	8:00
13	at Cincinnati	1:00
20	WASHINGTON	1:00
27	at New Orleans	4:00

November
3	TAMPA BAY	1:00
10	LOS ANGELES RAMS	1:00
18	at Washington	9:00
24	at St Louis	4:00

December
1	CLEVELAND	1:00
8	at Houston	4:00
15	at Dallas	1:00
21	at PITTSBURGH	12:30

VETERAN ROSTER

No.	Name	Pos.	Ht.	Wt.	NFL Year	College
67	Ard, Bill	G	6-3	250	5	Wake Forest
58	Banks, Carl	LB	6-4	232	2	Michigan State
	Battle, Ralph	S	6-2	205	2	Jacksonville State
73	Belcher, Kevin	G-C	6-3	255	3	Texas-El Paso
60	Benson, Brad	T	6-3	258	8	Penn State
64	Burt, Jim	NT	6-1	255	5	Miami
26	Carpenter, Rob	RB	6-1	230	9	Miami, Ohio
53	Carson, Harry	LB	6-2	235	10	South Carolina State
	Carthon, Maurice	RB	6-1	225	1	Arkansas State
31	Cephous, Frank	RB	5-10	205	2	UCLA
29	Currier, Bill	S	6-0	202	9	South Carolina
24	Daniel, Kenny	CB	5-11	190	2	San Jose State
37	Flowers, Larry	S	6 1	190	5	Texas Tech.
30	Galbreath, Tony	RB	6-0	228	10	Missouri
61	Godfrey, Chris	G	6-3	250	3	Michigan
62	Goode, Conrad	T	6-6	275	2	Missouri
83	Gray, Earnest	WR	6-3	195	7	Memphis State
6	Haji-Sheikh, Ali	K	6-0	172	3	Michigan
79	Hardison, Dee	DE	6-4	269	8	North Carolina
	Hasselbeck, Don	TE	6-7	245	9	Colorado
36	Haynes, Mark	CB	5-11	198	6	Colorado
54	Headen, Andy	LB	6-5	230	3	Clemson
48	Hill, Ken	S	6-0	195	5	Yale
15	Hostetler, Jeff	QB	6-3	215	2	West Virginia
57	Hunt, Byron	LB	6-5	230	5	Southern Methodist
13	Jennings, Dave	P	6-4	205	12	St Lawrence
88	Johnson, Bobby	WR	5-11	171	2	Kansas
51	Jones, Robbie	LB	6-2	230	2	Alabama
69	Jordan, David	G	6-6	267	2	Auburn
43	Kinard, Terry	S	6-1	190	3	Clemson
72	King, Gordon	T	6-6	275	8	Stanford
86	Manuel, Lionel	WR	5-11	175	2	Pacific
70	Marshall, Leonard	DE	6-3	285	3	Louisiana State
75	Martin, George	DE	6-4	245	11	Oregon
80	McConkey, Phil	WR-PR	5-10	170	2	Navy
33	McDaniel, LeCharls	CB	5-9	170	5	Cal Poly-SLO
76	McGriff, Curtis	DE	6-5	265	6	Alabama
52	McLaughlin, Joe	LB	6-1	235	7	Massachusetts
71	Merrill, Casey	DE	6-4	255	7	Cal-Davis
20	Morris, Joe	RB	5-7	190	4	Syracuse
84	Mowatt, Zeke	TE	6-3	238	3	Florida State
81	Mullady, Tom	TE	6-3	232	6	Southwestern Memphis
63	Nelson, Karl	T	6-6	272	2	Iowa State
9	Owen, Tom	QB	6-1	194	12	Wichita State
34	Patterson, Elvis	CB	5-11	190	2	Kansas
55	Reasons, Gary	LB	6-4	235	2	Northwest Louisiana
66	Roberts, Bill	T	6-5	275	2	Ohio State
17	Rutledge, Jeff	QB	6-1	190	7	Alabama
78	Sally, Jerome	NT	6-3	260	4	Missouri
44	Shaw, Pete	S	5-10	183	9	Northwestern
11	Simms, Phil	QB	6-3	216	7	Morehead State
56	Taylor, Lawrence	LB	6-3	237	5	North Carolina
38	Tuggle, John	RB	6-1	210	3	California
59	Umphrey, Rich	C	6-3	255	4	Colorado
87	Williams, Byron	WR	6-2	180	3	Texas-Arlington
23	Williams, Perry	CB	6-2	195	2	North Carolina State

PHILADELPHIA EAGLES NFC East

Address Philadelphia Veterans Stadium, Broad St. and Pattison Ave., Philadelphia, Pa. 19148.

Stadium Philadelphia Veterans Stadium, Philadelphia. *Capacity* 72,484 *Playing Surface* AstroTurf.

Team Colours Kelly Green, Silver and White.

Head Coach Marion Campbell – third year.

Championships Division 1980; Conference 1980; NFL 1948,'49,'60.

History NFL 1933-69, NFC 1970-

Offense

The Eagles don't look that good when measured by their numbers and yet that would be a long way from the truth. Certainly a 6-9-1 season is modest, but they play every Eastern division team twice and, these days, that alone adds up to a tough schedule. Even so, they could well have won games away to the Giants and St Louis (both were lost by one point), they tied with Detroit and came within a blocked extra point of tying in regulation time against Miami. Again, 60 quarterback sacks yielded would suggest a poor offensive line; but it's simply not that bad and will be given a boost by the arrival of first-round draftee tackle Kevin Allen. He should be an instant starter with Leonard Mitchell, Dean Miraldi and the returning veteran, Jerry Sisemore, competing for the other starting spot. The guards Steve Kenney and Ron Baker, and center Mark Dennard are secure at the heart of the line. Ron Jaworski's broken leg has healed and he will be back to start his twelfth NFL year. He's a wise quarterback with an eye for an open receiver but, like his reserve, Joe Pisarcik, is losing some of his sparkle, as the planners recognised by drafting Randall Cunningham in the second round. Cunningham represents the future and, for the present, Jaworski will continue to direct one of the league's better passing offenses. Wide receiver Mike Quick is highly dangerous, and tight end John Spagnola is only marginally less so after having enjoyed the best season of his five-year career. Last year's first-rounder, wide receiver Kenny Jackson, will be anxious to confirm his college pedigree. It has always been a probability that the dual-purpose backfield player, Wilbert Montgomery, would ease smoothly into the role of pass receiver and he gave the coaches a nudge with 60 receptions, third-best on the team. He also happens to be the Eagles' best running back and, until young players such as Michael Haddix and Michael Williams develop, he will have to soldier on.

Defense

Apart from a weakness against the run, the Eagles defense is good. Someone should think up a nickname for a line whose defensive ends Greg Brown and Dennis Harrison, and nose tackle Ken Clarke, registered 15.5, 12 and 10.5 quarterback sacks respectively. For a team which doesn't blitz that often, figures such as those are highly impressive. The great Jerry Robinson went to the 1982 Pro Bowl as an outside linebacker but has been converted to inside linebacker to use his formidable talents in defending against the run. Together with Anthony Griggs he forms a good partnership but they need a little more help from the outsides where ex-Falcon Joel Williams has yet to reproduce his form of 1980 when, amongst other things, he had 16 sacks. Wes Hopkins and Ray Ellis are two talented, hard-tackling safeties with a nose for the ball – they grabbed five and seven interceptions respectively. At left cornerback, the return of Roynell Young to full fitness is critical. Though intercepting four passes, Young's replacement, Elbert Foules, still has to develop a sense of position. On the other corner, veteran Herman Edwards may be under pressure from the 1984 rookie, Evan Cooper.

Special Teams

Rookie placekicker Paul McFadden broke the club single-season scoring record with 116 points. He missed only 2 of 12 field goal attempts from the 40-49 range and 1 of 4 from over 50 yards out – not bad for a 12th-round pick. Michael Horan, the punter, came as a first-year free agent and did well, averaging 42.2 yards with a hang time good enough to give his tacklers the time to get downfield. An 89-yard kickoff return for a touchdown by Andre Waters was the only bright spot in an otherwise sub-par year for the team as a whole. Neither Evan Cooper, who returned all the punts, nor Joe Hayes, who was the main kickoff returner, was particularly effective. There could well be changes.

1985 DRAFT

Round	Name	Pos.	Ht.	Wt.	College
1.	Allen, Kevin	T	6-5	275	Indiana
2.	Cunningham, Randall	QB	6-4	195	Nevada-Las Vegas
4.	Naron, Greg	G	6-4	265	North Carolina
5.	Jiles, Dwayne	LB	6-3	235	Texas Tech.
6.	Reeves, Ken	T	6-5	275	Texas A&M
8.	Polley, Thomas	LB	6-2	235	Nevada-Las Vegas
9.	Toub, Dave	C	6-3	282	Texas-El Paso
9.	Drake, Joe	DT	6-2	310	Arizona
10.	Kelso, Mark	DB	5-11	188	William & Mary
11.	Hunter, Herman	RB	6-0	190	Tennessee State
12.	Russell, Todd	DB	6-0	190	Boston College

1985 SCHEDULE

September

8	at New York Giants	1:00
15	LOS ANGELES RAMS	1:00
22	at Washington	1:00
29	NEW YORK GIANTS	1:00

October

6	at New Orleans	1:00
13	at St Louis	1:00
20	DALLAS	1:00
27	BUFFALO	1:00

November

3	at San Francisco	4:00
10	ATLANTA	1:00
17	ST LOUIS	1:00
24	at Dallas	4:00

December

1	MINNESOTA	1:00
8	WASHINGTON	1:00
15	at San Diego	4:00
22	at Minnesota	1:00

John Spagnola (#88) caught more passes than any other NFC tight end in 1984

VETERAN ROSTER

No.	Name	Pos.	Ht.	Wt.	NFL Year	College
96	Armstrong, Harvey	NT	6-2	255	4	Southern Methodist
63	Baker, Ron	G	6-4	250	8	Oklahoma State
98	Brown, Greg	DE	6-5	240	5	Kansas State
	Caldwell, Bryan	DE	6-4	248	2	Arizona State
	Christensen, Jeff	QB	6-3	203	3	Eastern Illinois
71	Clarke, Ken	NT	6-2	255	8	Syracuse
21	Cooper, Evan	DB-PR	5-11	180	2	Michigan
57	Cowher, Bill	LB	6-3	225	5	North Carolina State
94	Darby, Byron	DE	6-4	250	3	Southern California
65	Dennard, Mark	C	6-1	252	7	Texas A&M
46	Edwards, Herman	CB	6-0	190	9	San Diego State
24	Ellis, Ray	S	6-1	192	5	Ohio State
39	Everett, Major	RB	5-10	207	3	Mississippi College
67	Feehery, Gerry	C	6-2	268	3	Syracuse
29	Foules, Elbert	CB	5-11	185	3	Alcorn State
86	Garrity, Gregg	WR	5-10	171	3	Penn State
58	Griggs, Anthony	LB	6-3	230	4	Ohio State
26	Haddix, Michael	RB	6-2	225	3	Mississippi State
47	Hardy, Andre	RB	6-1	233	2	St Mary's, Ca.
68	Harrison, Dennis	DE	6-8	275	8	Vanderbilt
80	Hayes, Joe	WR-KR	5-9	185	2	Central State, Okla.
85	Hoover, Mel	WR	6-0	185	4	Arizona State
48	Hopkins, Wes	S	6-1	205	3	Southern Methodist
2	Horan, Mike	P	5-11	190	2	Long Beach State
81	Jackson, Kenny	WR	6-0	180	2	Penn State
7	Jaworski, Ron	QB	6-2	196	12	Youngstown State
	Jelesky, Tom	T	6-6	290	1	Purdue
84	Kab, Vyto	TE	6-5	240	4	Penn State
73	Kenney, Steve	G	6-4	262	6	Clemson
52	Kraynak, Rich	LB	6-1	221	3	Pittsburgh
5	May, Dean	QB	6-5	220	2	Louisville
8	McFadden, Paul	K	5-11	160	2	Youngstown State
64	Miraldi, Dean	T	6-5	254	3	Utah
74	Mitchell, Leonard	T	6-7	272	5	Houston
31	Montgomery, Wilbert	RB	5-10	195	9	Abilene Christian
34	Oliver, Hubert	RB	5-10	212	4	Arizona
62	Perot, Petey	G	6-2	261	6	Northwestern Louisiana
9	Pisarcik, Joe	QB	6-4	220	9	New Mexico State
82	Quick, Mike	WR	6-2	190	4	North Carolina State
55	Reichenbach, Mike	LB	6-2	235	2	East Stroudsburg
56	Robinson, Jerry	LB	6-2	225	7	UCLA
79	Russell, Rusty	T	6-5	295	2	South Carolina
87	Sampleton, Lawrence	TE	6-5	233	4	Texas
53	Schulz, Jody	LB	6-4	235	3	East Carolina
76	Sisemore, Jerry	T	6-4	265	13	Texas
88	Spagnola, John	TE	6-4	240	6	Yale
93	Strauthers, Thomas	DE	6-4	255	3	Jackson State
20	Waters, Andre	CB	5-11	182	2	Cheyney State
51	Wilkes, Reggie	LB	6-4	230	8	Georgia Tech.
59	Williams, Joel	LB	6-1	220	7	Wisconsin-LaCrosse
32	Williams, Michael	RB	6-2	217	3	Mississippi College
22	Wilson, Brenard	CB-S	6-0	175	7	Vanderbilt
83	Woodruff, Tony	WR	6-0	175	4	Fresno State
43	Young, Roynell	CB	6-1	181	6	Alcorn State

ST LOUIS CARDINALS NFC East

Address Busch Stadium, Box 888, St Louis, Missouri 63188.
Stadium Busch Memorial Stadium, St Louis.
   Capacity 51,392 *Playing Surface* AstroTurf.
Team Colours Cardinal Red, Black and White.
Head Coach Jim Hanifan – sixth year.
Championships Division 1974,'75; NFL 1925,'47.
History NFL 1920-69, NFC 1970-
   (Until 1960, they were known as the Chicago Cardinals.)

Offense

With slight improvement in one or two positions and a little luck, the Cardinals could win the Eastern division title, to which they came so close last season when losing by two points to the champion Redskins on Week Sixteen. First, however, they'll have to repair the damage done to the offensive line by the loss of left tackle Luis Sharpe to the USFL. Randy Clark, Joe Bostic and James 'Tootie' Robbins are steady at center, right guard and right tackle respectively but the eight-year veteran left guard, Terry Stieve, may lose his place for good to 1984 rookie Doug Dawson. Sharpe's replacement may well come from the 1985 draft in the form of either Scott Bergold or Lance Smith. There are no problems at quarterback except, that is, the lack of reserve strength. The starter, Neil Lomax, has turned out to be the pro flame-thrower the Cardinals expected him to be after an astonishing college career at Portland State. Last year, he threw for the fourth-highest yardage in NFL history on the way to a passer rating of 92.5, the latter which was good enough to earn selection to his first Pro Bowl as backup to Joe Montana. He's spoiled for choice at wide receiver, where Roy Green, last year's league leader in terms of receiving yardage, lines up with Pat Tilley. 1984's first-round pick, Clyde Duncan, must surely enter the picture after making a late start in his rookie season, and it would be no surprise to see former defensive back Cedric Mack emulate Green by making the conversion from defense to offense. Running back Ottis Anderson will doubtless power his way to a sixth 1,000-yard season and will cause more than a few problems filtering out of the backfield to catch passes. Anderson's backup, 'Stump' Mitchell, has rushed 219 times at a remarkable average of 5.3 yards over his four-year career. The other starter, three-year veteran Earl Ferrell, was regarded highly enough to enable the Cardinals to release Wayne Morris. Tight end Doug Marsh is expected to be even more productive, after two good seasons in a row, but beyond him there is no threat from this position.

Defense

Defensive left tackle Ramsey Dardar has eased smoothly into the line which, otherwise, is unchanged and confirmed its reputation with a repeat of 1983's good performance. Defensive right end Curtis Greer registered 14 of a team total 55 sacks, the latter which is still above average though down on last year's 59. The talented Mark Duda returns from injury to provide excellent reserve strength in both tackle positions. The versatile E.J. Junior had an outstanding year and was a starting inside linebacker in the Pro Bowl, despite playing ten games at outside linebacker for St Louis after an injury to Charles Baker. The unit could use some help against the run and it may have come with the drafting of Freddie Joe Nunn, who played defensive end in college but is just the right size for conversion to linebacker in the pros. The secondary will be good if the starters can stay healthy. Otherwise they could have difficulty against a good passing offense. Cornerback Lionel Washington has developed a good pass coverage technique and led the club with five interceptions. Free safety Benny Perrin, a crunching tackler, and cornerback Wayne Smith each chipped in with four. Former first-round pick Leonard Smith returns after injury and could challenge strong safety Lee Nelson for the starting job.

Special Teams

Neil O'Donoghue is an erratic placekicker but still pops over the occasional long field goal and, last year, equalled the club record with 117 points. Punter Carl Birdsong's gross average has dropped a touch but he's still the master of the 'coffin corner' delivery. 'Stump' Mitchell is by far the NFC's most valuable dual kickoff and punt returner – he ranked second and third respectively to round off a really fine year.

1985 DRAFT

Round	Name	Pos.	Ht.	Wt.	College
1.	Nunn, Freddie Joe	LB	6-3	230	Mississippi
2.	Bergold, Scott	T	6-7	260	Wisconsin
3.	Smith, Lance	T	6-2	255	Louisiana State
4.	Wolfley, Ron	RB	5-11	215	West Virginia
5.	Dunn, K.D.	TE	6-2	220	Clemson
5.	Wong, Louis	G	6-4	260	Brigham Young
6.	Novacek, Jay	WR	6-3	210	Wyoming
8.	Monaco, Rob	G	6-2	270	Vanderbilt
9.	Williams, Scott	TE	6-1	230	Georgia
10.	Williams, Dennis	RB	6-1	225	Furman
11.	Anderson, Ricky	K	6-1	190	Vanderbilt
12.	Young, Lonnie	DB	6-1	185	Michigan State

Benny Perrin, an underrated
free safety

1985 SCHEDULE

September

8	at Cleveland	1:00
15	CINCINNATI	1:00
22	at New York Giants	1:00
29	GREEN BAY	1:00

October

7	at Washington	9:00
13	PHILADELPHIA	1:00
20	at Pittsburgh	1:00
27	HOUSTON	1:00

November

4	DALLAS	9:00
10	at Tampa Bay	1:00
17	at Philadelphia	1:00
24	NEW YORK GIANTS	4:00
28	at Dallas	3:00

December

8	NEW ORLEANS	1:00
15	at Los Angeles Rams	4:00
21	WASHINGTON	4:00

VETERAN ROSTER

No.	Name	Pos.	Ht.	Wt.	NFL Year	College
58	Ahrens, Dave	LB	6-3	228	5	Wisconsin
51	Allerman, Kurt	LB	6-2	222	9	Penn State
32	Anderson, Ottis	RB	6-2	220	7	Miami
61	Audick, Dan	G	6-3	253	8	Hawaii
60	Baker, Al	DE	6-6	260	8	Colorado State
52	Baker, Charles	LB	6-2	217	6	New Mexico
18	Birdsong, Carl	P	6-0	192	5	S.W. Oklahoma State
71	Bostic, Joe	G	6-3	265	7	Clemson
64	Clark, Randy	C	6-3	254	6	Northern Illinois
62	Dardar, Ramsey	DT	6-2	264	2	Louisiana State
	Davis, Billy	S				
66	Dawson, Doug	G	6-3	267	2	Texas
73	Duda, Mark	DT	6-3	263	3	Maryland
86	Duncan, Clyde	WR	6-1	192	2	Tennessee
31	Ferrell, Earl	RB	6-0	215	4	East Tennessee State
65	Galloway, David	DT	6-3	277	4	Florida
84	Goode, John	TE	6-2	222	2	Youngstown State
81	Green, Roy	WR	6-0	195	7	Henderson State
75	Greer, Curtis	DE	6-4	252	6	Michigan
35	Griffin, Jeff	CB	6-0	185	4	Utah
78	Grooms, Elois	DT	6-4	250	10	Tennessee Tech.
39	Harrell, Willard	RB	5-8	182	11	Pacific
36	Harrington, Perry	RB	5-11	210	6	Jackson State
50	Harris, Bob	LB	6-2	205	3	Auburn
46	Heflin, Victor	CB	6-0	184	3	Delaware State
59	Howard, Thomas	LB	6-2	215	9	Texas Tech.
54	Junior, E.J.	LB	6-3	235	5	Alabama
89	LaFleur, Greg	TE	6-4	236	5	Louisiana State
15	Lomax, Neil	QB	6-3	215	5	Portland State
40	Love, Randy	RB	6-1	205	7	Houston
82	Mack, Cedric	WR	6-0	190	3	Baylor
12	Mackey, Kyle	QB	6-2	220	2	East Texas State
80	Marsh, Doug	TE	6-3	240	6	Michigan
76	Mays, Stafford	DE	6-2	250	6	Washington
87	McGill, Eddie	TE	6-6	225	3	Western Carolina
14	McIvor, Rick	QB	6-4	210	2	Texas
30	Mitchell, Stump	RB	5-9	188	5	Citadel
38	Nelson, Lee	S	5-10	185	10	Florida State
57	Noga, Falaniko	LB	6-1	230	2	Hawaii
11	O'Donoghue, Neil	K	6-6	210	9	Auburn
23	Perrin, Benny	S	6-2	178	4	Alabama
85	Pittman, Danny	WR	6-2	205	6	Wyoming
70	Plunkett, Art	T	6-7	270	5	Nevada-Las Vegas
72	Ralph, Dan	DT	6-4	268	2	Oregon
63	Robbins, Tootie	T	6-4	278	4	East Carolina
26	Schmitt, George	S	5-11	193	3	Delaware
56	Scott, Carlos	C	6-4	300	3	Texas-El Paso
45	Smith, Leonard	S	5-11	190	3	McNeese State
44	Smith, Wayne	CB	6-0	175	6	Purdue
68	Stieve, Terry	G	6-2	265	9	Wisconsin
83	Tilley, Pat	WR	5-10	178	10	Louisiana Tech.
33	Walker, Quentin	WR	6-1	200	2	Virginia
48	Washington, Lionel	CB	6-0	184	3	Tulane
42	Whitaker, Bill	S	6-0	182	5	Missouri

WASHINGTON REDSKINS NFC East

Address Redskin Park, P.O. Box 17247, Dulles International Airport, Washington, D.C. 20041.

Stadium Robert F. Kennedy Stadium, Washington. *Capacity* 55,363 *Playing Surface* Grass (Prescription Athletic Turf).

Team Colours Burgundy and Gold.

Head Coach Joe Gibbs – fifth year.

Championships Division 1972, '83, '84; Conference 1972, '82, '83; NFL 1937, '42; Super Bowl 1982.

History NFL 1932-69, NFC 1970-
(Originally named the Boston Braves for the 1932 season only, they were renamed the Boston Redskins until, in 1937, they moved to Washington.)

Offense

The Washington Redskins held off the challenge of their Eastern division opponents for the third consecutive year but not with quite the same style which had taken them to consecutive Super Bowls. And whilst their squad is of high quality in most positions, the reserve strength is a little thin. Without quarterback Joe Theismann they'd be in some trouble but, of course, with him they're in clover. Now entering his twelfth NFL year, he has lost none of his dynamism and remains one of pro football's great leaders. He had to play for much of last season without wide receiver 'Downtown' Charlie Brown who, thankfully, is fit to resume at full pace. In Brown's absence, Art Monk took the strain and established a new NFL single-season record for receptions. They were perhaps looking for a stopgap when the opportunity came to acquire Calvin Muhammad from the Raiders. He gave them a deep threat they had been missing, starting out with an 80-yard touchdown reception against Dallas, and will be difficult to displace. The Redskins are somewhat unusual in the minor contribution made by their backfield players to the passing offense. The arrival of running back George Rogers, from New Orleans, is unlikely to improve that aspect but he's certainly a first-class rusher and is the obvious replacement for the thirty-six-year-old John Riggins, who has had lower back problems. Joe Washington has been traded to Atlanta but, together with Riggins, second-year player Keith Griffin will provide adequate backup for Rogers. As always, Otis Wonsley will shoulder the burden of lead-blocking on short-yardage downs. The offensive line still has its powerful elements, particularly in left guard Russ Grimm and left tackle Joe Jacoby. It was asking a lot of Rick Donnalley to fill the shoes of the injured center, Jeff Bostic, and, though he did well, Bostic's return will be welcomed. As expected, Clint Didier remains as the leading tight end pass receiver on the roster, even though he missed the first five games. The other two, Don Warren and Rick Walker, will play a valuable part as blockers in what promises to be a formidable offense.

Defense

The Redskins defense is most ungenerous against the run but their problems defending against the pass are still unsolved – they ranked 25th in the league for passing yards conceded. The latter is surprising since the squad registered 66 sacks, 13.5 by defensive right end Dexter Manley and 10.5 by linebacker Monte Coleman. Furthermore, a total of 21 team interceptions is quite good (they shared fourth place in the NFC with Chicago and St Louis). However, they had to face more passes than any other NFC team (575) and over half of them found their mark. It's difficult to imagine this weakness remaining for much longer when one looks at the talent which the Redskins can assemble. The starting four-man line is really good and they will be given support by the return to fitness of two 1984 second-round draftees, defensive tackle Bob Slater and defensive end Steve Hamilton. Behind the front four, linebackers Mel Kaufman, Neal Olkewicz and Rich Milot have formed the starting trio in two Super Bowls. They are alert and tough. The secondary as a whole is not the fastest but Pro Bowl cornerback Darrell Green is, so they say, the fastest defensive back in the league, indeed. The other cornerback, Vernon Dean, fought his way ahead of Anthony Washington and led the team with seven pass interceptions. Draftee Tory Nixon could be a useful nickel back right away.

Special Teams

Providing the offense can place him inside the 30-yard line, veteran placekicker Mark Moseley will do a reliable job, as will punter Jeff Hayes, though perhaps lacking a couple of yards on his average. It would be good to see the Redskins' dual purpose returner reproduce his form of 1981 so that, once again, we could call him 'The Great' Mike Nelms.

1985 DRAFT

Round	Name	Pos.	Ht.	Wt.	College
2.	Nixon, Tory	DB	5-10	180	San Diego State
5.	Cherry, Raphel	RB	5-11	197	Hawaii
6.	Lee, Danzell	TE	6-2	214	Lamar
7.	Harris, Jamie	KR	5-7	160	Oklahoma State
7.	Vital, Lionel	RB	5-9	190	Nicholls State
8.	Wilburn, Barry	DB	6-2	190	Mississippi
9.	Geier, Mitch	G			Troy State
10.	Orr, Terry	RB	6-2	220	Texas
11.	McKenzie, Raleigh	G	6-1	258	Tennessee
11.	Kimble, Garry	DB	5-10	180	Sam Houston State
12.	Hamel, Dean	DT			Tulsa
12.	Winn, Bryant	LB	6-3	231	Houston

*Monster defensive tackle
Dave Butz*

1985 SCHEDULE

September

9	at Dallas	9:00
15	HOUSTON	1:00
22	PHILADELPHIA	1:00
29	at Chicago	1:00

October

7	ST LOUIS	9:00
13	DETROIT	1:00
20	at New York Giants	1:00
27	at Cleveland	1:00

November

3	at Atlanta	1:00
10	DALLAS	4:00
18	NEW YORK GIANTS	9:00
24	at Pittsburgh	1:00

December

1	SAN FRANCISCO	4:00
8	at Philadelphia	1:00
15	CINCINNATI	1:00
21	at St Louis	4:00

VETERAN ROSTER

No.	Name	Pos.	Ht.	Wt.	NFL Year	College
67	Beasley, Tom	DE	6-5	248	8	Virginia Tech.
53	Bostic, Jeff	C	6-2	250	6	Clemson
69	Brooks, Perry	DT	6-3	270	8	Southern University
87	Brown, Charlie	WR	5-10	179	4	South Carolina State
65	Butz, Dave	DT	6-7	295	13	Purdue
48	Coffey, Ken	S	6-0	190	3	Southwest Texas State
51	Coleman, Monte	LB	6-2	230	7	Central Arkansas
54	Cronan, Pete	LB	6-2	238	8	Boston College
32	Dean, Vernon	CB	5-11	178	4	San Diego State
86	Didier, Clint	TE	6-5	240	4	Portland State
76	Donnalley, Rick	C-G	6-2	257	4	North Carolina
77	Grant, Darryl	DT	6-1	275	5	Rice
28	Green, Darrell	CB	5-8	170	3	Texas A&I
35	Griffin, Keith	RB	5-8	185	2	Miami
68	Grimm, Russ	G	6-3	290	5	Pittsburgh
	Hamilton, Steve	DE	6-4	253	2	East Carolina
5	Hayes, Jeff	P	5-11	175	4	North Carolina
61	Huff, Ken	G	6-4	265	11	North Carolina
66	Jacoby, Joe	T	6-7	300	5	Louisville
82	Jones, Anthony	TE	6-3	248	2	Wichita State
22	Jordan, Curtis	S	6-2	205	9	Texas Tech.
56	Junkin, Trey	LB	6-2	221	3	Louisiana Tech.
55	Kaufman, Mel	LB	6-2	220	5	Cal Poly-SLO
63	Kimball, Bruce	C	6-2	260	4	Massachusetts
50	Kubin, Larry	LB	6-2	238	4	Penn State
12	Laufenberg, Babe	QB	6-2	195	3	Indiana
79	Liebenstein, Todd	DE	6-6	255	4	Nevada-Las Vegas
72	Manley, Dexter	DE	6-3	250	5	Oklahoma State
71	Mann, Charles	DE	6-6	250	3	Nevada-Reno
84	Mauti, Rich	WR	6-0	195	8	Penn State
73	May, Mark	G	6-6	288	5	Pittsburgh
78	McGee, Tony	DE	6-3	249	15	Bishop
83	McGrath, Mark	WR	5-11	175	4	Montana State
57	Milot, Rich	LB	6-4	237	7	Penn State
81	Monk, Art	WR	6-3	209	6	Syracuse
30	Moore, Jeff	RB	6-0	196	6	Jackson State
3	Moseley, Mark	K	6-0	204	14	Stephen F. Austin
89	Muhammad, Calvin	WR	5-11	190	4	Texas Southern
29	Murphy, Mark	S	6-4	210	9	Colgate
21	Nelms, Mike	KR-WR	6-1	185	6	Baylor
52	Olkewicz, Neal	LB	6-0	233	7	Maryland
23	Peters, Tony	S	6-1	190	10	Oklahoma
44	Riggins, John	RB	6-2	235	14	Kansas
	Rogers, George	RB	6-2	229	5	South Carolina
10	Schroeder, Jay	QB	6-4	215	2	UCLA
75	Slater, Bob	DE	6-4	265	2	Oklahoma
26	Smith, Ricky	CB	6-0	182	4	Alabama State
74	Starke, George	T	6-5	260	13	Columbia
	Sverchek, Paul	DT	6-3	256	2	Cal Poly-SLO
7	Theismann, Joe	QB	6-0	198	12	Notre Dame
70	Towns, Morris	T	6-4	263	9	Missouri
88	Walker, Rick	TE	6-4	235	9	UCLA
85	Warren, Don	TE	6-4	242	7	San Diego State
24	Washington, Anthony	CB	6-1	204	5	Fresno State
47	Williams, Greg	S	5-11	185	4	Mississippi State
	Williams, Mike	TE	6-4	251	4	Alabama A&M
39	Wonsley, Otis	RB	5-10	214	5	Alcorn State

CHICAGO BEARS NFC Central

Address 250 N. Washington, Lake Forest, Illinois 60045.
Stadium Soldier Field, Chicago.
  Capacity 65,790 *Playing Surface* AstroTurf.
Team Colours Navy Blue, Orange and White.
Head Coach Mike Ditka – fourth year.
Championships Division 1984; NFL
  1921,'32,'33,'40,'41,'43,'46,'63.
History NFL 1920-69, NFC 1970-
  (Before 1922, they were known as firstly the Decatur
  Staleys and then the Chicago Staleys.)

Offense

Last season the Bears were just a 'bit of passing offense' away from greatness. They say that you can't win a championship without a good quarterback. Of those, the Bears have two, Steve Fuller and Jim McMahon, of whom the latter might have entered the 'great' category when we look back on the 1985 season. But there are question marks over both players. Fuller has a problem with his passing shoulder and McMahon has yet to confirm that he can return after suffering a serious kidney injury against the Raiders on Week Ten. McMahon is a leader in the best Chicago traditions – as tough as old boots, even old Bears (and they were tough), brave and a winner. He has a good combination of wide receivers in the pairing of Willie Gault, a superb deep threat, and Dennis McKinnon, who goes for everything with abandon. They may well have found themselves another future starter in third-round draftee James Maness. In terms of pass receiving, the Bears haven't had much from the tight end position but former USFL player Tim Wrightman could change all that. Currently, Emery Moorehead is the most productive of the tight ends who are better known for their blocking. They certainly do expect, indeed they do get an outstanding contribution from the offensive backfield, where Walter Payton and Matt Suhey led the club with 45 and 42 receptions respectively. Payton could not be blamed for retiring to less-arduous surroundings, after having become the NFL's all-time leading rusher. But an important factor in achieving that status was his very enthusiasm when times were lean. He's on his way to 15,000 yards with no indications of slowing down. Behind Payton, Suhey is

reliable and Calvin Thomas is starting to punch out his yards with a greater sense of purpose. The offensive line has firmed up a little quicker than was expected of such a young unit. In terms of sacks given up (36), they were third-best in the NFC behind two great lines, those of San Francisco and the Rams respectively. Jimbo Covert, Mark Bortz, Jay Hilgenberg, Kurt Becker and Keith Van Horne (let's call them the 'Fearsome Fivesome') will take some handling in the coming season.

Defense

It's doubtful if even the late George Halas who, from 1920 until 1983, was the Bears guiding father, could have assembled a defensive squad better than that which now rates as the NFL's best. Looking at all the sensible categories, their lowest rating in the NFC was third in percentage interceptions. Four players, defensive tackle Dan Hampton, defensive end Richard Dent, linebacker Mike Singletary and safety Todd Bell, started in the 1985 Pro Bowl. Free safety Gary Fencik is a former Pro Bowler. Dent led the NFC with 17.5 sacks. Hampton had 11.5 and defensive left tackle Steve McMichael had 10. Collectively, the defense set an NFL record with 72 sacks. Ominously, there's just a possibility that first-round draftee defensive tackle William Perry could push McMichael for a starting spot. The starting linebackers, Otis Wilson, Singletary and Al Harris, are so consistently good that Wilber Marshall and Ron Rivera, 1984's first- and second-round picks respectively, can't break in. The secondary has a relative weakness in man-on-man coverage of the receivers and draftee Reggie Phillips may break into the lineup. Failing this, in Mike Richardson, Leslie Frazier, Bell and Gary Fencik, they're still in good shape.

Special Teams

Placekicker Bob Thomas missed only five field goal attempts from inside the 50-yard range and kicked two out of three beyond that distance, but will be challenged by draftee Kevin Butler. Dave Finzer improved as the season wore on and gradually established himself as a precision punter whose efforts were returned for just 4.8 yards on average. It's a different story in the kickoff return department, where none of the regulars had better than a 19-yard average. Punt returns are handled well by backup safety Jeff Fisher with Dennis McKinnon around for the odd shocker.

1985 DRAFT

Round	Name	Pos.	Ht.	Wt.	College
1.	Perry, William	DT	6-1	340	Clemson
2.	Phillips, Reggie	DB	5-9	170	Southern Methodist
3.	Maness, James	WR	5-11	170	Texas Christian
4.	Butler, Kevin	K	5-11	190	Georgia
7.	Bennett, Charles	DE	6-4	250	Southwestern Louisiana
8.	Buxton, Steve	T	6-6	262	Indiana State
9.	Sanders, Thomas	RB	5-10	195	Texas A&M
10.	Coryatt, Pat	DT	6-1	280	Baylor
11.	Morrissey, James	LB	6-2	212	Michigan State

Defensive end Mike Hartenstine, a key member of the 'Monsters of the Midway'

1985 SCHEDULE

September
8	TAMPA BAY	1:00
15	NEW ENGLAND	1:00
19	at Minnesota	8:00
29	WASHINGTON	1:00

October
6	at Tampa Bay	1:00
13	at San Francisco	4:00
21	GREEN BAY	9:00
27	MINNESOTA	1:00

November
3	at Green Bay	1:00
10	DETROIT	1:00
17	at Dallas	1:00
24	ATLANTA	1:00

December
2	at Miami	9:00
8	INDIANAPOLIS	1:00
14	at New York Jets	12:30
22	at Detroit	1:00

VETERAN ROSTER

No.	Name	Pos.	Ht.	Wt.	NFL Year	College
86	Anderson, Brad	WR	6-3	196	2	Arizona
60	Andrews, Tom	G	6-4	250	2	Louisville
84	Baschnagel, Brian	WR	6-0	184	10	Ohio State
79	Becker, Kurt	G	6-5	270	4	Michigan
25	Todd, Bell	S	6-0	207	5	Ohio State
62	Bortz, Mark	DT	6-5	267	3·	Iowa
97	Butkus, Mark	DT	6-4	261	1	Illinois
54	Cabral, Brian	LB	6-1	224	7	Colorado
30	Cameron, Jack	KR-WR	6-0	182	2	Winston-Salem State
74	Covert, Jimbo	T	6-4	271	3	Pittsburgh
95	Dent, Richard	DE	6-5	240	3	Tennessee State
22	Duerson, Dave	S	6-0	202	3	Notre Dame
88	Dunsmore, Pat	TE	6-2	230	3	Drake
64	Fada, Rob	G	6-2	258	3	Pittsburgh
45	Fencik, Gary	S	6-1	197	10	Yale
15	Finzer, David	P	6-0	195	2	De Pauw
24	Fisher, Jeff	S	5-10	195	5	Southern California
21	Frazier, Leslie	CB	6-0	189	5	Alcorn State
71	Frederick, Andy	T	6-6	265	9	New Mexico
4	Fuller, Steve	QB	6-4	198	7	Clemson
83	Gault, Willie	WR	6-0	178	3	Tennessee
23	Gayle, Shaun	CB	5-11	195	2	Ohio State
29	Gentry, Dennis	RB	5-8	173	4	Baylor
99	Hampton, Dan	DT	6-5	270	7	Arkansas
90	Harris, Al	LB	6-5	250	7	Arizona State
73	Hartenstine, Mike	DE	6-3	243	11	Penn State
63	Hilgenberg, Jay	C	6-3	260	5	Iowa
75	Humphries, Stefan	G	6-4	248	2	Michigan
32	Hutchison, Anthony	RB	5-10	180	3	Texas Tech.
49	Jordan, Donald	RB	6-0	201	2	Houston
98	Keys, Tyrone	DE	6-7	260	3	Mississippi State
89	Krenk, Mitch	TE	6-4	225	2	Nebraska
12	Lisch, Rusty	QB	6-3	213	6	Notre Dame
82	Margerum, Ken	WR	6-0	180	5	Stanford
58	Marshall, Wilber	LB	6-1	230	2	Florida
85	McKinnon, Dennis	WR	6-2	185	3	Florida State
9	McMahon, Jim	QB	6-0	187	4	Brigham Young
76	McMichael, Steve	DT	6-2	260	6	Texas
87	Moorehead, Emery	TE	6-2	220	9	Colorado
67	Norman, Tim	G	6-6	273	1	Illinois
34	Payton, Walter	RB	5-10	202	11	Jackson State
53	Rains, Dan	LB	6-1	220	4	Cincinnati
27	Richardson, Mike	CB	6-0	188	3	Arizona State
59	Rivera, Ron	LB	6-3	235	2	California
81	Saldi, Jay	TE	6-3	230	10	South Carolina
44	Schmidt, Terry	CB	6-0	177	12	Ball State
50	Singletary, Mike	LB	5-11	230	5	Baylor
26	Suhey, Matt	RB	5-11	217	6	Penn State
16	Thomas, Bob	K	5-10	175	10	Notre Dame
33	Thomas, Calvin	RB	5-11	220	4	Illinois
78	Van Horne, Keith	T	6-6	265	5	Southern California
70	Waechter, Henry	DT	6-6	260	4	Nebraska
80	Watts, Rickey	WR	6-1	203	7	Tulsa
55	Wilson, Otis	LB	6-2	222	6	Louisville
	Wrightman, Tim	TE	6-3	236	1	UCLA

DETROIT LIONS NFC Central

Address Pontiac Silverdome, 1200 Featherstone Road, Box 4200, Pontiac, Michigan 48057.

Stadium Pontiac Silverdome.

Capacity 80,638 *Playing Surface* AstroTurf.

Team Colours Honolulu Blue and Silver.

Head Coach Darryl Rogers – first year.

Championships Division 1983; NFL 1935, '52, '53, '57.

History NFL 1930-69, NFC 1970-

(Until 1934, they were known as the Portsmouth (Ohio) Spartans.)

Offense

After such a disappointing season it's best to look at the Lions' good points and, optimistically, at what might just happen if everything goes right. The best thing that could happen would be the return of a completely healthy Billy Sims, who was sorely missed over the second half of the season. Before then, he had clocked up four 100-yard rushing games, the last two on Weeks Seven and Eight, and was on a 1,350-yard schedule at an average of 5.3 per carry. With Sims in partnership with third-year fullback James Jones, supported by Ken Jenkins, the Lions would roll. Jones really came good when handed the main responsibility for offense, blasting for 532 yards and catching a club-record 77 passes. New head coach Darryl Rogers has sorted out the uncertainty over who would start at quarterback by trading Gary Danielson to Cleveland, leaving Eric Hipple to establish himself. Just to be on the safe side however, Rogers acquired the Buffalo veteran, Joe Ferguson. At wide receiver, the Lions have two who could cause more than a bit of trouble. Leonard Thompson has been regarded as a big-play threat for most of his ten-year career. Now, he has a bit of competition in this department from Mark Nichols, who averaged 21.9 yards over 34 receptions and is just beginning to wear the mantle of starter with confidence. Statistically, backup wide receiver Jeff Chadwick slipped a little but still looks like a bargain acquisition (he was a rookie free agent in 1983). There's not much coming from the tight end position where 1984's first-round pick, David Lewis, may need a little more time to learn the techniques. The offensive line was given a welcome boost by the drafting of tackle Lomas Brown and center Kevin Glover, two collegians noted for their speed and alertness. Brown could start immediately but Glover will be in competition with Amos Fowler and former starter Steve Mott, who is coming off injured reserve. Tackle Rich Strenger is another veteran returning from injury. A second-round pick in 1983, Strenger played well when standing in as a rookie for Pro Bowler Keith Dorney.

Defense

The defensive line which entered the 1984 season rated by many experts to be close to the NFL's best, took some time to crank into gear and was effective only in the later stages of the campaign. However, it is unlikely that there will be any changes in the starting quartet of Mike Cofer, Curtis Green, Doug English and William Gay. Both English and Gay will be anxious to regain their places on the Pro Bowl roster. Again, the starting linebacking trio of Garry Cobb, Ken Fantetti and Jimmy Williams, will remain undisturbed. James Johnson and Kevin Hancock were drafted in rounds three and four respectively but are best seen as long-term prospects. Completing a display of confidence it seems that last year's starters in the secondary will line up together in 1985. Three-year veteran cornerback Bobby Watkins brought his career interception total to 15 with a club-leading six, whilst left safety William Graham hauled in the first three of his career. Reserve cornerback Al Latimer is a former starter.

Special Teams

Eddie Murray, who currently has the longest sequence of successful extra point attempts with 153, is one of several very fine placekickers in the NFC. It is unfortunate for a kicker who, last year, was successful on 12 of 13 field goal attempts in the range 40-49 yards, that he is remembered for his failures, such as missing a 43-yarder that would have beaten San Francisco in the 1983 playoffs. Mike Black enhanced his punting average with a second good season. Unfortunately, his special-team tacklers have difficulty closing down on punt returners. On Detroit's behalf in that category, Robbie Martin does a good job but they could use a few more big plays from the kickoff returners.

1985 DRAFT

Round	Name	Pos.	Ht.	Wt.	College
1.	Brown, Lomas	T	6-3	280	Florida
2.	Glover, Kevin	C	6-1	262	Maryland
3.	Johnson, James	LB	6-2	220	San Diego State
4.	Hancock, Kevin	LB	6-1	225	Baylor
5.	McIntosh, Joe	RB	5-10	190	North Carolina State
6.	Short, Stan	G	6-3	270	Penn State
7.	Staten, Tony	DB	5-8	180	Angelo State
8.	Caldwell, Scott	RB	5-11	200	Texas-Arlington
9.	James, June	LB	6-0	215	Texas
10.	Beauford, Clayton	WR	5-10	180	Auburn
11.	Harris, Kevin	DB	6-0	193	Georgia
12.	Weaver, Mike	G	6-1	295	Georgia

1985 SCHEDULE

September
8	at Atlanta	1:00
15	DALLAS	1:00
22	at Indianapolis	1:00
29	TAMPA BAY	1:00

October
6	at Green Bay	1:00
13	at Washington	1:00
20	SAN FRANCISCO	1:00
27	MIAMI	1:00

November
3	at Minnesota	1:00
10	at Chicago	1:00
17	MINNESOTA	4:00
24	at Tampa Bay	1:00
28	NEW YORK JETS	12:30

December
8	at New England	1:00
15	GREEN BAY	1:00
22	CHICAGO	1:00

Running back Billy Sims, who is vital to the Lions' prospects

VETERAN ROSTER

No.	Name	Pos.	Ht.	Wt.	NFL Year	College
68	Baack, Steve	G	6-4	252	2	Oregon
54	Barnes, Roosevelt	LB	6-2	222	4	Purdue
11	Black, Mike	P	6-1	197	3	Arizona State
80	Bland, Carl	WR	5-11	180	2	Virginia Union
89	Chadwick, Jeff	WR	6-3	185	3	Grand Valley State
53	Cobb, Garry	LB	6-2	227	7	Southern California
66	Cofer, Mike	DE	6-5	245	3	Tennessee
50	Curley, August	LB	6-3	222	3	Southern California
44	D'Addio, Dave	RB	6-2	235	2	Maryland
72	Dieterich, Chris	T	6-3	255	6	North Carolina State
93	Dodge, Kirk	LB	6-1	231	2	Nevada-Las Vegas
58	Doig, Steve	LB	6-2	242	4	New Hampshire
70	Dorney, Keith	T	6-5	265	7	Penn State
61	Elias, Homer	G	6-2	255	8	Tennessee State
78	English, Doug	DT	6-5	258	10	Texas
57	Fantetti, Ken	LB	6-2	232	7	Wyoming
	Ferguson, Joe	QB	6-1	195	13	Arkansas
65	Fowler, Amos	C	6-3	253	8	Southern Mississippi
26	Frizzell, William	CB	6-2	195	2	North Carolina Central
79	Gay, William	DE-DT	6-5	255	8	Southern California
33	Graham, William	S	5-11	191	4	Texas
67	Greco, Don	G	6-3	255	4	Western Illinois
62	Green, Curtis	DE-DT	6-3	252	5	Alabama State
35	Hall, Alvin	S	5-10	184	5	Miami, Ohio
17	Hipple, Eric	QB	6-2	196	6	Utah State
31	Jenkins, Ken	RB	5-8	184	3	Bucknell
21	Johnson, Demetrious	S	5-11	190	3	Missouri
51	Jones, David	C	6-3	266	2	Texas
30	Jones, James	RB	6-2	228	3	Florida
	Kane, Rick	RB	6-0	200	9	San Jose State
92	King, Angelo	LB	6-1	230	5	South Carolina State
73	Laster, Don	T	6-5	285	3	Tennessee State
43	Latimer, Al	CB	5-11	177	6	Clemson
64	Lee, Larry	G-C	6-2	260	5	UCLA
87	Lewis, David	TE	6-4	230	2	California
14	Machurek, Mike	QB	6-1	205	4	Idaho State
82	Mandley, Pete	WR	5-10	183	2	Northern Arizona
83	Martin, Robbie	PR-WR	5-8	177	5	Cal Poly-SLO
81	McCall, Reese	TE	6-6	232	8	Auburn
29	McNorton, Bruce	CB	5-11	175	4	Georgetown, Ky.
36	Meade, Mike	RB	5-10	224	4	Penn State
63	Moss, Martin	DE	6-4	252	4	UCLA
52	Mott, Steve	C	6-3	260	3	Alabama
3	Murray, Ed	K	5-10	175	6	Tulane
86	Nichols, Mark	WR	6-2	208	5	San Jose State
84	Rubick, Rob	TE	6-2	228	4	Grand Valley State
20	Sims, Billy	RB	6-0	212	6	Oklahoma
71	Strenger, Rich	T	6-7	269	3	Michigan
55	Tautolo, Terry	LB	6-2	227	10	UCLA
39	Thompson, Leonard	WR	5-11	192	11	Oklahoma State
27	Watkins, Bobby	CB	5-10	184	4	Southwest Texas State
76	Williams, Eric	DT	6-4	265	2	Washington State
59	Williams, Jimmy	LB	6-2	222	4	Nebraska
18	Witkowski, John	QB	6-2	200	2	Columbia

GREEN BAY PACKERS NFC Central

Address 1265, Lombardi Avenue, Green Bay, Wisconsin 54303.

Stadium Lambeau Field, Green Bay and Milwaukee County Stadium, Milwaukee.
Capacity (Lambeau Field) 56,155, (Milwaukee County Stadium) 55,958 *Playing Surfaces* Grass, both stadia.

Team Colours Dark Green, Gold and White.

Head Coach Forrest Gregg – second year.

Championships Division 1972;
NFL 1929,'30,'31,'36,'39,'44,'61,'62,'65,'66,'67;
Super Bowl 1966,'67.

History NFL 1921-69, NFC 1970-

Offense

Every year we love to say, 'The Pack is back', but it is usually more in hope than anticipation. However, a 7-1 record over the second half of the 1984 season must tell us something. Packer detractors will be quick to point out that five of these victories were over non-playoff teams. But in this period they did beat the eventual NFC Central Division Champion, the Chicago Bears, after having blasted the Rams, 31-6. The resurgence had its origins in a good 1984 draft, which produced three defensive starters, and gathered momentum when Ron Hallstrom and Tim Huffman settled in at right and left guard respectively, complementing the steady veterans, center Larry McCarren and tackles Karl Swanke and Greg Koch. Eddie Lee Ivery returned to action on Week Nine and promptly ripped off 116 yards. Gerry Ellis, who before then had been labouring, quickly followed suit and, between them, they tore the opposition apart. The same combination of players will line up to start the 1985 season and, not having to draft for immediate need, the Packers could afford the luxury of planning for the future by picking tackle Ken Ruettgers and guard Rich Moran with their first two draft options. In addition, veteran running backs Jessie Clark and Harlan Huckleby, both of whom averaged over four yards per carry, will be itching to have a go. Quarterback Lynn Dickey had a fine season when not nursing injuries and is expected to continue in the same vein, though the acquisition of the former Giants and Denver quarterback, Scott Brunner, was a sensible move.

That man, wide receiver James Lofton, shows no signs of slowing down, but his mate in what used to be known as the All-World partnership, John Jefferson, has suffered a loss of form. It is conceivable that Phil Epps will start ahead of Jefferson, whose trade would spring no surprise. Tight end Paul Coffman, who together with Lofton, represented Green Bay in the Pro Bowl, is a clutch receiver, brave and sure-handed. Sadly, reserve tight end and kick-blocker par excellence, Gary Lewis, has a respiratory disorder and may have to hang up his boots.

Defense

The emergence of three defensive starters has to help and that's exactly what defensive ends Alphonso Carreker and Donnie Humphrey, and free safety Tom Flynn did. Carreker and Humphrey were subjectively assessed as having had a satisfactory year as rookie starters. The experts had no choice in their opinion of Flynn – he (objectively) led the NFC by intercepting nine passes and defensing a whole lot more. In linebackers John Anderson, Randy Scott, George Cumby and Mike Douglass, the Packers already had the nerve centre of a good defense and, quite suddenly, the other pieces began falling into place. Nose tackle Terry Jones firmed up against the run and, in the secondary, Tim Lewis, a 1983 first-rounder, started hanging onto passes meant for the other guy and finished up with seven interceptions. Cornerback Mark Lee has an eye for the errant pass (he intercepts it) and strong safety Mark Murphy does what those healthy lads are supposed to do, namely, he knocks down the man with the ball. There's a comfortable depth at defensive back in the form of Estus Hood, a good nickel back, and Daryll Jones.

Special Teams

Trading Jan Stenerud to Minnesota was a mistake – why? Because Stenerud subsequently went to the Pro Bowl as the NFC's best placekicker. After a poor performance by Eddie Garcia, placekicker Al Del Greco did enough to keep his place on the roster. Bucky Scribner puts plenty of leg into his punts and ended with the third-best gross average in the NFC. The versatile Tom Flynn displayed his class when pressed into punt return duty, and did alright, averaging 8.5 yards per attempt. Running back Del Rodgers does most of the kickoff returning and thoroughly deserved to spike the ball after his 97-yarder against Chicago.

1985 DRAFT

Round	Name	Pos.	Ht.	Wt.	College
1.	Ruettgers, Ken	T	6-5	270	Southern California
3.	Moran, Rich	G	6-2	270	San Diego State
4.	Stanley, Walter	WR	5-9	180	Mesa (Colorado)
5.	Noble, Brian	LB	6-3	237	Arizona State
6.	Lewis, Mark	TE	6-1	220	Texas A&M
7.	Wilson, Eric	LB	6-1	245	Maryland
7.	Ellerson, Gary	RB	5-11	207	Wisconsin
8.	Stills, Ken	DB			Wisconsin
9.	Johnson, Morris	G		314	Alabama A&M
10.	Burgess, Ronnie	DB	5-10	174	Wake Forest
11.	Shield, Joe	QB	6-1	190	Trinity, Conn.
12.	Meyer, Jim	P	6-4	210	Arizona State

Center Larry McCarren, a veteran of the 'trenches'

1985 SCHEDULE

September

8	at New England	1:00
15	NEW YORK GIANTS	4:00
22	NEW YORK JETS	
	(Milwaukee)	4:00
29	at St Louis	1:00

October

6	DETROIT	1:00
13	MINNESOTA	
	(Milwaukee)	1:00
21	at Chicago	9:00
27	at Indianapolis	1:00

November

3	CHICAGO	1:00
10	at Minnesota	1:00
17	NEW ORLEANS	
	(Milwaukee)	1:00
24	at Los Angeles Rams	4:00

December

1	TAMPA BAY	1:00
8	MIAMI	1:00
15	at Detroit	1:00
22	at Tampa Bay	1:00

VETERAN ROSTER

No.	Name	Pos.	Ht.	Wt.	NFL Year	College
59	Anderson, John	LB	6-3	229	8	Michigan
93	Brown, Robert	DE	6-2	250	4	Virginia Tech.
	Brunner, Scott	QB	6-5	200	6	Delaware
58	Cannon, Mark	C	6-3	258	2	Texas-Arlington
76	Carreker, Alphonso	DE	6-6	260	2	Florida State
88	Cassidy, Ron	WR	6-0	180	6	Utah State
33	Clark, Jessie	RB	6-0	233	3	Arkansas
82	Coffman, Paul	TE	6-3	225	8	Kansas State
21	Crouse, Ray	RB	5-11	214	2	Nevada-Las Vegas
52	Cumby, George	LB	6-1	224	6	Oklahoma
10	Del Greco, Al	K	5-10	180	2	Auburn
	DeLuca, Tony	NT	6-4	250	2	Rhode Island
12	Dickey, Lynn	QB	6-4	203	15	Kansas State
99	Dorsey, John	LB	6-2	235	2	Connecticut
53	Douglass, Mike	LB	6-0	214	8	San Diego State
61	Drechsler, Dave	G	6-2	264	3	North Carolina
31	Ellis, Gerry	RB	5-11	225	6	Missouri
85	Epps, Phillip	WR	5-10	155	4	Texas Christian
41	Flynn, Tom	S	6-10	195	2	Pittsburgh
11	Garcia, Eddie	K	5-8	178	3	Southern Methodist
65	Hallstrom, Ron	G-T	6-6	283	4	Iowa
69	Harris, Leotis	G	6-1	265	7	Arkansas
27	Hayes, Gary	CB	5-10	180	2	Fresno State
	Hoffman, Gary	T	6-7	282	2	Santa Clara
38	Hood, Estus	CB	5-11	189	8	Illinois State
25	Huckleby, Harlan	RB	6-1	201	6	Michigan
74	Huffman, Tim	G-T	6-5	282	5	Notre Dame
79	Humphrey, Donnie	DE	6-3	275	2	Auburn
40	Ivery, Eddie Lee	RB	6-1	214	6	Georgia Tech.
83	Jefferson, John	WR	6-1	204	8	Arizona State
90	Johnson, Ezra	DE	6-4	259	8	Morris Brown
43	Jones, Daryll	DB	6-0	190	2	Georgia
63	Jones, Terry	NT	6-2	253	7	Alabama
68	Koch, Greg	T	6-4	276	7	Arkansas
22	Lee, Mark	CB	5-11	188	6	Washington
56	Lewis, Cliff	LB	6-1	224	5	Southern Mississippi
81	Lewis, Gary	TE	6-5	234	5	Texas-Arlington
26	Lewis, Tim	CB	5-11	191	3	Pittsburgh
80	Lofton, James	WR	6-3	197	8	Stanford
94	Martin, Charles	DE	6-4	270	2	Livingston
54	McCarren, Larry	C	6-3	251	13	Illinois
29	McCoy, Mike	CB	5-11	190	10	Colorado
28	McLeod, Mike	S			2	
60	Moore, Blake	C-G	6-5	267	6	Wooster
37	Murphy, Mark	S	6-2	201	5	West Liberty, W. Va.
51	Prather, Guy	LB	6-2	229	5	Grambling
35	Rodgers, Del	RB	5-10	202	3	Utah
55	Scott, Randy	LB	6-1	222	5	Alabama
13	Scribner, Bucky	P	6-0	202	3	Kansas
67	Swanke, Karl	T	6-6	262	6	Boston College
	Taylor, Lenny	WR	5-10	173	2	Tennessee-Knoxville
70	Uecker, Keith	T	6-5	260	4	Auburn
86	West, Ed	TE	6-1	242	2	Auburn
50	Wingo, Rich	LB	6-1	227	6	Alabama
16	Wright, Randy	QB	6-2	194	2	Wisconsin

MINNESOTA VIKINGS NFC Central

Address 9520, Viking Drive, Eden Prairie, Minnesota 55344.

Stadium Hubert H. Humphrey Metrodome, Minneapolis. *Capacity* 62,212 *Playing Surface* Super Turf.

Team Colours Purple, Gold and White.

Head Coach Bud Grant – eighteenth year (he went into temporary retirement for last season).

Championships Division 1970,'71,'73,'74,'75,'76,'77,'78,'80; Conference 1973,'74,'76; NFL 1969.

History NFL 1961-69, NFC 1970-

Offense

Head coach Bud Grant has a man-sized task ahead of him, bringing the Vikings back into contention. And, if anything, the Central division opposition has become that bit tougher over the year he has been away. The first problem will be solved if veteran quarterback Tommy Kramer has recovered sufficiently from a shoulder injury which kept him out for the last four games of 1984. He wouldn't qualify for the description, 'great', but he's a neat, efficient pro who could expect a passer rating somewhere in the high 70s, and he'll complete a lot of the important passes. The 14-year veteran, Archie Manning, and Wade Wilson shared the load when Kramer was injured. In all fairness, Wilson is not yet ready to start and Manning may be past his best. Steve Bono was drafted in the sixth round but he is not likely to produce more than the existing reserves. Quite simply, it is imperative that Kramer returns. They could do with another wide receiver to complement Leo Lewis, who led the team with 47 receptions for 830 yards. He's improved significantly – he caught only 22 passes in the previous three years. Mike Jones, the other starter, moved ahead of the veteran Sammy White but tailed off towards the end of the campaign. Surprisingly, 'Buster' Rhymes was still available when it came to the Vikings' pick in the fourth round. He could turn out to be just the player they need. Tight end Joe Senser hasn't been match fit since the 1983 preseason. In his absence, Steve Jordan saw a lot more playing time and did well. Again, though, former Pro Bowler Senser is the man with the talents needed to bring the Vikings back. Rookie running back

Alfred Anderson was a pleasant surprise, rushing for 773 yards and with two early-season 100-yard games. He didn't catch many passes but completed three, two of which were for touchdowns. It's a mystery why running backs Ted Brown and the explosive Darrin Nelson aren't used more often. They averaged 4.5 and 5.1 yards respectively. With the arrival of the third-round draftees, center Kirk Lowdermilk and tackle Tim Long, there was some reinforcement for an offensive line which had its difficulties last year.

Defense

Let's get the worst bit over and done with. In 1984, in every major area of defense, the Vikings ranked last in the NFC, and in yardage given up they came bottom of the NFL. The reasons for this are difficult to identify. There are quality veterans available for most positions, particularly going from defensive left end all the way to right outside linebacker. Defensive ends Doug Martin and Neil Elshire really ought to be able to mount a pass rush – they certainly did in 1983 when they registered 22.5 sacks between them. Nose tackle Charlie Johnson and left outside linebacker Matt Blair have played in the Pro Bowl three and six times respectively. Right outside linebacker Fred McNeill has been a good pro for eleven years. Perhaps that's the explanation – the good players may have been around for too long. There are two excellent prospects just arriving, in the form of first-round draftee Chris Doleman and third-rounder Tim Meamber. Both play at linebacker, on the outside and inside respectively. The second-round draftee, safety Issiac Holt, could help out immediately in a defensive secondary, which is reinforced further by the return of a former starter, safety Keith Nord, after a year's absence.

Special Teams

Placekicker Jan Stenerud became the oldest man to play in the Pro Bowl (he was 41) when making his fourth appearance last January. He was an inspired acquisition from the Packers. Punter Greg Coleman just goes on improving (punting for at least half the time indoors may be a factor). Last year he was 2.2 yards better than his previous career average of 40.2. Darrin Nelson is a solid punt and kickoff returner, assisted in the latter category by the versatile Alfred Anderson.

1985 DRAFT

Round	Name	Pos.	Ht.	Wt.	College
1.	Doleman, Chris	LB	6-5	235	Pittsburgh
2.	Holt, Issiac	DB	6-1	190	Alcorn State
3.	Lowdermilk, Kirk	C	6-3	265	Ohio State
3.	Meamber, Tim	LB	6-2	225	Washington
3.	Long, Tim	T	6-6	285	Memphis State
4.	Rhymes, 'Buster'	WR	6-2	200	Oklahoma
4.	Morrell, Kyle	DB	6-0	190	Brigham Young
5.	MacDonald, Mark	G	6-4	265	Boston College
6.	Bono, Steve	QB	6-3	210	UCLA
6.	Newton, Tim	NT	5-11	280	Florida
8.	Blair, Nikita	LB	6-2	220	Texas-El Paso
9.	Covington, Jaime	RB	6-0	215	Syracuse
10.	Johnson, Juan	WR	5-11	185	Langston, Oklahoma
11.	Williams, Tim	DB	6-1	190	North Carolina A&T
12.	Jones, Byron	NT	6-4	270	Tulsa

Rookie success Alfred Anderson

1985 SCHEDULE

September

8	SAN FRANCISCO	1:00
15	at Tampa Bay	4:00
19	CHICAGO	8:00
29	at Buffalo	1:00

October

6	at Los Angeles Rams	4:00
13	vs. Green Bay	
	(Milwaukee)	1:00
20	SAN DIEGO	1:00
27	at Chicago	1:00

November

3	DETROIT	1:00
10	GREEN BAY	1:00
17	at Detroit	4:00
24	NEW ORLEANS	1:00

December

1	at Philadelphia	1:00
8	TAMPA BAY	4:00
15	at Atlanta	1:00
22	PHILADELPHIA	1:00

VETERAN ROSTER

No.	Name	Pos.	Ht.	Wt.	NFL Year	College
46	Anderson, Alfred	RB	6-0	214	2	Baylor
69	Arbubakrr, Hasson	DE	6-4	250	3	Texas Tech.
58	Ashley, Walker	LB	6-0	240	3	Penn State
21	Bess, Rufus	CB	5-9	185	7	South Carolina State
59	Blair, Matt	LB	6-5	235	12	Iowa State
62	Boyd, Brent	G	6-3	275	6	UCLA
23	Brown, Ted	RB	5-10	210	7	North Carolina State
47	Browner, Joey	CB-S	6-2	205	3	Southern California
82	Bruer, Bob	TE	6-5	240	7	Mankato State
63	Cobb, Robert	DE	6-4	250	3	Arizona
8	Coleman, Greg	P	6-0	185	9	Florida A&M
84	Collins, Dwight	WR	6-1	200	2	Pittsburgh
43	Colter, Jeff	CB	5-10	164	2	Kansas
73	Elshire, Neil	DE	6-6	260	5	Oregon
64	Feasel, Grant	T-C	6-8	267	3	Abilene Christian
50	Fowlkes, Dennis	LB	6-2	230	3	West Virginia
25	Green, Marcellus	CB	6-0	183	2	Arizona
90	Haines, John	DE	6-6	263	2	Texas
61	Hamilton, Wes	G	6-3	270	10	Tulsa
45	Hannon, Tom	S	5-11	195	9	Michigan State
60	Hernandez, Matt	T	6-6	260	3	Purdue
51	Hough, Jim	G	6-2	275	8	Utah State
76	Irwin, Tim	T	6-6	285	5	Tennessee
65	Johnson, Charlie	NT	6-3	275	9	Colorado
52	Johnson, Dennis	LB	6-3	235	6	Southern California
89	Jones, Mike	WR	5-11	176	3	Tennessee State
83	Jordan, Steve	TE	6-3	230	4	Brown
9	Kramer, Tommy	QB	6-2	205	9	Rice
39	Lee, Carl	S	5-11	185	3	Marshall
87	Lewis, Leo	WR	5-8	170	5	Missouri
4	Manning, Archie	QB	6-3	211	15	Mississippi
56	Martin, Chris	LB	6-2	220	3	Auburn
79	Martin, Doug	TE	6-3	255	6	Washington
54	McNeill, Fred	LB	6-2	230	12	UCLA
86	Mularkey, Mike	TE	6-4	245	3	Florida
77	Mullaney, Mark	DE	6-6	245	11	Colorado State
20	Nelson, Darrin	RB	5-9	180	4	Stanford
49	Nord, Keith	S	6-0	195	7	St Cloud State
36	Rice, Allen	RB	5-10	200	2	Baylor
78	Riley, Steve	T	6-6	260	12	Southern California
68	Rouse, Curtis	G	6-3	305	4	Tennessee-Chattanooga
67	Sams, Ron	C	6-3	269	3	Pittsburgh
57	Sendlein, Robin	LB	6-3	225	5	Texas
81	Senser, Joe	TE	6-4	235	6	West Chester State
91	Smith, Greg	NT	6-3	270	2	Kansas
3	Stenerud, Jan	K	6-2	190	19	Montana State
55	Studwell, Scott	LB	6-2	230	9	Illinois
29	Swain, John	CB	6-1	195	5	Miami
66	Tausch, Terry	T	6-5	275	4	Texas
37	Teal, Willie	CB	5-10	195	6	Louisiana State
24	Turner, Maurice	RB	5-11	200	2	Utah State
34	Wagoner, Dan	DB	5-10	180	3	Kansas
85	White, Sammy	WR	5-11	195	10	Grambling
11	Wilson, Wade	QB	6-3	210	5	East Texas State

TAMPA BAY BUCCANEERS NFC Central

Address One Buccaneer Place, Tampa, Florida 33607.
Stadium Tampa Stadium, Tampa.
   Capacity 74,270 *Playing Surface* Grass.
Team Colours Florida Orange, White and Red.
Head Coach Leeman Bennett – first year.
Championships Division 1979, '81.
History AFC 1976, NFC 1977-

Offense

There are lots of positives about the Buccaneers offense which was held to under ten points only twice last year. In all the furore surrounding Eric Dickerson's chase for O.J. Simpson's records, not many people noticed that Tampa Bay's brilliant dual-purpose runner, James Wilder, was homing in on the single-season record for combined yardage (rushing and pass receiving only). In the end, he fell 15 yards short of the record 2,244 newly established by Dickerson. Even though Wilder is the powerful heart of the offense it is by no means a one-man show. Certainly, last year, he was the only one who did any rushing of note, but the passing offense has its share of good and improving players. Quarterback Steve DeBerg could be starting at San Francisco, but for the presence of Joe Montana, and at Denver but for John Elway. He starts for the Buccaneers, despite the presence of reserve Jack Thompson, a former first-round pick of Cincinnati. Wide receiver Kevin House has been a good one for five years but, for the first time in their history, the Bucs now have a pair with the continued improvement of Gerald Carter. Wilder, House and Carter were placed 2nd, 5th and 12th in the NFC for number of pass receptions. The Buccaneers might expect a little more from the tight end position – around the league there are eight tight ends who each caught more than 50 passes, whereas Jerry Bell and former Pro Bowler Jimmie Giles caught just 53 between them. On the offensive line, the former Pittsburgh Steeler, left guard Steve Courson, made a significant contribution. Back in 1982, the Bucs were pleased with their number one draft pick, guard Sean Farrell, and they went to the same proving ground for tackle Ron Heller, who was drafted in round four last year. Together, the two former Penn State players take care of the right side of the line.

Defense

Injuries to starting linebackers Hugh Green and Cecil Johnson, and starting safety Cedric Brown, disturbed a defense which was beginning to look more like the 1979 version which was the best in pro football and played a major role in the team's advance to the NFC Championship Game. All three will be fit in 1985, and it is a measure of the existing strength that only Green can be certain of finding a place in the starting lineup. First-round draftee Ron Holmes is tremendously fast and will help a pass rush which, last year, sacked the quarterback just 32 times. Playing at defensive right end, Lee Roy Selmon is one of the game's most dominant players. He can look back on six consecutive Pro Bowl selections as a starter. Hugh Green lines up behind Selmon to form a partnership which the opposition likes to avoid. The arrival of third-round draftee Ervin Randle, who is an inside linebacker, could help a defense which just couldn't stop the run. Two youthful cornerbacks, Jeremiah Castille and John Holt, and a pair of tough veteran safeties, Mark Cotney and Beasley Reece, make up a good starting defensive secondary. Cotney, who was one of the original Buccaneers, back in 1976, had his best year for pass interceptions with a team-leading five.

Special Teams

Last year, Tampa Bay gave Nigerian-born Obed Ariri, a 1981 seventh-round pick of the Colts, his first opportunity to kick in the NFL. He responded by establishing a team scoring record with 95 points (field goals and PATs). Punter Frank Garcia was another who couldn't make the grade elsewhere – he has been released by five NFL teams since his entry in 1979. His gross average of 41.9 yards was good enough for sixth place in the NFC. Michael Morton continued as one of the NFC's better kickoff returners but Leon Bright was outside the top group in punt returning.

1985 DRAFT

Round	Name	Pos.	Ht.	Wt.	College
1.	Holmes, Ron	DE	6-3	255	Washington
3.	Randle, Ervin	LB	6-1	245	Baylor
4.	Heaven, Mike	DB	5-11	188	Illinois
7.	Prior, Mike	DB	5-11	190	Illinois State
8.	Freeman, Phil	WR			Arizona
9.	Calabria, Steve	QB	6-3	215	Colgate
10.	Igwebuike, Donald	K	5-8	172	Clemson
11.	Williams, James	RB	5-9	200	Memphis State
12.	Rockford, Jim	DB	5-10	185	Oklahoma
12.	Melka, Jim	LB	6-0	231	Wisconsin

Tampa Bay's All-Pro defensive end, Lee Roy Selmon (#63)

1985 SCHEDULE

September
8	at Chicago	1:00
15	MINNESOTA	4:00
22	at New Orleans	1:00
29	at Detroit	1:00

October
6	CHICAGO	1:00
13	LOS ANGELES RAMS	1:00
20	at Miami	4:00
27	NEW ENGLAND	1:00

November
3	at New York Giants	1:00
10	ST LOUIS	1:00
17	at New York Jets	1:00
24	DETROIT	1:00

December
1	at Green Bay	1:00
8	at Minnesota	4:00
15	INDIANAPOLIS	1:00
22	GREEN BAY	1:00

VETERAN ROSTER

No.	Name	Pos.	Ht.	Wt.	NFL Year	College
27	Acorn, Fred	CB	5-10	185	2	Texas
2	Ariri, Obed	K	5-8	170	2	Clemson
46	Armstrong, Adger	RB	6-0	225	6	Texas A&M
82	Bell, Jerry	TE	6-5	225	4	Arizona State
83	Bell, Theo	WR	6-0	190	9	Arizona
71	Braggs, Byron	DE	6-4	270	5	Alabama
52	Brantley, Scot	LB	6-1	230	6	Florida
29	Bright, Leon	RB-PR	5-9	192	5	Florida State
34	Brown, Cedric	S	6-2	200	9	Kent State
57	Browner, Keith	LB	6-5	225	2	Southern California
77	Bujnoch, Glenn	G	6-6	265	10	Texas A&M
78	Cannon, John	DE	6-5	260	4	William & Mary
86	Carroll, Jay	TE	6-4	230	2	Minnesota
87	Carter, Gerald	WR	6-1	190	6	Texas A&M
28	Carver, Mel	RB	5-11	215	4	Nevada-Las Vegas
23	Castille, Jeremiah	CB	5-10	175	3	Alabama
33	Cotney, Mark	S	6-0	205	10	Cameron, Oklahoma
72	Courson, Steve	G	6-1	270	8	South Carolina
31	Curry, Craig	S	6-0	187	2	Texas
58	Davis, Jeff	LB	6-0	230	4	Clemson
17	DeBerg, Steve	QB	6-3	205	9	San Jose State
25	Dierking, Scott	RB	5-10	220	9	Purdue
81	Dixon, Dwayne	WR	6-1	199	2	Florida
62	Farrell, Sean	G	6-3	260	4	Penn State
5	Garcia, Frank	P	6-0	205	3	Arizona
88	Giles, Jimmie	TE	6-3	240	9	Alcorn State
53	Green, Hugh	LB	6-2	225	5	Pittsburgh
60	Grimes, Randy	C	6-4	265	3	Baylor
24	Harvey, Maurice	DB	5-9	187	7	Ball State
73	Heller, Ron	T	6-6	265	2	Penn State
21	Holt, John	CB	5-11	175	5	West Texas State
89	House, Kevin	WR	6-1	175	6	Southern Illinois
56	Johnson, Cecil	LB	6-2	235	9	Pittsburgh
79	Kaplan, Ken	T	6-4	275	2	New Hampshire
16	Kiel, Blair	QB	6-0	200	2	Notre Dame
76	Logan, Dave	NT	6-2	250	7	Pittsburgh
67	Morgan, Karl	NT	6-1	255	2	UCLA
20	Morton, Michael	KR-RB	5-8	180	4	Nevada-Las Vegas
26	Owens, James	RB	5-11	200	7	UCLA
38	Peoples, George	RB	6-0	215	4	Auburn
43	Reece, Beasley	S	6-1	195	10	North Texas State
74	Sanders, Eugene	T	6-3	280	7	Texas A&M
63	Selmon, Lee Roy	DE	6-3	250	10	Oklahoma
55	Spradlin, Danny	LB	6-1	235	5	Tennessee
70	Thomas, Kelly	T	6-6	270	3	Southern California
41	Thomas, Norris	CB	6-0	180	9	Southern Mississippi
	Thomas, Zack	WR-KR	6-0	182	3	South Carolina State
14	Thompson, Jack	QB	6-3	220	6	Washington State
59	Thompson, Robert	LB	6-3	225	3	Michigan
	Tyler, Andre	WR	6-0	180	4	Stanford
51	Washington, Chris	LB	6-4	220	2	Iowa State
40	Washington, Mike	CB	6-2	200	10	Alabama
32	Wilder, James	RB	6-3	220	5	Missouri
50	Wilson, Steve	C	6-4	270	10	Georgia
85	Witte, Mark	TE	6-3	235	3	North Texas State
54	Wood, Richard	LB	6-2	230	11	Southern California

ATLANTA FALCONS NFC West

Address Suwanee Road at I-85, Suwanee, Georgia 30174.
Stadium Atlanta-Fulton County Stadium.
Capacity 60,748 *Playing Surface* Grass.
Team Colours Red, Black, White and Silver.
Head Coach Dan Henning – third year.
Championships Division 1980.
History NFL 1966-69, NFC 1970-

Offense

The offensive line is normally considered an Atlanta strength. Center Jeff Van Note, tackle Mike Kenn and guard R.C. Thielemann have thirteen Pro Bowl appearances between them and lined up together in both the 1982 and 1983 games. Overall, however, the unit has slipped a little. At the end of 1983 the lack of mobility at quarterback was an easy explanation for having given up 55 sacks. Last year, they yielded 67 (for a loss of almost 500 yards), ranking dead last in the league. First-round draftee Bill Fralic was the best offensive lineman in college and should be an instant starter. The news on William Andrews, who is probably the NFL's best dual-purpose backfield player, is gloomy. And, even if he comes back after his serious knee injury of August, 1984, he is unlikely ever to be a danger. It's as well for Atlanta that Gerald Riggs is around. Stepping into the limelight, he blasted out 1,486 yards in a season when he, too, was slowed by injuries. He is supported by Lynn Cain, who used to partner Andrews in the pro set formation, but will give Riggs a rest from time to time in Atlanta's H-Back formation (it uses only one running back). Quarterback Steve Bartkowski is coming off a disappointing season in which his best single-game passing yardage was 299 and only once did he pass for three touchdowns in a game. He missed five of the last six games with injury. He's still the best man for the starting job but David Archer may move ahead of Mike Moroski as the senior reserve. Yet another setback came when Billy 'White Shoes' Johnson was sidelined on Week Six. He's a really important part of this Atlanta offense, catching passes at wide receiver, returning punts or just simply for his enthusiasm. In his third NFL season, Stacey Bailey became the club's premier wide receiver, catching passes for over 1,000 yards for the first time. Alfred Jackson, too, is coming off the best of several good pro years. Of the two players one might call tight ends, Arthur Cox is the more likely to catch passes but the other, H-back Cliff Benson, who was one of two rookies to start, developed well as a blocker and seems to be just right for the system.

Defense

Last year the Falcons used their first five draft choices for defense. Of these, defensive tackle Rick Bryan became a starter of real class and three others made the squad. Again the Falcons have looked for players in positions throughout the defense and, by drafting second-rounder Mike Gann, have a sound backup for the returning Mike Pitts. Last year they never were able to put opposing quarterbacks under much pressure – defensive end Don Smith led with six out of a team total 38 sacks – and the need for outside pass rushing is clear. It's not likely to come from the existing outside linebackers, Al Richardson and David Frye, who are better against the run. Buddy Curry, playing in the middle position, remains the pick of the three starters. The defensive secondary contains three experienced starters, Bobby Butler, Tom Pridemore and Kenny Johnson. The fourth, right cornerback James Britt, was a second-round pick in 1983. They need perhaps a little more aggression in going for the ball – left safety Johnson was responsible for five of a modest team total of twelve interceptions on the year.

Special Teams

Kicker Mick Luckhurst is now established in the NFL. Last year he missed only one field goal attempt below 40 yards and kicked three of four over 50 yards. Punter Ralph Giacomarro improved in his second year as a pro – his gross average was up 1.7 yards per attempt to 42.0. 'White Shoes' averages 12.3 yards over a career 240 punt returns and regularly places the team in scoring position with his elusive running. His rehabilitation from injury is crucial. Sylvester 'Zip Code' Stamps shares the kick returning with Kenny Johnson but is more productive by almost five yards per return.

1985 DRAFT

Round	Name	Pos.	Ht.	Wt.	College
1.	Fralic, Bill	T	6-5	285	Pittsburgh
2.	Gann, Mike	DE	6-5	255	Notre Dame
4.	Harry, Emile	WR	5-10	170	Stanford
6.	Pleasant, Reggie	DB			Clemson
8.	Lee, Ashley	DB	6-1	195	Virginia Tech.
8.	Washington, Ronnie	LB	6-0	230	Northeastern Louisiana
9.	Moon, Micah	LB	6-0	225	North Carolina
10.	Martin, Brent	C	6-3	265	Stanford
11.	Ayres, John	DB			Illinois
12.	Whisenhunt, Ken	TE	6-2	228	Georgia Tech.

1985 SCHEDULE

September

8	DETROIT	1:00
15	at San Francisco	4:00
22	DENVER	1:00
29	at Los Angeles Rams	4:00

October

6	SAN FRANCISCO	1:00
13	at Seattle	4:00
20	NEW ORLEANS	1:00
27	at Dallas	1:00

November

3	WASHINGTON	1:00
10	at Philadelphia	1:00
17	LOS ANGELES RAMS	1:00
24	at Chicago	1:00

December

1	LOS ANGELES RAIDERS	4:00
8	at Kansas City	1:00
15	MINNESOTA	1:00
22	at New Orleans	1:00

Gerald Riggs (#42) has taken over as Atlanta's main rushing threat

VETERAN ROSTER

No.	Name	Pos.	Ht.	Wt.	NFL Year	College
31	Andrews, William	RB	6-0	213	7	Auburn
16	Archer, David	QB	6-1	200	2	Iowa State
39	Austin, Cliff	RB	6-0	190	3	Clemson
82	Bailey, Stacey	WR	6-1	160	4	San Jose State
10	Bartkowski, Steve	QB	6-4	218	11	California
69	Benish, Dan	DT-DE	6-5	265	3	Clemson
87	Benson, Cliff	TE	6-3	237	2	Purdue
53	Benson, Thomas	LB	6-2	235	2	Oklahoma
26	Britt, James	DB	6-0	185	3	Louisiana State
77	Bryan, Rick	DT	6-4	260	2	Oklahoma
73	Burley, Gary	DT	6-3	282	10	Pittsburgh
23	Butler, Bobby	CB	5-11	175	5	Florida State
21	Cain, Lynn	RB	6-1	205	8	Southern California
25	Case, Scott	S	6-0	178	2	Oklahoma
70	Chapman, Mike	T-G	6-3	250	2	Texas
88	Cox, Arthur	TE	6-3	245	3	Texas Southern
89	Curran, Willie	WR	5-10	175	4	UCLA
50	Curry, Buddy	LB	6-4	228	6	North Carolina
71	Dufour, Dan	G-T	6-5	280	3	UCLA
58	Frye, David	LB	6-2	205	3	Purdue
34	Gaison, Blane	S	6-1	188	6	Hawaii
1	Giacomarro, Ralph	P	6-0	190	3	Penn State
75	Harris, Roy	DT	6-2	261	2	Florida
83	Hodge, Floyd	WR	6-0	190	4	Utah
85	Jackson, Alfred	WR	6-0	185	8	Texas
51	Jackson, Jeff	LB	6-0	235	2	Auburn
81	Johnson, Billy	WR	5-9	170	10	Widener
37	Johnson, Kenny	S	5-11	172	6	Mississippi State
20	Jones, Earl	CB	6-1	175	6	Norfolk State
78	Kenn, Mike	T	6-7	255	8	Michigan
54	Kuykendall, Fulton	LB	6-4	228	11	UCLA
80	Landrum, Mike	TE	6-2	231	2	Southern Mississippi
55	Levenick, Dave	LB	6-3	220	3	Wisconsin
18	Luckhurst, Mick	K	6-0	180	5	California
52	Malancon, Rydell	LB	6-2	219	2	Louisiana State
49	Matthews, Allama	TE	6-3	230	3	Vanderbilt
62	Miller, Brett	T	6-7	275	3	Iowa
15	Moroski, Mike	QB	6-4	200	7	Cal-Davis
64	Pellegrini, Joe	C-G	6-4	252	4	Harvard
74	Pitts, Mike	DE	6-5	260	3	Alabama
27	Pridemore, Tom	S	5-11	186	8	West Virginia
72	Provence, Andrew	DE	6-3	265	3	South Carolina
59	Rade, John	LB	6-1	220	3	Boise State
	Radloff, Wayne	C	6-5	265	1	Georgia
56	Richardson, Al	LB	6-3	220	6	Georgia Tech.
42	Riggs, Gerald	RB	6-1	230	4	Arizona State
67	Sanders, Eric	T	6-7	270	5	Nevada-Reno
61	Scully, John	G	6-6	255	5	Notre Dame
41	Seay, Virgil	WR	5-9	175	5	Troy State
48	Small, Gerald	CB	5-11	192	8	San Jose State
65	Smith, Don	DT-DE	6-5	260	7	Miami
84	Stamps, Sylvester	WR	5-7	166	2	Jackson State
96	Taylor, Johnny	LB	6-2	234	2	Hawaii
68	Thielemann, R.C.	G	6-4	252	9	Arkansas
86	Tuttle, Perry	WR	6-0	180	4	Clemson
32	Tyrrell, Tim	RB	6-1	201	2	Northern Illinois
57	Van Note, Jeff	C	6-2	250	17	Kentucky
	Washington, Joe	RB	5-10	179	9	Oklahoma

LOS ANGELES RAMS NFC West

Address 2327 West Lincoln Avenue, Anaheim, California 92801.

Stadium Anaheim Stadium, Anaheim.
Capacity 69,007 *Playing Surface* Grass.

Team Colours Royal Blue, Gold and White.

Head Coach John Robinson – third year.

Championships Division 1973, '74, '75, '76, '77, '78, '79; Conference 1979; NFL 1945, '51.

History NFL 1937-69, NFC 1970-
(Until 1946, they were known as the Cleveland Rams.)

Offense

The Rams are steadily re-establishing the reputation which always meant that they would be pencilled in for postseason competition, even before they had thrown a block in anger. Ever mindful of that description applied increasingly to his offense, namely, 'one-dimensional', coach John Robinson acquired the former CFL quarterback, Dieter Brock, to service his array of fleet-footed wide receivers. Each of Drew Hill, Ron Brown and Henry Ellard, have the speed to go deep and make the difficult receptions. Robinson is hoping that Brock will be able to find them more consistently than last year's stand-in, Jeff Kemp, and the former starter, Vince Ferragamo, who has lost some of the bite in his passes and will almost certainly look for a new home. David Hill, formerly an orthodox tight end with Detroit, has developed into a useful U-back in the Rams' Single-Back formation and could spend more time in this role, given a return to form by Mike Barber. And what of that single back? Eric Dickerson is already a legend after only two seasons in the league. Jim Brown, O.J. Simpson and the like never played in this widely-used formation, one refinement of which enhances the effectiveness of a great backfield player. So we can't make comparisons. But, for sure, not one current running back compares with Dickerson, accelerating up to the line bristling with the certainty of impending success. The offensive line has played a major part in springing Dickerson out of the backfield. Left guard Kent Hill, right guard Dennis Harrah, center Doug Smith and tackle Jackie Slater, are Pro Bowlers. Slater is coming back after injury but will find it difficult to displace right tackle Bill Bain. Russ Bolinger, who was a valuable acquisition from Detroit in 1983, is a versatile reserve able to fit in at either guard or tackle. It all adds up to the best Rams offensive unit for some years. The games with their upstate rivals, the Super Bowl Champion 49ers, are eagerly anticipated.

Defense

The loss of several defensive stars was a critical factor in the Rams' premature exit from the 1984 playoffs. Earlier in the season, they had been without starting free safety Johnnie Johnson and Gary Jeter, the latter who starts at defensive tackle when the Rams use a four-man line and otherwise is a reserve defensive end. Starting cornerback Eric Harris and the four-time Pro Bowler, strong safety Nolan Cromwell, both went down and out as did starting outside linebacker George Andrews. The final straw was a late-season back injury to the indomitable defensive end, Jack Youngblood. He's the sort who will play despite such trifles but, in his case, bravery might not be enough – he may have to retire after fourteen glorious years, seven of them as a Pro Bowler. The rest should be back to give the Rams a defense to rate with the best. Pro Bowler Gary Green, for whom the Rams gave Kansas City their 1984 first- and a fifth-round draft option, has a lock on the left cornerback spot and LeRoy Irvin, interception returner extraordinaire, will be difficult to displace on the right corner. English-born Vince Newsome will be an excellent reserve for Nolan Cromwell at strong safety. They are joined by the best college safety available in the draft, Jerry Gray, who accordingly was selected in round one. Andrews will replace Mike Wilcher at right outside linebacker bringing the team back to full strength.

Special Teams

Kicker Mike Lansford secured his tenure with the Rams by finishing the season with a flourish, including a club record 13 consecutive field goals. But punter John Misko will be under pressure from draftee Dale Hatcher. Henry Ellard returned the punts for two touchdowns and an NFC-best average of 13.4 yards. The kickoff return department is in the safe hands of Drew Hill and Barry Redden, who tied with Stump Mitchell for the NFC lead.

1985 DRAFT

Round	Name	Pos.	Ht.	Wt.	College
1.	Gray, Jerry	DB	6-0	185	Texas
2.	Scott, Chuck	WR	6-1	205	Vanderbilt
3.	Hatcher, Dale	P	6-0	200	Clemson
5.	Greene, Kevin	LB	6-2	240	Auburn
6.	Young, Mike	WR	6-0	190	UCLA
6.	Johnson, Damone	TE	6-4	228	Cal Poly-SLO
7.	Bradley, Danny	RB	5-10	185	Oklahoma
8.	McIntyre, Marlon	RB	5-11	210	Pittsburgh
9.	Swanson, Gary	LB	6-1	226	Cal Poly-SLO
10.	Love, Duval	G	6-2	265	UCLA
11.	Flutie, Doug	QB	5-9	177	Boston College
11.	Brown, Kevin	DB			Northwestern

1985 SCHEDULE

September

8	DENVER	4:00
15	at Philadelphia	1:00
23	at Seattle	9:00
29	ATLANTA	4:00

October

6	MINNESOTA	4:00
13	at Tampa Bay	1:00
20	at Kansas City	1:00
27	SAN FRANCISCO	4:00

November

3	NEW ORLEANS	4:00
10	at New York Giants	1:00
17	at Atlanta	1:00
24	GREEN BAY	4:00

December

1	at New Orleans	1:00
9	at San Francisco	9:00
15	ST LOUIS	4:00
23	LOS ANGELES RAIDERS	9:00

Linebacker Jim Collins (#50)

VETERAN ROSTER

No.	Name	Pos.	Ht.	Wt.	NFL Year	College
52	Andrews, George	LB	6-3	225	7	Nebraska
62	Bain, Bill	T	6-4	290	11	Southern California
86	Barber, Mike	TE	6-3	237	10	Louisiana Tech.
96	Barnett, Doug	DE	6-3	250	4	Azusa Pacific
73	Bolinger, Russ	G	6-5	255	9	Cal St-Long Beach
90	Brady, Ed	LB	6-2	228	2	Illinois
	Brock, Dieter	QB			1	
89	Brown, Ron	WR	5-11	181	2	Arizona State
50	Collins, Jim	LB	6-2	230	5	Syracuse
21	Cromwell, Nolan	S	6-1	200	9	Kansas
28	Croudip, David	CB-S	5-9	183	2	San Diego State
45	Crutchfield, Dwayne	RB	6-0	235	4	Iowa State
70	DeJurnett, Charles	NT	6-4	260	9	San Jose State
29	Dickerson, Eric	RB	6-3	220	3	Southern Methodist
8	Dils, Steve	QB	6-1	195	6	Stanford
71	Doss, Reggie	DE	6-4	263	8	Hampton
55	Ekern, Carl	LB	6-3	222	9	San Jose State
80	Ellard, Henry	WR	5-11	170	3	Fresno State
84	Farmer, George	WR	5-10	175	4	Southern U.
88	Faulkner, Chris	TE	6-4	260	2	Florida
15	Ferragamo, Vince	QB	6-3	212	8	Nebraska
82	Grant, Otis	WR	6-3	197	3	Michigan State
27	Green, Gary	CB	5-11	191	9	Baylor
44	Guman, Mike	RB	6-2	218	6	Penn State
60	Harrah, Dennis	G	6-5	265	11	Miami
26	Harris, Eric	CB	6-3	202	6	Memphis State
81	Hill, David	TE	6-2	228	10	Texas A&I
87	Hill, Drew	WR	5-9	170	7	Georgia Tech.
72	Hill, Kent	G	6-5	260	7	Georgia Tech.
47	Irvin, LeRoy	CB	5-11	184	6	Kansas
59	Jerue, Mark	LB	6-3	229	3	Washington
77	Jeter, Gary	DE	6-4	260	9	Southern California
20	Johnson, Johnnie	S	6-1	183	6	Texas
24	Jones, A.J.	RB	6-1	202	4	Texas
46	Kamana, John	RB	6-2	215	2	Southern California
9	Kemp, Jeff	QB	6-0	201	5	Dartmouth
76	Kowalski, Gary	T	6-5	275	3	Boston College
1	Lansford, Mike	K	6-0	183	4	Washington
57	Laughlin, Jim	LB	6-1	222	6	Ohio State
83	McDonald, James	TE	6-5	230	3	Southern California
63	McDonald, Mike	LB	6-1	235	2	Southern California
69	Meisner, Greg	NT	6-3	253	5	Pittsburgh
98	Miller, Shawn	DE	6-4	255	2	Utah State
6	Misko, John	P	6-5	207	4	Oregon State
22	Newsome, Vince	S	6-1	179	3	Washington
58	Owens, Mel	LB	6-2	224	5	Michigan
75	Pankey, Irv	T	6-4	267	5	Penn State
43	Pleasant, Mike	S	6-1	195	2	Oklahoma
30	Redden, Barry	RB	5-10	205	4	Richmond
93	Reed, Doug	DE	6-3	250	2	San Diego State
66	Reese, Booker	DE	6-6	260	4	Bethune-Cookman
64	Shearin, Joe	C	6-4	250	3	Texas
78	Slater, Jackie	T	6-4	271	10	Jackson State
61	Slaton, Tony	C	6-3	269	2	Southern California
56	Smith, Doug	C-G	6-3	253	8	Bowling Green
37	Sully, Ivory	S	6-0	200	7	Delaware
51	Vann, Norwood	LB	6-2	225	2	East Carolina
54	Wilcher, Mike	LB	6-3	235	3	North Carolina
85	Youngblood, Jack	DE	6-4	242	15	Florida

NEW ORLEANS SAINTS NFC West

Address 1500 Poydras Street, New Orleans, Louisiana 70112.

Stadium Louisiana Superdome, New Orleans. *Capacity* 71,647 *Playing Surface* AstroTurf.

Team Colours Old Gold, Black and White.

Head Coach O.A. 'Bum' Phillips — fifth year.

Championships None.

History NFL 1967-69, NFC 1970-

Offense

The Saints' offense is a puzzle, the solution to which will only become apparent when head coach 'Bum' Phillips reveals his hand – and that's not likely until after the preseason games. George Rogers, one of the very best running backs in the league, was traded to Washington, just before the collegiate draft, as part of a deal which gave New Orleans the Redskins' first-round option. The Saints had traded away their own first-round position to Houston (halfway through 1984) in exchange for running back Earl Campbell, whom Phillips drafted when he was head coach of the Oilers, way back in 1978. There's little to choose between the two players but the 30-year-old Campbell is closer to four than three years older than Rogers and, of late, has shown signs of the extra defensive attention he has received over seven NFL years. Campbell must expect to share time with Hokie Gajan, who is too good to be overlooked. Gajan ripped off his 615 yards rushing at a big-time average of 6.0, and he was the club leader with 35 pass receptions. Wayne Wilson, too, has had his moments, notably when rushing for 108, 160 and 103 yards on consecutive weeks when Rogers was injured in 1983. Richard Todd, who was acquired from the Jets, was not the answer at quarterback and is likely to be displaced by the younger Dave Wilson, who saw a great deal of playing time in the last four weeks of 1984 and left a good impression. If wide receiver Lindsay Scott, a former number one pick, was a little disappointing, the play of 1983 free agent Tyrone Young was a pleasant surprise. He's a genuine deep threat and now starts ahead of Scott,

in partnership with Jeff Groth. Tight end Hoby Brenner has begun to spread his wings, catching his 28 passes at the average of 19.8 yards. The offensive line will be hoping for a 1985 campaign with fewer injuries. There's the nucleus of a good front five but the departed center, John Hill, will be missed after ten years with the club. Draftee tackle Daren Gilbert was a sensible choice in round two.

Defense

There are excellent players spread throughout a defensive unit which, last year, ranked second in the NFC in fewest yards given up. They're particularly good against the pass. With the defensive line applying the pressure, outside linebackers Rickey Jackson and Whitney Paul home in for the kill – they registered 12 and 9.5 sacks respectively. Defensive end Bruce Clark, a former first-round pick of the Green Bay Packers, now plays up to that standard and, in particular, collared the quarterback 10.5 times. It earned his first selection to the Pro Bowl. The Saints signalled their determination to maintain an excellent defensive standard by using the pick they obtained from Washington to draft linebacker Alvin Toles, who was an inside specialist in college and could well displace Dennis Winston, who has given great service since coming from the Steelers in 1982. The Saints' third-round pick, outside linebacker Jack Del Rio, is especially tough and could be the best to come out of that round of the draft. The starting secondary of cornerbacks Dave Waymer and Johnnie Poe, and safeties Russell Gary and Frank Wattelet are all veterans, secure in their positions. They don't make many interceptions but are noted for their close coverage of receivers.

Special Teams

Morten Andersen is a good, consistent kicker, who is due for a couple of really long ones. Brian Hansen, a ninth-round draftee in 1984, was a sensation, averaging a gross 43.8 over 69 punts and being selected to the Pro Bowl. Jitter Fields holds down a roster spot, returning both punts and kickoffs. He's in charge of the former, averaging a respectable 8.7 yards, and may take over Tyrone Young's load in the kickoff return department, partnering Kenny Duckett.

1985 DRAFT

Round	Name	Pos.	Ht.	Wt.	College
1.	Toles, Alvin	LB	6-1	215	Tennessee
2.	Gilbert. Daren	T	6-5	268	Cal State-Fullerton
3.	Del Rio, Jack	LB	6-3	235	Southern California
4.	Allen, Billy	DB	5-11	205	Florida State
7.	Martin, Eric	WR	6-0	198	Louisiana State
8.	Kohlbrand, Joe	DE	6-4	228	Miami
9.	Johnson, Earl	DB	6-0	190	South Carolina
12.	Songy, Treg	DB	6-1	195	Tulane

The reliable Hokie Gajan (#46)

1985 SCHEDULE

September
8	KANSAS CITY	1:00
15	at Denver	4:00
22	TAMPA BAY	1:00
29	at San Francisco	4:00

October
6	PHILADELPHIA	1:00
13	at Los Angeles Raiders	4:00
20	at Atlanta	1:00
27	NEW YORK GIANTS	4:00

November
3	at Los Angeles Rams	4:00
10	SEATTLE	1:00
17	vs. Green Bay (Milwaukee)	1:00
24	at Minnesota	1:00

December
1	LOS ANGELES RAMS	1:00
8	at St Louis	1:00
15	SAN FRANCISCO	1:00
22	ATLANTA	1:00

VETERAN ROSTER

No.	Name	Pos.	Ht.	Wt.	NFL Year	College
7	Andersen, Morten	K	6-2	210	4	Michigan State
22	Anthony, Tyrone	RB	5-11	200	2	North Carolina
85	Brenner, Hoby	TE	6-4	240	5	Southern California
67	Brock, Stan	T	6-6	285	6	Colorado
35	Campbell, Earl	RB	5-11	238	8	Texas
65	Carter, David	C	6-2	260	9	Western Kentucky
75	Clark, Bruce	DE	6-3	275	4	Penn State
68	Clark, Kelvin	G	6-3	265	7	Nebraska
83	Duckett, Kenny	WR	6-0	187	4	Wake Forest
63	Edelman, Brad	G	6-6	265	4	Missouri
99	Elliot, Tony	NT	6-2	265	4	North Texas State
26	Fields, Jitter	CB	5-8	185	2	Texas
46	Gajan, Hokie	RB	5-11	220	4	Louisiana State
20	Gary, Russell	S	5-11	195	5	Nebraska
97	Geathers, James	DE	6-7	263	2	Wichita State
88	Goodlow, Eugene	WR	6-2	190	3	Kansas State
86	Groth, Jeff	WR	5-10	175	7	Bowling Green
10	Hansen, Brian	P	6-3	207	2	Sioux Falls, S.D.
28	Harding, Greg	S	6-2	202	2	Nicholls State
87	Hardy, Larry	TE	6-3	230	8	Jackson State
92	Haynes, James	LB				
61	Hilgenberg, Joel	C	6-3	250	2	Iowa
24	Hoage, Terry	S	6-3	197	2	Georgia
57	Jackson, Rickey	LB	6-2	240	5	Pittsburgh
34	Johnson, Bobby	S	6-0	191	3	Texas
60	Korte, Steve	G	6-2	270	3	Arkansas
52	Kovach, Jim	LB	6-2	225	7	Kentucky
64	Lafary, Dave	T	6-7	280	9	Purdue
93	Lewis, Gary	NT	6-3	260	3	Oklahoma State
98	Lewis, Reggie	DE	6-2	260	4	San Diego State
29	Lewis, Rodney	CB	5-11	190	3	Nebraska
19	Merkens, Guido	QB	6-1	195	8	Sam Houston State
84	Miller, Junior	TE	6-4	240	6	Nebraska
74	Moore, Derland	NT	6-4	270	13	Oklahoma
66	Oubre, Louis	G	6-4	262	4	Oklahoma
51	Paul, Whitney	LB	6-3	220	10	Colorado
53	Pelluer, Scott	LB	6-2	220	5	Washington State
25	Poe, Johnnie	CB	6-1	185	5	Missouri
58	Redd, Glen	LB	6-1	225	4	Brigham Young
41	Rogers, Jimmy	RB	5-10	190	6	Oklahoma
80	Scott, Lindsay	WR	6-1	190	4	Georgia
96	Thorp, Don	NT	6-4	248	2	Illinois
82	Tice, John	TE	6-5	242	3	Maryland
11	Todd, Richard	QB	6-2	206	10	Alabama
72	Ward, Chris	T	6-3	269	8	Ohio State
73	Warren, Frank	DE	6-4	275	5	Auburn
49	Wattelet, Frank	S	6-0	185	5	Kansas
44	Waymer, Dave	CB	6-1	195	6	Notre Dame
94	Wilks, Jim	DE	6-5	260	5	San Diego State
18	Wilson, Dave	QB	6-3	210	4	Illinois
45	Wilson, Tim	RB	6-3	235	9	Maryland
30	Wilson, Wayne	RB	6-3	220	7	Shepherd, W. Va.
56	Winston, Dennis	LB	6-0	230	9	Arkansas
89	Young, Tyrone	WR	6-6	190	3	Florida

SAN FRANCISCO 49ers NFC West

Address 711, Nevada Street, Redwood City, California 94061.

Stadium Candlestick Park, San Francisco. *Capacity* 61,185 *Playing Surface* Grass.

Team Colours Forty Niners Gold and Scarlet.

Head Coach Bill Walsh – seventh year.

Championships Division 1970,'71,'72,'81,'83,'84; Conference 1981,'84. Super Bowl 1981,'84.

History AAFC 1946-49, NFL 1950-69, NFC 1970-

Offense

It has become a tradition to attach invincibility to the reigning Super Bowl Champion. It was easy for both Washington and, subsequently, the Raiders. And after the way the 49ers dismissed the challenge of Miami, they become genuine contenders for immortality. Neither the Raiders nor Washington had quite the strength in depth to repeat their championships but that could hardly be said about the 49ers. Even at quarterback there is quality reserve support. Matt Cavanaugh showed that he could cope when standing in for Joe 'Big Sky' Montana on Weeks Four and Fifteen. Montana retained his position as the NFL's all-time leading passer over the regular season and finished off by dominating Super Bowl XIX. The amazing thing is that he is not a particularly gifted athlete – there are several around the league who could out-pass him. But there is none as inventive under pressure or with the nerve to wait for the right moment to let fly. His wide receivers have thrived on a supply of perfectly-timed passes. As expected, Dwight Clark led the pure pass receivers with 52 receptions, Freddie Solomon came second with a better average and caught the most touchdown passes, and Renaldo Nehemiah's cameo appearances were at a club-best average of 19.8 yards. Either Solomon or, more probably, Nehemiah, will have to yield time to first-round draftee Jerry Rice, a real burner whom the 49ers wanted badly enough to pay the price for trading up. The offensive backfield pairing of Wendell Tyler and Roger Craig is the envy of most clubs around the league. Tyler is a blue-chipper and yet Craig, who led the club with 71 pass receptions, may turn out to be even

better. A slight weakness was the absence of fullback power but along came draftee Ricky Moore in round three to solve that problem. Currently, Earl Cooper is the more productive tight end but Russ Francis is quickly re-establishing the reputation he carried with ease when with the Patriots. The starting offensive line remains intact, once more to establish the platform for the NFC's most prolific scoring machine.

Defense

The 49ers have given new meaning to the term 'situational substitution' which, roughly translated, means wholesale confusion for the opposition. They've made tactical use of specialists such as the pass-rushing defensive end, Fred Dean, for some time. But now any seven of a dozen players, linemen and linebackers, could line up on any one down. Nominally, they'll use a 3-4 formation with Jim Stuckey and Dwaine Board at defensive end, flanking nose tackle Manu Tuiasosopo, the latter who was an inspired acquisition from Seattle. Fred Dean and Gary 'Big Hands' Johnson, both former San Diego players, are pass rush specialists. Board led the team with ten sacks but Dean, who did not play until the 12th game of the season, will be anxious to regain his title of sack leader. At line-backer, Riki Ellison enhanced his status as a starter and, on the outsides, starting veterans Keena Turner and Dan Bunz maintained a standard which held off the challenges of the talented young players, Milt McColl, Blanchard Montgomery and first-round pick Todd Shell. The quartet made up by cornerbacks Ronnie Lott and Eric Wright, and safeties Carlton Williamson and Dwight Hicks, came together in 1981. Collectively, they have been a major factor in two victorious Super Bowls. It was just reward when all four were selected to the 1985 Pro Bowl.

Special Teams

Placekicker Ray Wersching is steady as a rock. He doesn't land a lot of long ones but kicks the ones which matter. Punter Max Runager had a better gross average than the man he replaced, Tom Orosz, but puts rather too many into the end zone. Dana McLemore is a speedy, elusive punt returner who came second in the NFC to Henry Ellard. Derrick Harmon may see more action returning kickoffs, after averaging 27.5 yards on limited opportunities.

1985 DRAFT

Round	Name	Pos.	Ht.	Wt.	College
1.	Rice, Jerry	WR	6-2	190	Mississippi Valley State
3.	Moore, Ricky	RB	5-10	245	Alabama
5.	Collie, Bruce	T	6-5	275	Texas-Arlington
6.	Barry, Scott	QB	6-1	190	Cal-Davis
11.	Wood, David	DE	6-3	255	Arizona
12.	Chumley, Donald	DT	6-4	252	Georgia

Roger Craig

1985 SCHEDULE

September

8	at Minnesota	1:00
15	ATLANTA	4:00
22	at Los Angeles Raiders	4:00
29	NEW ORLEANS	4:00

October

6	at Atlanta	1:00
13	CHICAGO	4:00
20	at Detroit	1:00
27	at Los Angeles Rams	4:00

November

3	PHILADELPHIA	4:00
11	at Denver	9:00
17	KANSAS CITY	4:00
25	SEATTLE	9:00

December

1	at Washington	4:00
9	LOS ANGELES RAMS	9:00
15	at New Orleans	1:00
22	DALLAS	4:00

VETERAN ROSTER

No.	Name	Pos.	Ht.	Wt.	NFL Year	College
68	Ayers, John	G	6-5	265	9	West Texas State
76	Board, Dwaine	DE	6-5	250	6	North Carolina A&T
57	Bunz, Dan	LB	6-4	225	7	Cal State-Long Beach
95	Carter, Michael	NT	6-2	281	2	Southern Methodist
6	Cavanaugh, Matt	QB	6-2	212	8	Pittsburgh
87	Clark, Dwight	WR	6-4	210	7	Clemson
29	Clark, Mario	CB	6-2	195	10	Oregon
47	Collier, Tim	CB	6-0	176	10	East Texas State
89	Cooper, Earl	TE	6-2	227	6	Rice
33	Craig, Roger	RB	6-1	222	3	Nebraska
51	Cross, Randy	G	6 3	265	10	UCLA
74	Dean, Fred	DE	6-2	236	11	Louisiana Tech.
50	Ellison, Riki	LB	6-2	220	3	Southern California
55	Fahnhorst, Jim	LB	6-4	235	2	Minnesota
71	Fahnhorst, Keith	T	6-6	273	12	Minnesota
54	Ferrari, Ron	LB	6-0	212	4	Illinois
81	Francis, Russ	TE	6-6	242	10	Oregon
86	Frank, John	TE	6-3	225	2	Ohio State
49	Fuller, Jeff	S	6-2	216	2	Texas A&M
	Gervais, Rick	S	5-11	190	5	Stanford
24	Harmon, Derrick	RB	5-10	202	2	Cornell
75	Harty, John	DT	6-4	263	5	Iowa
22	Hicks, Dwight	S	6-1	189	7	Michigan
28	Holmoe, Tom	S	6-2	180	3	Brigham Young
97	Johnson, Gary	DE	6-2	255	11	Grambling
94	Kelcher, Louie	NT	6-5	310	11	Southern Methodist
66	Kennedy, Allan	T	6-7	275	4	Washington State
42	Lott, Ronnie	CB	6-0	199	5	Southern California
53	McColl, Milt	LB	6-6	220	5	Stanford
62	McIntyre, Guy	G	6-3	271	2	Georgia
43	McLemore, Dana	KR-CB	5-10	183	4	Hawaii
32	Monroe, Carl	RB	5-8	166	3	Utah
16	Montana, Joe	QB	6-2	200	7	Notre Dame
52	Montgomery, Blanchard	LB	6-2	236	3	UCLA
83	Nehemiah, Renaldo	WR	6-1	177	4	Maryland
77	Paris, Bubba	T	6-6	293	3	Michigan
65	Pillers, Lawrence	DE-NT	6-4	250	10	Alcorn State
56	Quillan, Fred	C	6-5	266	8	Oregon
64	Reynolds, Jack	LB	6-1	232	16	Tennessee
30	Ring, Bill	RB	5-10	215	5	Brigham Young
4	Runager, Max	P	6-1	189	7	South Carolina
61	Sapolu, Jesse	G	6-4	260	3	Hawaii
90	Shell, Todd	LB	6-4	225	2	Brigham Young
67	Shields, Billy	T	6-8	284	11	Georgia Tech.
88	Solomon, Freddie	WR	5-11	185	11	Tampa
72	Stover, Jeff	NT	6-5	275	4	Oregon
79	Stuckey, Jim	DE	6-4	251	6	Clemson
78	Tuiasosopo, Manu	NT	6-3	250	7	UCLA
58	Turner, Keena	LB	6-2	219	6	Purdue
26	Tyler, Wendell	RB	5-10	198	8	UCLA
99	Walter, Mike	LB	6-3	238	3	Oregon
14	Wersching, Ray	K	5-11	210	13	California
27	Williamson, Carlton	S	6-0	204	5	Pittsburgh
85	Wilson, Mike	WR	6-3	210	5	Washington State
21	Wright, Eric	CB	6-1	180	5	Missouri

1985 NATIONAL FOOTBALL LEAGUE SCHEDULE

(All times local)

FIRST WEEK

Sunday, September 8 — Kickoff

Denver at Los Angeles Rams	1:00
Detroit at Atlanta	1:00
Green Bay at New England	1:00
Indianapolis at Pittsburgh	1:00
Kansas City at New Orleans	12:00
Miami at Houston	12:00
New York Jets at Los Angeles Raiders	1:00
Philadelphia at New York Giants	1:00
St Louis at Cleveland	1:00
San Diego at Buffalo	4:00
San Francisco at Minnesota	12:00
Seattle at Cincinnati	1:00
Tampa Bay at Chicago	12:00

Monday, September 9

Washington at Dallas	8:00

SECOND WEEK

Thursday, September 12

Los Angeles Raiders at Kansas City	7:00

Sunday, September 15

Atlanta at San Francisco	1:00
Buffalo at New York Jets	1:00
Cincinnati at St Louis	12:00
Dallas at Detroit	1:00
Houston at Washington	1:00
Indianapolis at Miami	4:00
Los Angeles Rams at Philadelphia	1:00
Minnesota at Tampa Bay	4:00
New England at Chicago	12:00
New Orleans at Denver	2:00
New York Giants at Green Bay	3:00
Seattle at San Diego	1:00

Monday, September 16

Pittsburgh at Cleveland	9:00

THIRD WEEK

Thursday, September 19

Chicago at Minnesota	7:00

Sunday, September 22

Cleveland at Dallas	12:00
Denver at Atlanta	1:00
Detroit at Indianapolis	12:00
Houston at Pittsburgh	1:00
Kansas City at Miami	4:00
New England at Buffalo	1:00
New York Jets vs Green Bay at Milwaukee	3:00
Philadelphia at Washington	1:00
St Louis at New York Giants	1:00
San Diego at Cincinnati	1:00
San Francisco at Los Angeles Raiders	1:00
Tampa Bay at New Orleans	12:00

Monday, September 23

Los Angeles Rams at Seattle	6:00

FOURTH WEEK

Sunday, September 29

Atlanta at Los Angeles Rams	1:00
Cleveland at San Diego	1:00
Dallas at Houston	12:00
Green Bay at St Louis	12:00
Indianapolis at New York Jets	4:00
Los Angeles Raiders at New England	1:00
Miami at Denver	2:00
Minnesota at Buffalo	1:00
New Orleans at San Francisco	1:00
New York Giants at Philadelphia	1:00
Seattle at Kansas City	12:00
Tampa Bay at Detroit	1:00
Washington at Chicago	12:00

Monday, September 30

Cincinnati at Pittsburgh	9:00

FIFTH WEEK

Sunday, October 6

Buffalo at Indianapolis	12:00
Chicago at Tampa Bay	1:00
Dallas at New York Giants	8:00
Detroit at Green Bay	12:00
Houston at Denver	2:00

Kansas City at Los Angeles Raiders	1:00
Minnesota at Los Angeles Rams	1:00
New England at Cleveland	1:00
New York Jets at Cincinnati	4:00
Philadelphia at New Orleans	12:00
Pittsburgh at Miami	1:00
San Diego at Seattle	1:00
San Francisco at Atlanta	1:00

Monday, October 7
St Louis at Washington	9:00

SIXTH WEEK
Sunday, October 13
Atlanta at Seattle	1:00
Buffalo at New England	1:00
Chicago at San Francisco	1:00
Cleveland at Houston	12:00
Denver at Indianapolis	12:00
Detroit at Washington	1:00
Kansas City at San Diego	1:00
Los Angeles Rams at Tampa Bay	1:00
Minnesota vs Green Bay at Milwaukee	12:00
New Orleans at Los Angeles Raiders	1:00
New York Giants at Cincinnati	1:00
Philadelphia at St Louis	12:00
Pittsburgh at Dallas	12:00

Monday, October 14
Miami at New York Jets	9:00

SEVENTH WEEK
Sunday, October 20
Cincinnati at Houston	12:00
Dallas at Philadelphia	1:00
Indianapolis at Buffalo	1:00
Los Angeles Raiders at Cleveland	1:00
Los Angeles Rams at Kansas City	12:00
New Orleans at Atlanta	1:00
New York Jets at New England	4:00
St Louis at Pittsburgh	1:00
San Diego at Minnesota	12:00
San Francisco at Detroit	1:00
Seattle at Denver	2:00
Tampa Bay at Miami	4:00
Washington at New York Giants	1:00

Monday, October 21
Green Bay at Chicago	8:00

EIGHTH WEEK
Sunday, October 27
Atlanta at Dallas	12:00
Buffalo at Philadelphia	1:00
Denver at Kansas City	12:00
Green Bay at Indianapolis	1:00
Houston at St Louis	12:00
Miami at Detroit	1:00
Minnesota at Chicago	12:00
New England at Tampa Bay	1:00

New York Giants at New Orleans	3:00
Pittsburgh at Cincinnati	4:00
San Francisco at Los Angeles Rams	1:00
Seattle at New York Jets	1:00
Washington at Cleveland	1:00

Monday, October 28
San Diego at Los Angeles Raiders	6:00

NINTH WEEK
Sunday, November 3
Chicago at Green Bay	12:00
Cincinnati at Buffalo	1:00
Cleveland at Pittsburgh	1:00
Denver at San Diego	1:00
Detroit at Minnesota	12:00
Kansas City at Houston	12:00
Los Angeles Raiders at Seattle	1:00
Miami at New England	1:00
New Orleans at Los Angeles Rams	1:00
New York Jets at Indianapolis	4:00
Philadelphia at San Francisco	1:00
Tampa Bay at New York Giants	1:00
Washington at Atlanta	1:00

Monday, November 4
Dallas at St Louis	8:00

TENTH WEEK
Sunday, November 10
Atlanta at Philadelphia	1:00
Cleveland at Cincinnati	1:00
Dallas at Washington	4:00
Detroit at Chicago	12:00
Green Bay at Minnesota	12:00
Houston at Buffalo	1:00
Indianapolis at New England	1:00
Los Angeles Raiders at San Diego	1:00
Los Angeles Rams at New York Giants	1:00
New York Jets at Miami	4:00
Pittsburgh at Kansas City	12:00
St Louis at Tampa Bay	1:00
Seattle at New Orleans	12:00

Monday, November 11
San Francisco at Denver	7:00

ELEVENTH WEEK
Sunday, November 17
Buffalo at Cleveland	1:00
Chicago at Dallas	12:00
Cincinnati at Los Angeles Raiders	1:00
Kansas City at San Francisco	1:00
Los Angeles Rams at Atlanta	1:00
Miami at Indianapolis	1:00
Minnesota at Detroit	4:00
New England at Seattle	1:00
New Orleans vs Green Bay at Milwaukee	12:00
Pittsburgh at Houston	12:00
St Louis at Philadelphia	1:00
San Diego at Denver	2:00

Tampa Bay at New York Jets   1:00

Monday, November 18
New York Giants at Washington   9:00

TWELFTH WEEK
Sunday, November 24
Atlanta at Chicago   12:00
Cincinnati at Cleveland   1:00
Denver at Los Angeles Raiders   1:00
Detroit at Tampa Bay   1:00
Green Bay at Los Angeles Rams   1:00
Indianapolis at Kansas City   3:00
Miami at Buffalo   1:00
New England at New York   1:00
New Orleans at Minnesota   12:00
New York Giants at St Louis   3:00
Philadelphia at Dallas   3:00
San Diego at Houston   12:00
Washington at Pittsburgh   1:00

Monday, November 25
Seattle at San Francisco   6:00

THIRTEENTH WEEK
Thursday, November 28 (Thanksgiving Day)
New York Jets at Detroit   12:30
St Louis at Dallas   3:00

Sunday, December 1
Buffalo at San Diego   1:00
Cleveland at New York Giants   1:00
Denver at Pittsburgh   1:00
Houston at Cincinnati   1:00
Kansas City at Seattle   1:00
Los Angeles Raiders at Atlanta   4:00
Los Angeles Rams at New Orleans   12:00
Minnesota at Philadelphia   1:00
New England at Indianapolis   1:00
San Francisco at Washington   4:00
Tampa Bay at Green Bay   12:00

Monday, December 2
Chicago at Miami   9:00

FOURTEENTH WEEK
Sunday, December 8
Atlanta at Kansas City   12:00
Cleveland at Seattle   1:00
Dallas at Cincinnati   1:00
Detroit at New England   1:00
Indianapolis at Chicago   12:00
Los Angeles Raiders at Denver   2:00
Miami at Green Bay   12:00
New Orleans at St Louis   12:00
New York Giants at Houston   3:00
New York Jets at Buffalo   1:00
Pittsburgh at San Diego   6:00
Tampa Bay at Minnesota   3:00
Washington at Philadelphia   1:00

Monday, December 9
Los Angeles Rams at San Francisco   6:00

FIFTEENTH WEEK
Saturday, December 14
Chicago at New York Jets   12:30
Kansas City at Denver   2:00

Sunday, December 15
Buffalo at Pittsburgh   1:00
Cincinnati at Washington   1:00
Green Bay at Detroit   1:00
Houston at Cleveland   1:00
Indianapolis at Tampa Bay   1:00
Minnesota at Atlanta   1:00
New York Giants at Dallas   12:00
Philadelphia at San Diego   1:00
St Louis at Los Angeles Rams   1:00
San Francisco at New Orleans   12:00
Seattle at Los Angeles Raiders   1:00

Monday, December 16
New England at Miami   9:00

SIXTEENTH WEEK
Friday, December 20
Denver at Seattle   5:00

Saturday, December 21
Pittsburgh at New York Giants   12:00
Washington at St Louis   3:00

Sunday, December 22
Atlanta at New Orleans   12:00
Buffalo at Miami   1:00
Chicago at Detroit   1:00
Cincinnati at New England   1:00
Cleveland at New York Jets   1:00
Dallas at San Francisco   1:00
Green Bay at Tampa Bay   1:00
Houston at Indianapolis   4:00
Philadelphia at Minnesota   12:00
San Diego at Kansas City   12:00

Monday, December 23
Los Angeles Raiders at Los Angeles Rams   6:00

Postseason

Sunday, Dec 29   AFC and NFC First Round Playoffs
Saturday, Jan 4   AFC and NFC Divisional Playoffs
Sunday, Jan 5   AFC and NFC Divisional Playoffs
Sunday, Jan 12   AFC and NFC Championship Games
Sunday, Jan 26   Super Bowl XX at Louisiana
                  Superdome, New Orleans, Louisiana
Sunday, Feb 2   AFC-NFC Pro Bowl, Honolulu, Hawaii

WASHINGTON

Seattle Seahawks

OREGON

MONTANA

NORTH DAKOTA

IDAHO

SOUTH DAKOTA

WYOMING

NEBRASKA

San Francisco 49ers

NEVADA

UTAH

Denver Broncos

CALIFORNIA

COLORADO

KANSAS

Ka

Los Angeles Raiders

Los Angeles Rams

ARIZONA

NEW MEXICO

OKLA

San Diego Chargers

Dallas Cowbo

TEXAS

Hou